Word-to-word (Bilingual) DICTIONARY

ENGLISH-TURKISH
TURKISH-ENGLISH

Word-to-word Dictionaries

English-Urdu / Urdu-English (compiled by Dr Khurshid Alam)
English-Hindi / Hindi-English (compiled by Joseph W. Raker)
English-Punjabi / Punjabi-English (compiled by Prakash Singh Gill)
English-Farsi / Farsi-English (compiled by Maryam Zamankhani)
English-Arabic / Arabic-English (compiled by Abdulla Hasan Al-Jabre)
English-Somali / Somali-English (compiled by Mohamud Korshel)
English-Spanish / Spanish-English (compiled by Candido Sesma)
English-Gujarati / Gujarati-English (compiled by Nehal Mehta)
English-Chinese / Chinese-English (compiled by Weixuan Liao)
English-Korean / Korean-English (compiled by Mindy Kim Christlieb)
English-Russian / Russian-English (compiled by Ekaterina Strieby)
English-Portuguese / Portuguese-English (compiled by Suzana Santos)
English-Vietnamese / Vietnamese-English (compiled by Terry Gwenn)
English-German / German-English (compiled by Hella Bell)
English-Turkish / Turkish-English (compiled by Nagme Yazgin)
English-Bengali / Bengali-English (compiled by Prodip Kumar Dutta)
English-Tagalog / Tagalog-English (compiled by Norma Smith)
English-Haitian Creole / Haitian Creole-English (compiled by Karine Gentil)
English-Cambodian / Cambodian-English (compiled by Hak Sokleang)
English-French / French-English (compiled by Vanessa Munsch)
English-Pashto / Pashto-English (compiled by Sobia Kattak)
English-Romanian / Romanian-English (compiled by Ana Cristana Dobrin)
English-Thai / Thai-English (compiled by Kesorn Kawila)

More languages in print

STAR PUBLICATIONS PVT.LTD
New Delhi 110 002

Word-to-word (Bilingual) DICTIONARY

ENGLISH-TURKISH
TURKISH-ENGLISH

Compiled by
Nagme Yazgin

Yazgin, Nagme
ENGLISH-TURKISH / TURKISH-ENGLISH
Word-to-word (Bilingual) Dictionary

First Edition : 2009

Published in India by :
Star Publications Pvt. Ltd.
4/5B Asaf Ali Road
New Delhi-110 002 (India)
(e-mail:starpub@satyam.net.in)

under arrangement with
Bilingual Dictionaries Inc, USA

Printed at: Star Print O Bind, New Delhi 110 020

List of Irregular Verbs

present - past - past participle

arise - arose - arisen
awake - awoke - awoken, awaked
be - was - been
bear - bore - borne
beat - beat - beaten
become - became - become
begin - began - begun
behold - beheld - beheld
bend - bent - bent
beseech - besought - besought
bet - bet - betted
bid - bade (bid) - bidden (bid)
bind - bound - bound
bite - bit - bitten
bleed - bled - bled
blow - blew - blown
break - broke - broken
breed - bred - bred
bring - brought - brought
build - built - built
burn - burnt - burnt *
burst - burst - burst
buy - bought - bought
cast - cast - cast
catch - caught - caught
choose - chose - chosen
cling - clung - clung
come - came - come
cost - cost - cost
creep - crept - crept
cut - cut - cut
deal - dealt - dealt
dig - dug - dug
do - did - done
draw - drew - drawn
dream - dreamt - dreamed
drink - drank - drunk
drive - drove - driven
dwell - dwelt - dwelt
eat - ate - eaten
fall - fell - fallen
feed - fed - fed
feel - felt - felt
fight - fought - fought
find - found - found
flee - fled - fled
fling - flung - flung
fly - flew - flown
forebear - forbore - forborne
forbid - forbade - forbidden
forecast - forecast - forecast
forget - forgot - forgotten
forgive - forgave - forgiven
forego - forewent - foregone
foresee - foresaw - foreseen
foretell - foretold - foretold

forget - forgot - forgotten
forsake - forsook - forsaken
freeze - froze - frozen
get - got - gotten
give - gave - given
go - went - gone
grind - ground - ground
grow - grew - grown
hang - hung * - hung *
have - had - had
hear - heard - heard
hide - hid - hidden
hit - hit - hit
hold - held - held
hurt - hurt - hurt
hit - hit - hit
hold - held - held
keep - kept - kept
kneel - knelt * - knelt *
know - knew - known
lay - laid - laid
lead - led - led
lean - leant * - leant *
leap - lept * - lept *
learn - learnt * - learnt *
leave - left - left
lend - lent - lent
let - let - let
lie - lay - lain
light - lit * - lit *
lose - lost - lost
make - made - made
mean - meant - meant
meet - met - met
mistake - mistook - mistaken
must - had to - had to
pay - paid - paid
plead - pleaded - pled
prove - proved - proven
put - put - put
quit - quit * - quit *
read - read - read
rid - rid - rid
ride - rode - ridden
ring - rang - rung
rise - rose - risen
run - ran - run
saw - sawed - sawn
say - said - said
see - saw - seen
seek - sought - sought
sell - sold - sold
send - sent - sent
set - set - set
sew - sewed - sewn
shake - shook - shaken
shear - sheared - shorn
shed - shed - shed

shine - shone - shone
shoot - shot - shot
show - showed - shown
shrink - shrank - shrunk
shut - shut - shut
sing - sang - sung
sink - sank - sunk
sit - sat - sat
slay - slew - slain
sleep - sleep - slept
slide - slid - slid
sling - slung - slung
smell - smelt * - smelt *
sow - sowed - sown *
speak - spoke - spoken
speed - sped * - sped *
spell - spelt * - spelt *
spend - spent - spent
spill - spilt * - spilt *
spin - spun - spun
spit - spat - spat
split - split - split
spread - spread - spread
spring - sprang - sprung
stand - stood - stood
steal - stole - stolen
stick - stuck - stuck
sting - stung - stung
stink - stank - stunk
stride - strode - stridden
strike - struck - struck (stricken)
strive - strove - striven
swear - swore - sworn
sweep - swept - swept
swell - swelled - swollen *
swim - swam - swum
take - took - taken
teach - taught - taught
tear - tore - torn
tell - told - told
think - thought - thought
throw - threw - thrown
thrust - thrust - thrust
tread - trod - trodden
wake - woke - woken
wear - wore - worn
weave - wove * - woven *
wed - wed * - wed *
weep - wept - wept
win - won - won
wind - wound - wound
wring - wrung - wrung
write - wrote - written

Those tenses with an * also have regular forms.

English-Turkish

Abbreviations

English - Turkish

a - article - nesne
adj - adjective - sıfat
adv - adverb - belirteç
c - conjunction - bağlaç
e - exclamation - ünlem
n - noun - ad
pre - preposition - edat
pro - pronoun - zamir
v - verb - eylem

A

a *a* bir
abandon *v* terketmek
abandonment *n* terk
abbey *n* manastır
abbot *n* başrahip
abbreviate *v* kısaltmak
abbreviation *n* kısaltmak
abdicate *v* çekilmek
abdication *n* çekilme
abdomen *n* karın
abduct *v* kaçırmak
abduction *n* kaçırma
aberration *n* sapma
abhor *v* iğrenmek
abide by *v* itaat
ability *n* yetenek
ablaze *adj* ışıltılı
able *adj* muktedir
abnormal *adj* anormal
abnormality *n* anormallik
aboard *adv* içinde
abolish *v* feshetmek
abort *v* durdurmak
abortion *n* kürtaj
abound *v* bol olmak
about *pre* civarında
about *adv* hakkında
above *pre* üstünde
abreast *adv* yanyana
abridge *v* özetlemek
abroad *adv* yurtdışında
abrogate *v* feshetmek
abruptly *adv* birdenbire
absence *n* eksiklik
absent *adj* eksik
absolute *adj* tam
absolution *n* af
absolve *v* bağışlamak
absorb *v* emmek
absorbent *adj* emici
abstain *v* kaçınmak
abstinence *n* rizayet
abstract *adj* soyut
absurd *adj* saçma
abundance *n* bolluk
abundant *adj* bol
abuse *v* kötüye kullanmak
abuse *n* suistimal
abusive *adj* kötüleyici
abysmal *adj* dipsiz
abyss *n* uçurum
academic *adj* akademik
academy *n* akademi

accelerate *v* hızlandırmak
accelerator *n* hızlandırıcı
accent *n* aksan
accept *v* kabul etmek
acceptable *adj* kabul edilebilir
acceptance *n* kabul
access *n* erişim
accessible *adj* erişilebilir
accident *n* kaza
accidental *adj* yanlışlıkla
acclaim *v* övmek
acclimatize *v* alıştırmak
accommodate *v* yerleştirmek
accompany *v* eşlik etmek
accomplice *n* suç ortağı
accomplish *v* başarmak
accomplishment *n* başarı
accord *n* anlaşma
according to *pre* e göre
accordion *n* akordeon
account *n* hesap
account for *v* hesap vermek
accountable *adj* sorumlu
accountant *n* muhasebeci
accumulate *v* biriktirmek
accuracy *n* doğruluk
accurate *adj* doğru
accusation *n* suçlama
accuse *v* suçlamak
accustom *v* alıştırmak
ace *n* as
ache *n* ağrı
achieve *v* başarmak
achievement *n* başarı
acid *n* asit
acidity *n* asitlik
acknowledge *v* kabul etmek
acorn *n* meşe palamudu
acoustic *adj* akustik
acquaint *v* haberdar olmak
acquaintance *n* haberdar
acquire *v* elde etmek
acquisition *n* kazanım
acquit *v* aklamak
acquittal *n* beraat
acre *n* akre
acrobat *n* akrobat
across *pre* öbür tarafına
act *v* davranmak
action *n* eylem
activate *v* etkinleştirmek
activation *n* etkinleştirme
active *adj* faal
activity *n* faaliyet
actor *n* aktör
actress *n* aktris

actual *adj* asıl
actually *adv* aslında
acute *adj* keskin; akut
adamant *adj* kararlı
adapt *v* uyarlamak
adaptable *adj* uyarlanabilen
adaptation *n* adaptasyon
adapter *n* adaptör
add *v* eklemek
addicted *adj* bağımlı
addiction *n* bağımlılık
addition *n* ekleme
additional *adj* ek
address *n* adres
address *v* hitap etmek
addressee *n* muhatap
adequate *adj* yeterli
adhere *v* e yapışmak
adhesive *adj* yapışkan
adjacent *adj* bitişik
adjective *n* sıfat
adjoin *v* bitiştirmek
adjoining *adj* yanyana
adjourn *v* sona ermek
adjust *v* düzenlemek
adjustable *adj* düzenlenebilir
adjustment *n* düzenleme
administer *v* yönetmek
admirable *adj* takdire değer
admiral *n* amiral
admiration *n* takdir
admire *v* beğenmek
admirer *n* hayran
admissible *adj* makbul
admission *n* kabul; itiraf
admit *v* kabul etmek
admittance *n* kabul
admonish *v* tembih etmek
admonition *n* tembih
adolescence *n* ergenlik
adolescent *n* ergen
adopt *v* edinmek
adoption *n* benimseme
adoptive *adj* üvey
adorable *adj* tapılası
adoration *n* tapınma
adore *v* tapmak
adorn *v* süslemek
adrift *adv* sürüklenmiş
adulation *n* dalkavukluk
adult *n* yetişkin
adulterate *v* karıştırmak
adultery *n* zina
advance *v* ilerlemek
advance *n* ilerleme
advantage *n* avantaj

Advent *n* Advent
adventure *n* macera
adverb *n* zarf
adversary *n* düşman
adverse *adj* karşıt
adversity *n* zorluk
advertising *n* tanıtım
advice *n* nasihat
advisable *adj* makul
advise *v* tavsiye etmek
adviser *n* danışman
advocate *v* savunmak
aeroplane *n* uçak
aesthetic *adj* estetik
afar *adv* uzakta
affable *adj* cana yakın
affair *n* iş; aşk ilişkisi
affect *v* etkilemek
affection *n* düşkünlük
affectionate *adj* düşkün
affiliate *v* birleştirmek
affiliation *n* yakın ilişki
affinity *n* benzerlik
affirm *v* doğrulamak
affirmative *adj* olumlu
affix *v* sonek
afflict *v* acı vermek
affliction *n* dert
affluence *n* refah
affluent *adj* zengin
afford *v* karşılamak
affordable *adj* karşılanabilir
affront *v* hakaret etmek
affront *n* hakaret
afloat *adv* yüzen
afraid *adj* korkmuş
afresh *adv* yeniden
after *pre* sonra
afternoon *n* öğleden sonra
afterwards *adv* daha sonra
again *adv* tekrar
against *pre* karşı
age *n* yaş
agency *n* ajans
agenda *n* ajanda
agent *n* ajan
agglomerate *v* yığışmak
aggravate *v* kötüleştirmek
aggravation *n* kötüleştirme
aggregate *v* toplamak
aggression *n* toplanma
aggressive *adj* saldırgan
aggressor *n* saldırgan
aghast *adj* donakalmış
agile *adj* çevik
agitator *n* kışkırtıcı

agnostic *n* bilinemezci
agonize *v* ıstırap çekmek
agonizing *adj* ıstırap verici
agony *n* ıstırap
agree *v* anlaşmak
agreeable *adj* uygun
agreement *n* anlaşma
agricultural *adj* tarımsal
agriculture *n* tarım
ahead *pre* ileride
aid *n* yardım
aid *v* yardımcı olmak
aide *n* yardımcı
ailing *adj* rahatsız
ailment *n* hastalık
aim *v* amaçlamak
aimless *adj* amaçsız
air *n* hava
air *v* havalandırmak
aircraft *n* uçak
airfare *n* uçuş ücreti
airfield *n* havaalanı
airline *n* havayolu
airliner *n* yolcu uçağı
airmail *n* uçak postası
airplane *n* uçak
airport *n* havalimanı
airspace *n* hava boşluğu
airstrip *n* uçak pisti
airtight *adj* hava geçirmez
aisle *n* koridor
ajar *adj* aralık
akin *adj* benzer
alarm *n* alarm
alarm clock *n* çalar saat
alarming *adj* endişe verici
alcoholic *adj* alkolik
alcoholism *n* alkolizm
alert *n* uyarı
alert *v* uyarmak
algebra *n* cebir
alien *n* yabancı
alight *adv* yanan
align *v* hizaya getirmek
alignment *n* hiza
alike *adj* benzer
alive *adj* canlı
all *adj* hepsi
allegation *n* iddia
allege *v* iddia etmek
allegedly *adv* sözde
allegiance *n* sadakat
allegory *n* kinaye
allergic *adj* alerjik
allergy *n* alerji
alleviate *v* azaltmak

alley *n* patika
alliance *n* ittifak
allied *adj* müttefik
alligator *n* timsah
allocate *v* ayırmak
allot *v* pay etmek
allotment *n* tahis
allow *v* izin vermek
allowance *n* harçlık
alloy *n* alaşım
allure *n* cazibe
alluring *adj* cazibeli
allusion *n* ima
ally *n* müttefik
ally *v* ittifak etmek
almanac *n* almanak
almighty *adj* yüce
almond *n* badem
almost *adv* neredeyse
alms *n* sadaka
alone *adj* yalnız
along *pre* yanında
aloof *adj* ilgisiz; soğuk
aloud *adv* yüksek ses
alphabet *n* alfabe
already *adv* zaten
alright *adv* peki
also *adv* bir de
altar *n* sunak
alter *v* değiştirmek
alteration *n* değişim
altercation *n* çekişme
alternate *adj* karşılıklı
alternative *n* alternatif
although *c* rağmen
altitude *n* yükseklik
altogether *adj* hep beraber
aluminum *n* alüminyum
always *adv* her zaman
amass *v* yığmak
amateur *adj* amatör
amaze *v* şaşırtmak
amazement *n* hayret
amazing *adj* şaşırtıcı
ambassador *n* büyükelçi
ambiguous *adj* belirsiz
ambition *n* hırs
ambitious *adj* hırslı
ambivalent *adj* kararsız
ambulance *n* ambulans
ambush *v* pusuya düşürmek
amenable *adj* uysal
amend *v* düzeltmek
amendment *n* düzeltme
amenities *n* rahatlıklar
American *adj* Amerikan

amiable *adj* sevimli
amicable *adj* dostane
amid *pre* ortasına
ammonia *n* amonyak
ammunition *n* cephane
amnesia *n* hafıza kaybı
amnesty *n* genel af
among *pre* arasında
amoral *adj* ahlak dışı
amorphous *adj* şekilsiz
amortize *v* amorti etmek
amount *n* miktar
amount to *v* kadar etmek
amphibious *adj* amfibi
amphitheater *n* amfiteatr
ample *adj* bol
amplifier *n* yükselteç
amplify *v* yükseltmek
amputate *v* ampute etmek
amputation *n* amputasyon
amuse *v* eğlendirmek
amusement *n* eğlence
amusing *adj* eğlenceli
an *a* bir
analogy *n* analoji
analysis *n* analiz
analyze *v* analiz etmek
anarchist *n* anarşist
anarchy *n* anarşi
anatomy *n* anatomi
ancestor *n* ata
ancestry *n* soy
anchor *n* çapa
anchovy *n* ancüez
ancient *adj* antik
and *c* ve
anecdote *n* anekdot
anemia *n* anemi
anemic *adj* anemik
anesthesia *n* anestezi
anew *adv* yeniden
angel *n* melek
angelic *adj* meleksi
anger *v* sinirlenmek
anger *n* sinir
angina *n* anjin
angle *n* açı
Anglican *adj* Anglikan
angry *adj* sinirli
anguish *n* ıstırap
animal *n* hayvan
animate *v* canlandırmak
animation *n* animasyon
animosity *n* husumet
ankle *n* ayak bileği
annex *n* ilhak

annexation *n* istila
annihilate *v* imha etmek
annihilation *n* imha
anniversary *n* yıldönümü
annotate *v* not eklemek
annotation *n* açıklayıcı not
announce *v* duyurmak
announcement *n* duyuru
announcer *n* sunucu
annoy *v* kızdırmak
annoying *adj* kızdırıcı
annual *adj* yıllık
annul *v* feshetmek
annulment *n* fesih
anoint *v* yağlamak
anonymity *n* yazarı bilinmeyiş
anonymous *adj* anonim
another *adj* başka
answer *v* cevaplamak
answer *n* cevap
ant *n* karınca
antagonize *v* düşman etmek
antecedent *n* önce gelen
antecedents *n* atalar
antelope *n* antilop
antenna *n* anten
anthem *n* marş
antibiotic *n* antibiyotik
anticipate *v* beklemek
anticipation *n* beklenti
antidote *n* panzehir; antidot
antipathy *n* antipati
antiquated *adj* çağdışı
antiquity *n* antikite
anvil *n* örs
anxiety *n* endişe
anxious *adj* endişeli
any *adj* herhangi bir
anybody *pro* kimse
anyhow *pro* bir şekilde
anyone *pro* hiç biri
anything *pro* herhangi bir şey
apart *adv* ayrı
apartment *n* apartman
apathy *n* ilgisizlik
ape *n* maymun
aperitif *n* aperitif
apex *n* zirve
aphrodisiac *adj* afrodizyak
apiece *adv* parça başına
apocalypse *n* kıyamet
apologize *v* özür dilemek
apology *n* özür
apostle *n* havari
apostolic *adj* papaya ait
apostrophe *n* kesme işareti

appall *v* dehşete düşmek
appalling *adj* dehşet verici
apparel *n* kuşam
apparent *adj* belli
apparently *adv* belli ki
apparition *n* hayalet
appeal *n* temyiz; cazibe
appeal *v* temyiz etmek
appealing *adj* cazip
appear *v* görünmek
appearance *n* görünüm
appease *v* yatıştırmak
appeasement *n* yatıştırma
appendicitis *n* apandisit
appendix *n* apandis
appetite *n* iştah
appetizer *n* meze
applaud *v* alkışlamak
applause *n* alkış
apple *n* elma
appliance *n* cihaz
applicable *adj* uygulanabilir
applicant *n* aday
application *n* uygulama
apply *v* uygulamak
apply for *v* müracaat etmek
appoint *v* tayin etmek
appointment *n* atama; randevu
appraisal *n* kıymet tahmini
appraise *v* değer biçmek
appreciate *v* takdir etmek
appreciation *n* takdir etmek
apprehend *v* idrak etmek
apprehensive *adj* evhamlı
apprentice *n* çırak
approach *v* yakınlaşmak
approach *n* yakınlaşma
approachable *adj* yaklaşılabilir
approbation *n* tasvip
appropriate *adj* uygun
approval *n* onay
approve *v* onaylamak
approximate *adj* yaklaşık
apricot *n* kayısı
April *n* Nisan
apron *n* önlük
aptitude *n* kabiliyet
aquarium *n* akvaryum
aquatic *adj* suda yaşayan
aqueduct *n* sukemeri
Arabic *adj* Arap
arable *adj* tarıma elverişli
arbiter *n* arabulucu
arbitrary *adj* keyfi
arbitration *n* hakemlik
arc *n* yay

arch *n* kemer
archaeology *n* arkeoloji
archaic *adj* arkaik
archbishop *n* başpiskopos
architect *n* mimar
architecture *n* mimari
archive *n* arşiv
arctic *adj* arktik
ardent *adj* gayretli
ardor *n* gayret
arduous *adj* güç
area *n* alan
arena *n* arena; saha
argue *v* tartışmak
argument *n* tartışma
arid *adj* kuru
arise *iv* ortaya çıkmak
aristocracy *n* aristokrasi
aristocrat *n* aristokrat
arithmetic *n* aritmetik
ark *n* sandık
arm *n* kol; silah
arm *v* silahlanmak
armaments *n* silahlanma
armchair *n* koltuk
armed *adj* silahlı
armistice *n* ateşkes
armor *n* zırh
armpit *n* koltukaltı
army *n* ordu
aromatic *adj* aromatik
around *pre* etrafında
arouse *v* ortaya çıktı
arrange *v* düzenlemek
arrangement *n* düzenleme
array *n* düzen
arrest *v* tutuklamak
arrest *n* tutuklama
arrival *n* varış
arrive *v* varmak
arrogance *n* kibir
arrogant *adj* kibirli
arrow *n* ok
arsenal *n* cephanelik
arsenic *n* arsenik
arson *n* kundakçılık
arsonist *n* kundakçı
art *n* sanat
artery *n* atardamar
arthritis *n* artrit
artichoke *n* enginar
article *n* makale
articulate *v* ifade etmek
articulation *n* anlaşılır
artificial *adj* yapay
artillery *n* ağır silah

artisan *n* artizan
artist *n* sanatçı
artistic *adj* artistik
artwork *n* sanat çalışması
as *c* olarak
as *adv* gibi
ascend *v* yukarı çıkmak
ascendancy *n* hüküm
ascertain *v* keşfetmek
ascetic *adj* sofu
ash *n* kül; dilbudak ağacı
ashamed *adj* mahcup
ashore *adv* kıyıda
ashtray *n* küllük; tabla
aside *adv* kenara
aside from *adv* dışında
ask *v* sormak; istemek
asleep *adj* uykuda
asparagus *n* kuşkonmaz
aspect *n* görünüş
asphalt *n* asfalt
asphyxiate *v* boğmak
asphyxiation *n* boğulma
aspiration *n* nefes almak
aspire *v* talip olmak
aspirin *n* aspirin
assail *v* saldırmak
assailant *n* saldırgan
assassin *n* suikastçı
assassinate *v* öldürmek
assassination *n* suikast
assault *n* saldırı
assault *v* saldırmak
assemble *v* toplanmak
assembly *n* toplantı; montaj
assent *v* razı olmak
assert *v* öne sürmek
assertion *n* iddia
assess *v* talep etmek
assessment *n* değerlendirme
asset *n* mal
assets *n* malvarlıkları
assign *v* tayin etmek
assignment *n* tayin
assimilate *v* asimile etmek
assimilation *n* asimilasyon
assist *v* yardım etmek
assistance *n* yardım
associate *v* ilişkilendirmek
association *n* ilişki; dernek
assorted *adj* çeşitli
assortment *n* karışım
assume *v* varsaymak
assumption *n* varsayım
assurance *n* güvence
assure *v* temin etmek

asterisk *n* yıldız imi
asteroid *n* asteroit
asthma *n* astım
asthmatic *adj* astımlı
astonish *v* şaşırtmak
astonishing *adj* şaşırtıcı
astound *v* şoke etmek
astounding *adj* hayret verici
astray *v* doğru yoldan sapmış
astrologer *n* astrolog
astrology *n* astroloji
astronaut *n* astronot
astronomer *n* astronom
astronomic *adj* astronomik
astronomy *n* astronomi
astute *adj* kurnaz
asunder *adv* parçalar halinde
asylum *n* akıl hastanesi
at *pre* de; da
atheism *n* ateizm
atheist *n* ateist
athlete *n* atlet
athletic *adj* atletik
atmosphere *n* atmosfer
atmospheric *adj* atmosferik
atom *n* atom
atomic *adj* atomik
atone *v* kefaret etmek
atonement *n* kefaret
atrocious *adj* zalim
atrocity *n* vahşet
atrophy *v* körelmek
attach *v* iliştirmek
attached *adj* ilişik
attachment *n* ek; bağlılık
attack *n* saldırı
attack *v* saldırmak
attacker *n* saldırgan
attain *v* ulaşmak
attainable *adj* ulaşılır
attainment *n* ulaş
attempt *v* teşebbüs etmek
attempt *n* teşebbüs
attend *v* katılmak
attendance *n* katılım
attendant *n* görevli
attention *n* uyarı
attentive *adj* dikkatli
attenuate *v* hafifletmek
attenuating *adj* hafifletici
attest *v* doğrulamak
attic *n* tavanarası
attitude *n* tutum
attorney *n* vukat
attract *v* cezbetmek
attraction *n* cazibe

attractive *adj* çekici
attribute *v* vasıf
auction *n* müzayede
auctioneer *n* mezatçi
audacious *adj* yürekli
audacity *n* cesaret
audible *adj* duyulur
audience *n* seyirci
audit *v* denetlemek
auditorium *n* toplantı salonu
augment *v* ilave
August *n* Ağustos
aunt *n* hala; teyze
auspicious *adj* hayırlı
austere *adj* sade
austerity *n* sadelik
authentic *adj* otantik
authenticate *v* belgelemek
authenticity *n* otantiklik
author *n* yazar
authoritarian *adj* otoriter
authority *n* otorite
authorization *n* yetki; izin
authorize *v* yetkilendirmek
auto *n* oto
autograph *n* imza
automatic *adj* otomatik
automobile *n* otomobil
autonomous *adj* otonom
autonomy *n* otonomi
autopsy *n* otopsi
autumn *n* Sonbahar
auxiliary *adj* yardımcı
avail *v* fayda
availability *n* kullanılırlık
available *adj* mevcut
avalanche *n* heyelan
avarice *n* para hırsı
avaricious *adj* tamahkar
avenge *v* intikam almak
avenue *n* cadde
average *n* ortalama
averse *adj* isteksiz
aversion *n* isteksizlik
avert *v* yön değiştirmek
aviation *n* havacılık
aviator *n* havacı
avid *adj* coşkun
avoidable *adj* kaçınılabilir
avowed *adj* tasdikli
await *v* gözlemek
awake *iv* uyandırmak
awake *adj* uyanık
awakening *n* uyanış
award *v* ödüllendirmek
award *n* ödül

aware *adj* farkında
awareness *n* farkındalık
away *adv* uzakta
awe *n* huşu
awesome *adj* korkunç
awful *adj* berbat
awkward *adj* uygunsuz
awning *n* tente
ax *n* balta
axiom *n* belit
axis *n* eksen
axle *n* dingil

B

babble *v* gevezelik etmek
baby *n* bebek
babysitter *n* çocuk bakıcısı
bachelor *n* bekar
back *n* arka
back *adv* arkasında
back *v* desteklemek
back down *v* boyun eğmek
back up *v* desteklemek
backbone *n* omurga
backdoor *n* arka kapı; yasadışı
backfire *v* geri tepmek
background *n* arkaplan
backing *n* destek
backlash *n* geri tepme
backlog *n* birikim
backpack *n* sırt çantası
backup *n* yedek
backward *adj* arkaya doğru
backwards *adv* arkaya doğru
backyard *n* avlu
bacon *n* domuz pastırması
bacteria *n* bakteri
bad *adj* kötü
badge *n* rozet
badly *adv* kötü bir şekilde
baffle *v* şaşırtmak
bag *n* çanta
baggage *n* bagaj
baggy *adj* bol; sarkık
baguette *n* baget
bail *n* kefalet
bailiff *n* mübaşir
bait *n* yem
bake *v* fırında pişirmek
baker *n* fırıncı
bakery *n* fırın
balance *v* dengelemek

balance *n* denge; bakiye
balcony *n* balkon
bald *adj* kel
bale *n* balya; denek
ball *n* top; balo
balloon *n* balon
ballot *n* oy pusulası
ballroom *n* dans balo salonu
balm *n* merhem
balmy *adj* yumuşak; iyileştirici
bamboo *n* bambu
ban *n* yasak
ban *v* yasaklamak
banality *n* bayağı
banana *n* muz
band *n* band; müzik grubu
bandage *n* bandaj
bandage *v* bandajlamak
bang *v* vurmak
bandit *n* haydut
banish *v* sürgüne yollamak
banishment *n* sürgün
bank *n* bank
bankrupt *v* iflas etmek
bankrupt *adj* iflas etmiş
bankruptcy *n* iflas
banner *n* ilan; bayrak
banquet *n* ziyafet
baptism *n* vaftiz
baptize *v* vaftiz etmek
bar *n* bar; çubuk
bar *v* sokmamak
barbarian *n* barbar
barbaric *adj* barbarca
barbarism *n* barbarlık
barbecue *n* mangal
barber *n* berber
bare *adj* çıplak; açık
barefoot *adj* çıplak ayak
barely *adv* güçbela
bargain *n* pazarlık
bargain *v* pazarlık etmek
bargaining *n* ucuz fiyat
barge *n* mavna
bark *v* havlamak
bark *n* hav hav; çığırtkanlık
barley *n* arpa
barmaid *n* bayan barmen
barman *n* barmen
barn *n* ahır
barometer *n* barometre
barracks *n* kışla
barrage *n* baraj
barrel *n* fıçı
barren *adj* meyvesiz; çorak
barricade *n* barikat

barrier *n* bariyer
barring *pre* haricinde
bartender *n* barmen
barter *v* takas yapmak
base *n* temel
base *v* dayanmak
baseball *n* beyzbol
baseless *adj* asılsız; temelsiz
basement *n* bodrum; zemin
bashful *adj* utangaç
basic *adj* temel
basics *n* temel bilgiler
basin *n* leğen
basis *n* kaynak
bask *v* güneşlenmek
basket *n* sepet
basketball *n* basketbol
bastard *n* piç
bat *n* yarasa; sopa
batch *n* yığın
bath *n* banyo
bathe *v* banyo yapmak
bathrobe *n* bornoz
bathroom *n* banyo
bathtub *n* banyo küveti
baton *n* değnek; baton
battalion *n* tabur
batter *v* dövmek
battery *n* pil
battle *n* savaş
battle *v* savaşmak
battleship *n* savaş gemisi
bay *n* körfez
bayonet *n* süngü
bazaar *n* pazar
be *iv* olmak
be born *v* doğmak
beach *n* plaj
beacon *n* fener
beak *n* gaga
beam *n* ışın
bean *n* fasulye
bear *n* ayı
bear *iv* dayanmak; taşımak
bearable *adj* dayanılır
beard *n* sakal
bearded *adj* sakallı
bearer *n* taşıyıcı
beast *n* canavar
beat *iv* dövmek; yenmek
beat *n* vuruş; ritm
beaten *adj* mağlup
beating *n* yenilgi; mağlubiyet
beautiful *adj* güzel
beautify *v* güzelleştirmek
beauty *n* güzellik

beaver *n* kunduz
because *c* çünkü
because of *pre* nedeniyle
beckon *v* işaretle çağırmak
become *iv* olmak
bed *n* yatak; nehir yatağı
bedding *n* yatak takımı
bedroom *n* yatak odası
bedspread *n* yatak örtüsü
bee *n* arı
beef *n* sığır eti
beef up *v* yakınmak
beehive *n* arı kovanı
beer *n* bira
beet *n* pancar
beetle *n* böcek
before *adv* önce
before *pre* önce
beforehand *adv* önceden
befriend *v* arkadaş olmak
beg *v* yalvarmak
beggar *n* dilenci
begin *iv* başlamak
beginner *n* acemi
beginning *n* başlangıç
beguile *v* aklını çelmek
behalf (on) *adv* birinin namına
behave *v* davranmak
behavior *n* davranış
behead *v* başını kesmek
behind *pre* arkasında
behold *iv* dikkatle bakmak
being *n* varlık
belated *adj* geç kalmış
belch *v* geğirmek
belch *n* geğirti
belfry *n* çan kulesi
Belgian *adj* Belçikalı
Belgium *n* Belçika
belief *n* inanç
believable *adj* inanılır
believe *v* inanmak
believer *n* inanan; mümin
belittle *v* küçümsemek
bell *n* zil; çan
bell pepper *n* dolmalık biber
belligerent *adj* kavgacı
belly *n* göbek
belly button *n* göbek deliği
belong *v* ait olmak
belongings *n* eşyalar
beloved *adj* sevgili; aziz
below *adv* altında
below *pre* aşağısında
belt *n* kemer
bench *n* bank; benç

bend *iv* eğmek
bend down *v* aşağıya eğilmek
beneath *pre* altında; sonda
benediction *n* kutsama
benefactor *n* bağışçı
beneficial *adj* yararlı
beneficiary *n* faydalanan kişi
benefit *n* fayda
benefit *v* faydası olmak
benevolence *n* iyi niyet
benevolent *adj* iyi niyetli
benign *adj* iyi kalpli
bequeath *v* vasiyet etmek
bereavement *n* matem
beret *n* bere
berserk *adv* çılgına dönmüş
berth *n* ranza
beseech *iv* yalvarmak
beset *iv* etrafını sarmak
beside *pre* yanında
besides *pre* bunun yanında
besiege *iv* kuşatmak
best *adj* en iyi
best man *n* sağdıç
bestial *adj* hayvani
bestow *v* armağan etmek
bet *iv* bahse girmek
bet *n* bahis
betray *v* aldatmak
betrayal *n* ihanet
better *adj* daha iyi
between *pre* arasında
beverage *n* içecek
beware *v* sakınmak
bewilder *v* şaşırtmak
bewitch *v* büyü yapmak
beyond *adv* ardında
bias *n* önyargı
bible *n* incil
biblical *adj* incilden
bibliography *n* kaynakça
bicycle *n* bisiklet
bid *n* fiyat teklifi
big *adj* büyük
bigamy *n* ikieşlilik
bigot *adj* bağnaz; yobaz
bigotry *n* yobazlık
bike *n* bisiklet
bile *n* garaz
bilingual *adj* iki dilli
bill *n* fatura; gaga
billion *n* milyar
billionaire *n* milyarder
billiards *n* bilardo
bimonthly *adj* iki ayda bir
bin *n* çöp

bind *iv* bağlamak
binding *adj* zorlayıcı; geçerli
binoculars *n* dürbün
biography *n* biyografi
biological *adj* biyolojik
biology *n* biyoloji
bird *n* kuş
birth *n* doğum
birthday *n* doğum günü
biscuit *n* bisküvi
bishop *n* piskopos
bison *n* bizon
bit *n* parça; kücük kısım
bite *iv* ısırmak
bite *n* ısırık; lokma
bitter *adj* acı
bitterly *adv* acı; keskin
bitterness *n* acılık
bizarre *adj* acayip
black *adj* siyah
blackberry *n* böğürtlen
blackboard *n* karatahta
blackmail *n* şantaj
blackmail *v* şantaj yapmak
blackness *n* karalık
blackout *n* elektrik kesintisi
blacksmith *n* demirci
bladder *n* mesane
blade *n* kılıç
blame *n* kınama
blame *v* suçlamak
blameless *adj* suçsuz
bland *adj* mülayim
blank *adj* boş
blanket *n* battaniye
blasphemy *n* tanrıya küfür
blast *n* infilak
blaze *v* parlamak
bleach *v* ağartmak
bleach *n* beyazlatıcı
bleak *adj* kasvetli
bleed *iv* kanamak
bleeding *n* kanayan
blemish *n* kusur
blemish *v* lekelemek
blend *n* harman
blend *v* harmanlamak
blender *n* mikser
bless *v* kutsamak
blessed *adj* kutsanmış
blessing *n* kutsama
blind *v* göz kamaştırmak
blind *adj* kör; âmâ
blindfold *n* gözleri bağlı
blindly *adv* kör gibi
blindness *n* gözü kapalı

blink *v* göz kırpmak
bliss *n* neşe
blissful *adj* neşeli
blister *n* kabarcık
blizzard *n* tipi
bloat *v* şişirmek
bloated *adj* şiş
block *n* büyük parça; blok
block *v* bloke etmek
blockade *v* abluka etmek
blockade *n* abluka
blockage *n* tıkanma
blond *adj* sarışın
blood *n* kan
bloodthirsty *adj* kana susamış
bloody *adj* kanlı
bloom *v* çiçek açmak
blossom *v* çiçeklenmek
blot *n* kusur
blot *v* lekelemek
blouse *n* bluz
blow *n* esinti
blow *iv* esmek; üflemek
blow out *iv* üfleyip söndürmek
blow up *iv* patlatmak
blowout *n* lastik patlaması
bludgeon *v* coplamak
blue *adj* mavi
blueprint *n* mavi kopya
bluff *v* blöf yapmak
blunder *n* gaf
blunt *adj* körelmiş; dobra
bluntness *n* körlük; pervasız
blur *v* bulanıklaştırmak
blurred *adj* bulanık
blush *v* yüzü kızarmak
blush *n* pembeleşmiş
boar *n* yabandomuzu
board *n* tahta; yönetim kurulu
board *v* yemek vermek; binmek
boast *v* böbürlenmek
boat *n* gemi
bodily *adj* maddi
body *n* beden; kütle
bog *n* bataklık
bog down *v* çıkmaza girmek
boil *v* kaynamak
boil down to *v* anlamına gelmek
boil over *v* taşmak
boiler *n* kazan
boisterous *adj* gürültülü
bold *adj* koyu; cesur
boldness *n* koyuluk; cüret
bolster *v* minder
bolt *n* sürgü; cıvata
bolt *v* sürgülemek

bomb *n* bomba
bomb *v* bombalamak
bombing *n* bombalama
bombshell *n* bomba mermisi
bond *n* senet; bono
bondage *n* kölelik
bone *n* kemik
bone marrow *n* kemik iliği
bonfire *n* şenlik ateşi
bonus *n* bonus
book *n* kitap
bookcase *n* kitaplık
bookkeeper *n* muhasebeci
bookkeeping *n* muhasebe
booklet *n* kitapçık
bookseller *n* kitapçı
bookstore *n* kitap evi
boom *n* gümbürtü; çıkış
boom *v* gümbürdemek
boost *v* güçlendirmek
boost *n* kuvvet
boot *n* çizme
booth *n* çadır; kabin
booty *n* ganimet
booze *n* içki
border *n* hudut; kenar
border on *v* ulaşmak
borderline *adj* sınır
bore *v* usandırmak
bored *adj* bıkkın
boredom *n* bıkkınlık
boring *adj* sıkıcı
born *adj* doğmuş
borough *n* kasaba
borrow *v* ödünç almak
bosom *n* bağır
boss *n* patron
bossy *adj* amirane
botany *n* botanik
botch *v* berbat etmek
both *adj* her ikisi de
bother *v* uğraşmak
bothersome *adj* uğraştırıcı
bottle *n* şişe
bottle *v* şişelemek
bottleneck *n* dar geçit
bottom *n* alt
bottomless *adj* dipsiz
bough *n* dal
boulder *n* kaya
boulevard *n* bulvar
bounce *v* yansıma
bounce *n* sıçramak
bound *adj* gidici
bound for *adj* gitmek üzere
boundary *n* sınır

boundless *adj* sınırsız
bounty *n* cömertlik
bourgeois *adj* burjuva
bow *n* reverans; yay
bow *v* reverans yapmak
bow out *v* başından savmak
bowels *n* bağırsaklar
bowl *n* kase; çanak
box *n* kutu
boxer *n* bokser
boxing *n* boks
box office *n* gişe
boy *n* oğlan
boycott *v* boykot etmek
boyfriend *n* erkek arkadaş
boyhood *n* erkeklik
bra *n* sütyen
brace for *v* sağlamlaştırmak
bracelet *n* bilezik
bracket *n* ayraç
brag *v* yüksekten atmak
braid *n* kordon
brain *n* beyin
brainwash *v* beyin yıkamak
brake *n* fren
brake *v* frenlemek
branch *n* dal
branch office *n* şube
branch out *v* dal salmak
brand *n* marka
brand-new *adj* yepizyeni
brandy *n* konyak
brat *n* afacan
brave *adj* cesur
bravely *adv* cesurca
bravery *n* yiğitlik
brawl *n* arbede
breach *n* ihlal; yarık
bread *n* ekmek
breadth *n* genişlik
break *n* aralık; şans
break *iv* kırmak
break away *v* ayrılmak
break down *v* bozulmak
break free *v* kaçmak
break in *v* hırsızlık yapmak
break off *v* bozmak; kesmek
break open *v* kırıp açmak
break up *v* ayrılmak
break out *v* patlak vermek
breakable *adj* kırılır
breakdown *n* sinir bozukluğu
breakfast *n* kahvaltı
breakthrough *n* büyük buluş
breast *n* göğüs
breath *n* nefes

breathe *v* nefes almak
breathing *n* nefes alma
breathtaking *adj* nefes kesici
breed *iv* üremek; yol açmak
breed *n* cins; damızlık
breeze *n* meltem
brethren *n* din kardeşi
brevity *n* kısalık; özlük
brew *v* demlemek
brewery *n* birahane
bribe *v* rüşvet vermek
bribe *n* rüşvet
bribery *n* rüşvet
brick *n* tuğla
bricklayer *n* duvarcı
bridal *adj* düğüne ait
bride *n* gelin
bridegroom *n* damat
bridesmaid *n* nedime
bridge *n* köprü
bridle *n* at başlığı
brief *adj* özlü
brief *v* özetlemek
briefcase *n* evrak çantası
briefing *n* brifing
briefly *adv* kısaca
briefs *n* özet
brigade *n* tugay
bright *adj* parlak
brighten *v* parlatmak
brightness *n* parlaklık
brilliant *adj* mükemmel
brim *n* bardak ağzı
bring *iv* getirmek
bring back *v* geri getirmek
bring down *v* kibrini kırmak
bring up *v* yetiştirmek
brink *n* eşik
brisk *adj* hareketli
Britain *n* Britanya
British *adj* Britanyalı
brittle *adj* kırılgan
broad *adj* engin
broadcast *v* yayımlamak
broadcast *n* yayın
broadcaster *n* yayımcı
broaden *v* genişletmek
broadly *adv* genişçe
broadminded *adj* geniş görüşlü
brochure *n* broşür
broil *v* ızgara yapmak
broiler *n* ızgara
broke *adj* beş parasız
broken *adj* kırık
bronchitis *n* bronşit
bronze *n* bronz

broom *n* süpürge
broth *n* etsuyu
brothel *n* genelev
brother *n* kardeş; abi
brotherhood *n* kardeşlik
brother-in-law *n* kayınbirader
brotherly *adj* kardeşçe
brow *n* kaş
brown *adj* kahverengi
browse *v* göz atmak
browser *n* listeleyici
bruise *n* bere; ezik
bruise *v* berelemek
brunch *n* geç kahvaltı
brunette *adj* kumral
brush *n* fırça
brush *v* fırçalamak
brush aside *v* önemsememek
brush up *v* tazelemek
brusque *adj* düşüncesiz
brutal *adj* zorba
brutality *n* zorbalık
brutalize *v* zorbalık etmek
brute *adj* hayvan
bubble *n* kabarcık
bubble gum *n* sakız
buck *n* antilop
bucket *n* kova
buckle *n* toka
buckle up *v* bağlamak
bud *n* tomurcuk; varlık
buddy *n* ahbap
budge *v* kımıldamak
budget *n* bütçe
buffalo *n* bufalo
bug *n* böcek
bug *v* can sıkmak
build *iv* inşaa etmek
builder *n* inşaat işçisi
building *n* inşaat
buildup *n* büyüme
built-in *adj* yerleşik
bulb *n* ampul
bulge *n* bel vermek
bulk *n* yığın; hacim
bulky *adj* hacimli
bull *n* boğa
bullet *n* kurşun
bulletin *n* tebliğ; bildiri
bull fight *n* boğa güreşi
bull fighter *n* boğa güreşçisi
bully *adj* zorba
bulwark *n* siper
bum *n* kıç; serseri
bump *n* şiş; darbe
bump into *v* karşılaşmak

bumper *n* tampon
bumpy *adj* tümsekli
bun *n* sıkıntı; çörek
bunch *n* salkım
bundle *n* bohça
bundle *v* bohçalamak
bunk bed *n* ranza
bunker *n* yeraltı sığınağı
buoy *n* şamandıra
burden *n* yük
burden *v* yüklemek
burdensome *adj* yüklü
bureau *n* büro
bureaucracy *n* bürokrasi
bureaucrat *n* bürokrat
burger *n* hamburger
burglar *n* hırsız
burglarize *v* hırsızlık yapmak
burglary *n* hırsızlık
burial *n* cenaze töreni
burly *adj* iriyarı
burn *iv* yanmak
burn *n* yanık
burp *v* geğirmek
burp *n* geğirti
burrow *n* oyuk
burst *iv* patlamak
burst into *v* aceleyle girmek
bury *v* gömmek
bus *n* otobüs
bus *v* otobüsle götürmek
bush *n* çalı
busily *adv* meşgul
business *n* iş
businessman *n* iş adamı
bust *n* büst
bustling *adj* telaşlı
busy *adj* meşgul
but *c* ama
butcher *n* kasap
butchery *n* mezbaha
butler *n* kilerci
butt *n* göt; kurban
butter *n* tereyağı
butterfly *n* kelebek
button *n* düğme
buttonhole *n* düğme iliği
buy *iv* satın almak
buy off *v* para yedirmek
buyer *n* müşteri
buzz *n* vızıltı
buzz *v* vızıldamak
buzzard *n* akbaba
buzzer *n* vızıldayan alet
by *pre* yanında; yakın
bye *e* eyvallah

bypass *n* güle güle
bypass *v* atlamak
by-product *n* yan ürün
bystander *n* seyirci kalan

C

cab *n* taksi
cabbage *n* lahana
cabin *n* kabin
cabinet *n* dolap; kabine
cable *n* kablo
cafeteria *n* kafeterya
caffeine *n* kafein
cage *n* kafes
cake *n* kek; pasta
calamity *n* felaket
calculate *v* hesaplamak
calculation *n* hesaplama
calculator *n* hesap makinesi
calendar *n* takvim
calf *n* dana
caliber *n* kalibre
calibrate *v* ayarlamak
call *n* çağrı; deklare
call *v* aramak; istemek
call off *v* iptal etmek
call on *v* uğramak
call out *v* devreye sokmak
calling *n* lüzum; davet
callous *adj* hissiz
calm *adj* sakin
calm *n* sakin
calm down *v* sakinleşmek
calorie *n* kalori
calumny *n* iftira
camel *n* deve
camera *n* fotoğraf makinesi
camouflage *v* kamufle etmek
camouflage *n* kamuflaj
camp *n* kamp
camp *v* kamp yapmak
campaign *n* kampanya
campfire *n* kamp ateşi
can *iv* yapabilmek
can *v* yapabilmek
can *n* teneke kutu
canal *n* kanal
canary *n* kanarya
cancel *v* iptal etmek
cancellation *n* iptal
cancer *n* kanser
cancerous *adj* kanser

candid *adj* dürüst
candidacy *n* adaylık
candidate *n* aday
candle *n* mum
candlestick *n* mum
candor *n* tarafsızlık
candy *n* şekerleme
cane *n* baston; silah
canister *n* teneke kuru
canned *adj* konserve
cannibal *n* yamyam
cannon *n* toplu silah
canoe *n* kano
canonize *v* aziz saymak
cantaloupe *n* kavun
canteen *n* kantin
canvas *n* çadır bezi; tuval
canyon *n* kanyon
cap *n* kapak; doruk
capability *n* yetenek
capable *adj* yetenekli
capacity *n* kapasite
cape *n* pelerin; burun
capital *n* başkent; sermaye
capital letter *n* büyük harf
capitalism *n* kapitalizm
capitulate *v* teslim olmak
capsize *v* alabora olmak
capsule *n* kapsül
captain *n* kaptan
captivate *v* tutsak etmek
captive *n* tutsak
captivity *n* tutsaklık
capture *v* ele geçirmek
capture *n* yakalarnak
car *n* araba
carat *n* karat
caravan *n* karavan
carburetor *n* karbüratör
carcass *n* ceset
card *n* kart; kartvizit
cardboard *n* mukavva
cardiac *adj* kalbe ait
cardiac arrest *n* kalp krizi
cardiology *n* kardiyoloji
care *n* dert
care *v* umrunda olmak
care about *v* merak etmek
care for *v* hoşlanmak
career *n* kariyer
carefree *adj* tasasız
careful *adj* dikkatli
careless *adj* dikkatsiz
carelessness *n* dikkatsizlik
caress *n* okşama
caress *v* okşamak

caretaker *n* bakıcı
cargo *n* kargo
caricature *n* karikatür
caring *adj* yardımsever
carnage *n* katliam
carnal *adj* cinsel
carnation *n* karanfil
carol *n* Noel ilahisi
carpenter *n* marangoz
carpentry *n* marangozluk
carpet *n* halı
carriage *n* at arabası
carrot *n* havuç
carry *v* taşımak
carry on *v* devam etmek
carry out *v* uygulamak
cart *n* el arabası
cart *v* taşımak
cartoon *n* çizgi film
cartridge *n* kutucuk
carve *v* uymak
cascade *n* basamaklamak
case *n* çanta; dava
cash *n* nakit para
cashier *n* kasiyer
casino *n* gazino
casket *n* tabut; küçük kutu
casserole *n* güveç
cassock *n* cübbe
cast *iv* fırlatmak
castaway *n* kazazede
caste *n* kast
castle *n* kale
casual *adj* tesadüfen
casualty *n* kazazede
cat *n* kedi
cataclysm *n* tufan
catacomb *n* katakomb
catalog *n* katalog
catalog *v* katalog yapmak
cataract *n* şelale; katarakt
catastrophe *n* afet
catch *iv* yakalamak
catch up *v* yetişmek
catching *adj* nefesini tutmak
catchword *n* slogan
catechism *n* ilmihal
category *n* kategori
caterpillar *n* tırtıl
cathedral *n* katedral
catholic *adj* katolik
Catholicism *n* Katolik
cattle *n* sığır
cauliflower *n* karnabahar
cause *n* neden
cause *v* yol açmak

caution *n* uyarı
cautious *adj* ihtiyatlı
cavalry *n* süvari
cave *n* mağara
cave in *v* çökmek
cavern *n* mağara
cavity *n* çürük
cease *v* durdurmak
cease-fire *n* ateşkes
ceaselessly *adv* durmadan
ceiling *n* tavan
celebrate *v* kutlamak
celebration *n* kutlama
celebrity *n* ünlü
celery *n* kereviz
celestial *adj* kutsal
celibacy *n* bekarlık
celibate *adj* bekar
cellar *n* bodrum
cellphone *n* cep telefonu
cement *n* çimento
cemetery *n* mezarlık
censorship *n* sansür
censure *v* kınamak
census *n* nüfus sayımı
cent *n* sent
center *n* merkez
center *v* ortalamak
centimeter *n* santimetre
central *adj* merkezi
centralize *v* merkezleştirmek
century *n* yüzyıl
ceramic *n* seramik
cereal *n* gevrek
cerebral *adj* beyinsel
ceremony *n* seremoni
certain *adj* kesin
certainty *n* kesinlik
certificate *n* sertifika
certify *v* tasdik etmek
chagrin *n* utanç
chain *n* zincir
chain *v* zincirlemek
chainsaw *n* zincirli testere
chair *n* sandalye
chair *v* sandalye
chairman *n* kurul başkanı
chalet *n* küçük kösk
chalice *n* kadeh
chalk *n* tebeşir
chalkboard *n* karatahta
challenge *v* meydan okumak
challenge *n* meydan okuma
chamber *n* meclis
champ *n* şampiyon
champion *n* şampiyon

champion *v* savunmak
chance *n* şans; olasılık
chancellor *n* rektör
chandelier *n* avize
change *v* değiştirmek
change *n* değişim
channel *n* kanal
chant *n* ilahi
chaos *n* kaos
chaotic *adj* karmakarışık
chapel *n* şapel
chaplain *n* vaiz
chapter *n* bölüm
char *v* karakter
character *n* karakter
characteristic *adj* karakteristik
charade *n* maskaralık
charbroiled *adj* ızgara
charcoal *n* mangal kömürü
charge *v* şarj etmek
charge *n* şarj; görev
charisma *n* karizma
charismatic *adj* karizmatik
charitable *adj* hayırsever
charity *n* hayırseverlik
charm *v* büyülemek
charm *n* cazibe
charming *adj* cazibeli
chart *n* grafik; çizelge
charter *n* dolmuş uçak
charter *v* kiralamak
chase *n* av
chase *v* kovalamak
chase away *v* peşine düşmek
chasm *n* kanyon
chaste *adj* namuslu
chastise *v* cezalandırmak
chastisement *n* ceza
chastity *n* iffet
chat *v* sohbet etmek
chauffeur *n* özel soför
cheap *adj* ucuz
cheat *v* dolandırmak
cheater *n* hilekar
check *n* denetim; adisyon
check *v* kontrol etmek
check in *v* kaydını yaptırmak
check up *n* muayene
checkbook *n* çek defteri
cheek *n* yanak
cheekbone *n* elmacık kemiği
cheeky *adj* yüzsüz
cheer *v* tezahürat yapmak
cheer up *v* neşelendirmek
cheerful *adj* neşeli
cheers *n* şerefe

cheese *n* peynir
chef *n* şef
chemical *adj* kimyasal
chemist *n* kimyager
chemistry *n* kimya
cherish *v* üzerine titremek
cherry *n* kiraz
chess *n* satranç
chest *n* göğüs; sandık
chestnut *n* kestane
chew *v* çiğnemek
chick *n* civciv; genç kız
chicken *n* tavuk
chicken out *v* tırsmak
chicken pox *n* suçiçeği
chide *v* kusur bulmak
chief *n* şef
chiefly *adv* başlıca
child *n* çocuk
childhood *n* çocukluk
childish *adj* çocukça
childless *adj* çocuksuz
children *n* çocuklar
chill *n* soğuk; ürperti
chill *v* soğutmak
chill out *v* rahatlamak
chilly *adj* serin
chimney *n* baca
chimpanzee *n* şempanze
chin *n* çene
chip *n* yonga; çip
chisel *n* keski
chocolate *n* çikolata
choice *n* seçim
choir *n* koro
choke *v* boğmak
cholera *n* kolera
cholesterol *n* kolestorol
choose *iv* seçmek
choosy *adj* müşkülpesent
chop *v* doğramak
chop *n* pirzola
chopper *n* helikopter
chore *n* küçük iş
chorus *n* koro
christen *v* vaftiz etmek
christening *n* vaftiz
christian *adj* Hristiyan
Christianity *n* Hristiyanlık
Christmas *n* Noel
chronic *adj* müzmin
chronicle *n* kronik
chronology *n* kronoloji
chubby *adj* tombul
chuckle *v* kıkırdamak
chunk *n* külçe

church *n* kilise
chute *n* paraşüt
cider *n* elma şarabı
cigar *n* puro
cigarette *n* sigara
cinder *n* kül
cinema *n* sinema
cinnamon *n* tarçın
circle *n* yuvarlak
circle *v* kuşatmak
circuit *n* devre
circular *adj* yuvarlak
circulate *v* havanın akması
circulation *n* hava akımı
circumcise *v* sünnet etmek
circumcision *n* sünnet
circumstance *n* durum
circus *n* sirk
cistern *n* sarnıç
citizen *n* vatandaş
citizenship *n* vatandaşlık
city *n* şehir
city hall *n* belediye
civic *adj* şehirli
civil *adj* medeni
civilization *n* medeniyet
civilize *v* medenileştirmek
claim *v* talep etmek
claim *n* talep; iddia
clam *n* deniztarağı
clamor *v* yaygara
clamp *n* kıskaç
clan *n* kabile
clandestine *adj* el altından
clap *v* el çırpmak
clarification *n* açıklama
clarify *v* açıklama getirmek
clarinet *n* klarnet
clarity *n* netlik
clash *v* çarpmak
clash *n* çarpış
class *n* sınıf; zümre
classic *adj* klasik
classify *v* sınıflandırmak
classmate *n* sınıf arkadaşı
classroom *n* sınıf
classy *adj* klas
clause *n* tümce
claw *n* pençe
claw *v* tırmalamak
clay *n* kil
clean *adj* temiz
clean *v* temizlemek
cleanliness *n* temizlik
cleanse *v* temizlemek
cleanser *n* temizleyici madde

clear *adj* şeffaf; pürüzsüz
clear *v* temizlemek
clearance *n* temizlik
clear-cut *adj* kesin
clearly *adv* açıkça; net
clearness *n* açıklık; netlik
cleft *n* yarık
clemency *n* merhamet
clench *v* sıkmak
clergy *n* ruhban
clergyman *n* papaz
clerical *adj* yazıcıya ait
clerk *n* katip
clever *adj* akıllı; zeki
click *v* tıklamak
client *n* müşteri
clientele *n* müvekkiller
cliff *n* uçurum
climate *n* iklim
climatic *adj* iklimsel
climax *n* zirve
climb *v* tırmanmak
climbing *n* tırmanma
clinch *v* perçinlemek
cling *iv* tutunmak
clinic *n* klinik
clip *v* kırpmak
clipping *n* kırpma; kesme
cloak *n* pelerin
clock *n* saat
clog *v* tıkamak
cloister *n* manastır
clone *v* klonlamak
cloning *n* klon
close *v* kapatmak
close *adj* kapalı
close to *pre* yakın
closed *adj* kapalı
closely *adv* yakından
closet *n* klozet
closure *n* kapanış
clot *n* pıhtı
cloth *n* kumaş parçası; bez
clothe *v* giydirmek
clothes *n* giysi
clothing *n* kıyafet
cloud *n* bulut
cloudless *adj* bulutsuz
cloudy *adj* bulutlu
clown *n* palyaço
club *n* kulüp; disko
club *v* dövmek
clue *n* ipucu
clumsiness *n* beceriksizlik
clumsy *adj* beceriksiz
cluster *n* küme

cluster *v* kümelenmek
clutch *n* debriyaj
coach *v* çalıştırmak
coach *n* antrenör
coaching *n* antrenörlük etmek
coagulate *v* pıhtılaşmak
coagulation *n* pıhtılaşma
coal *n* kömür
coalition *n* koalisyon
coarse *adj* kaba; görgüsüz
coast *n* sahil
coastal *adj* kıyı boyunca
coastline *n* kıyı
coat *n* palto; tabaka
coax *v* dil dökmek
cob *n* mısır koçanı
cobblestone *n* parke taşı
cobweb *n* örümcek ağı
cocaine *n* kokain
cock *n* horoz
cockpit *n* kokpit
cockroach *n* hamamböceği
cocktail *n* kokteyl
cocky *adj* kibirli
cocoa *n* kakao
coconut *n* hindistancevizi
cod *n* morina
code *n* kod; kanun
codify *v* kodlamak
coefficient *n* katsayı
coerce *v* zorlamak
coercion *n* baskı; zorlama
coexist *v* birlikte varolmak
coffee *n* kahve
coffin *n* tabut
coherent *adj* mantıklı
cohesion *n* uyum
coin *n* madeni para
coincide *v* tesadüf etmek
coincidence *n* tesadüf
coincidental *adj* tesadüfen
cold *adj* soğuk
coldness *n* soğukluk
colic *n* kolik
collaboration *n* işbirliği
collaborator *n* işbirlikçi
collapse *v* yıkılmak
collapse *n* çöküş
collar *n* yaka
collarbone *n* anat
collateral *adj* kollateral
colleague *n* iş arkadaşı
collect *v* toplamak
collection *n* kolleksiyon
collector *n* kolleksiyoncu
college *n* kolej

collide *v* çarpmak
collision *n* çarpış
cologne *n* kolonya
colon *n* kolon
colonel *n* albay
colonial *adj* sömürgeci
colony *n* sömürge
color *n* renk
color *v* renklendirmek
colorful *adj* renkli
colossal *adj* muazzam
colt *n* tay
column *n* sütun
coma *n* koma
comb *n* tarak
comb *v* taramak
combat *n* mücadele
combat *v* mücadele etmek
combatant *n* dövüşçü
combination *n* birleşim
combine *v* birleştirmek
combustible *n* yanıcı
combustion *n* tutuşma
come *iv* gelmek
come about *v* doğmak
come across *v* karşılaşmak
come apart *v* kopuvermek
come back *v* geri gelmek
come down *v* aşağı inmek
come forward *v* ilerlemek
come from *v* bir yerden gelmek
come in *v* içeri girmek
come out *v* dışarı çıkmak
come over *v* ulaşmak
come up *v* ortaya çıkmak
comeback *n* dönüş
comedian *n* komedyen
comedy *n* komedi
comet *n* kuyrukluyıldız
comfort *n* konfor
comfortable *adj* konforlu
comforter *n* yorgan
comical *adj* komik
coming *n* varış
coming *adj* gelen
comma *n* virgül
command *v* emir
commander *n* kumandan
commandment *n* emir
commemorate *v* anmak
commence *v* başlamak
commend *v* tavsiye etmek
commendation *n* övgü
comment *v* yorum yapmak
comment *n* yorum
commerce *n* ticaret

commercial *adj* ticari
commission *n* komisyon
commit *v* adamak
commitment *n* vaat
committed *adj* söz vermiş
committee *n* komite
common *adj* ortak; genel
commotion *n* şamata
communicate *v* iletişim kurmak
communication *n* iletişim
communion *n* paylaşma
communism *n* komünizm
communist *adj* komünist
community *n* toplum
commute *v* seyahat etmek
compact *adj* kompakt
compact *v* sıkıştırmak
companion *n* yoldaş
companionship *n* yoldaşlık
company *n* şirket; arkadaşlık
comparable *adj* karşılanabilir
comparative *adj* karşılaştırmalı
compare *v* karşılaştırmak
comparison *n* karşılaştırma
compartment *n* bölme
compass *n* pusula
compassion *n* şefkat
compassionate *adj* şefkatli
compatibility *n* uygun
compatible *adj* uyumlu
compatriot *n* vatandaş
compel *v* zorlamak
compelling *adj* zorlayıcı
compendium *n* hülasa; özet
compensate *v* telafi etmek
compensation *n* tazminat
compete *v* rekabet etmek
competence *n* kabiliyet
competent *adj* ehil; yeterli
competition *n* yarşıma
competitive *adj* rakip
competitor *n* rakip; yarışmacı
compile *v* derlemek
complain *v* şikayet etmek
complaint *n* şikayet
complement *n* tümleyici
complete *adj* tam
complete *v* tamarnlamak
completely *adv* tamamen
completion *n* tamamlama
complex *adj* karmaşık
complexion *n* ten rengi
complexity *n* karmaşıklık
compliance *n* itaat
compliant *adj* uysal
complication *n* komplikasyon

C

complicity *n* suç ortaklığı
compliment *n* iltifat
complimentary *adj* övgü dolu
comply *v* razı olmak
component *n* bileşen
compose *v* bestelemek
composed *adj* oluşmuş
composer *n* besteci
composition *n* kompozisyon
compost *n* komposto
composure *n* soğukkanlılık
compound *n* bileşik
compound *v* halletmek
comprehend *v* kavramak
comprehensive *adj* kapsamlı
compress *v* sıkıştırmak
compression *n* kompresyon
comprise *v* ihtiva etmek
compromise *n* uzlaşma
compromise *v* uzlaşmak
compulsion *n* baskı
compulsive *adj* kompülsif
compulsory *adj* mecburi
compute *v* hesaplamak
computer *n* bilgisayar
comrade *n* komrad
con man *n* hilekar
conceal *v* gizlemek
concede *v* teslim etmek
conceited *adj* kibir
conceive *v* gebe kalmak
concentrate *v* konsantre olmak
concentration *n* konsantrasyon
concentric *adj* ortak merkezli
concept *n* konsept
conception *n* gebe kalma
concern *v* endişe
concern *n* ilgilendiren şey
concerning *pre* alaka
concert *n* konser
concession *n* kabul; teslim
conciliate *v* gönlünü almak
conciliatory *adj* yatıştırıcı
concise *adj* özlü
conclude *v* sonuç çıkarmak
conclusion *n* sonuç; son kısım
conclusive *adj* kesin
concoct *v* tertip etmek
concoction *n* karışım; tertip
concrete *n* somut; beton
concrete *adj* somut
concur *v* uyuşmak
concurrent *adj* koşutzamanlı
concussion *n* şiddetli sarsıntı
condemn *v* kınamak
condemnation *n* kınama

C

condensation *n* buğu
condense *v* yoğunlaştırmak
condescend *v* tenezzül etmek
condiment *n* baharat
condition *n* koşul
conditional *adj* koşullu
conditioner *n* artırıcı; düzeltici
condo *n* mülk
condone *v* göz yummak
conducive *adj* yardımcı
conduct *n* idare
conduct *v* idare etmek
conductor *n* iletken; lider
cone *n* koni
confer *v* müzakere etmek
conference *n* konferans
confess *v* itiraf etmek
confession *n* itiraf
confidant *n* sırdaş
confide *v* sırrını söylemek
confidence *n* itimat; güven
confident *adj* kendinden emin
confidential *adj* gizli
confine *v* hapsetmek
confinement *n* hapis
confirm *v* onaylamak
confirmation *n* onay
confiscate *v* el koymak
confiscation *n* haczetmek
conflict *n* itilaf; uyuşmazlık
conflict *v* uyuşmamak
conflicting *adj* çelişkili
conform *v* itaat etmek
conformist *adj* konformist
conformity *n* uygunluk
confound *v* şaşırtmak
confront *v* yüz yüze gelmek
confrontation *n* yüzleşme
confuse *v* kafasını karıştırmak
confusing *adj* kafa karıştıran
confusion *n* karışıklık
congenial *adj* sempatik
congested *adj* tıklım tıklım
congestion *n* tıkanıklık; izdiham
congratulate *v* tebrik etmek
congratulations *n* tebrikler
congregate *v* toplamak
congregation *n* toplama
congress *n* kongre
conjecture *n* varsayım
conjugal *adj* evlilikle ilgili
conjugate *v* birleşmek
conjunction *n* birleşme
conjure up *v* anımsatmak
connect *v* bağlamak
connection *n* bağ

connote *v* akla getirmek
conquer *v* fethetmek
conqueror *n* fatih
conquest *n* fetih
conscience *n* vicdan
conscious *adj* vicdanlı
conciousness *n* bilinçlilik
conscript *n* askere alınmış
consecrate *v* kutsamak
consecration *n* kutsama
consecutive *adj* ardıl
consensus *n* oybirliği
consent *v* rızasını almak
consent *n* rıza
consequence *n* sonuç
consequent *adj* netice
conservation *n* konuşma
conservative *adj* tutucu
conserve *v* muhafaza etmek
conserve *n* muhafaza; reçel
consider *v* dikkate almak
considerable *adj* önemli oranda
considerate *adj* düşünceli
consideration *n* düşünce
consignment *n* sevkiyat
consist *v* meydana gelmek
consistency *n* tutarlılık
consistent *adj* tutarlı; istikrarlı
consolation *n* teselli
console *v* teselli etmek
consolidate *v* pekiştirmek
consonant *n* ünsüz
conspicuous *adj* göstermelik
conspiracy *n* komplo
conspirator *n* komplocu
conspire *v* komplo kurmak
constancy *n* vefa
constant *adj* sabit
constellation *n* takımyıldız
consternation *n* dehşet
constipate *v* kabızlık vermek
constipated *adj* kabız
constipation *n* kabızlık
constitute *v* teşkil etmek
constitution *n* anayasa; yapı
constrain *v* sınırlamak
constraint *n* kısıt; sıkıntı
construct *v* inşa etmek
construction *n* inşaat
constructive *adj* yapıcı
consul *n* konsolos
consulate *n* konsolosluk
consult *v* danışmak
consultation *n* danışma
consume *v* tüketmek
consumer *n* tüketici

C

consumption *n* tüketim
contact *v* temas etmek
contact *n* temas
contagious *adj* bulaşıcı
contain *v* içermek
container *n* konteyner
contaminate *v* bulaştırmak
contamination *n* pislik
contemplate *v* düşünmek
contemporary *adj* geçici
contempt *n* zillet
contend *v* çekişmek
contender *n* yarışmacı
content *adj* içerik
content *v* memnun olmak
contentious *adj* kavgacı
contents *n* memnuniyet
contest *n* mücadele; itiraz
contestant *n* yarışmacı
context *n* bağlam
continent *n* kıta
continental *adj* kıtasal
contingency *n* durumsallık
contingent *adj* olası
continuation *n* devamı
continue *v* devam etmek
continuity *n* süreklilik
continuous *adj* sürekli
contour *n* dış hatlar; kontur
contraband *n* kaçak
contract *v* sözleşmek
contract *n* sözleşme
contraction *n* kasılma
contradict *v* çelişmek
contradiction *n* çelişki
contrary *adj* karşıt
contrast *v* karşılaştırma
contrast *n* karşıtlık
contribute *v* katkıda bulunmak
contribution *n* katkı; makale
contributor *n* yardımcı
contrition *n* pişmanlık
control *n* kontrol
control *v* kontrol etmek
controversial *adj* tartışmalı
controversy *n* tartışma
convalescent *adj* iyileşen
convene *v* toplanmak
convenience *n* elverişlilik
convenient *adj* elverişli
convent *n* manastır
convention *n* toplantı
conventional *adj* geleneksel
converge *v* yakınsamak
conversation *n* muhabbet
converse *v* konuşmak

conversely *adv* tersine
conversion *n* çevrim
convert *v* dönüştürmek
convert *n* dönüşüm
convey *v* taşımak; nakletmek
convict *v* mahkum etmek
conviction *n* mahkumiyet; inanç
convince *v* ikna etmek
convincing *adj* ikna edici
convoluted *adj* sarılmış
convoy *n* konvoy
convulse *v* sarsmak
convulsion *n* sarsıntı
cook *v* pişirmek
cook *n* aşçı
cookie *n* kurabiye
cooking *n* yemek yapma
cool *adj* soğuk; serinkanlı
cool *v* soğutmak
cool down *v* soğutmak
cooling *adj* soğutucu
coolness *n* soğukluk
cooperate *v* işbirliği yapmak
cooperation *n* işbirliği
cooperative *adj* kooperatif
coordinate *v* eşgüdümlemek
coordination *n* koordinasyon
coordinator *n* koordinatör
cop *n* polis
cope *v* uğraşmak
copier *n* fotokopi makinası
copper *n* bakır
copy *v* kopyalamak
copy *n* kopya
copyright *n* telif hakkı
cord *n* kablo; kordon
cordial *adj* samimi
cordless *adj* kablosuz
cordon *n* kordon
cordon off *v* kuşatmak
core *n* öz
cork *n* tapa
corn *n* mısır; nasır
corner *n* köşe; korner
cornerstone *n* köşe taşı
cornet *n* kornet
corollary *n* doğal sonuç
coronary *adj* kalple ilgili
coronation *n* taç giyme töreni
corporal *adj* bedeni; onbaşı
corporal *n* onbaşı
corporation *n* anonim şirket
corpse *n* ceset
corpulent *adj* şişman
corpuscle *n* anat
correct *v* doğrulamak

C

correct *adj* doğru
correction *n* doğrulama
correspond *v* mektuplaşmak
correspondent *n* muhabir
corresponding *adj* mutabık
corridor *n* koridor
corroborate *v* pekiştirmek
corrode *v* aşındırmak
corrupt *v* yozlaşmış
corrupt *adj* yoz; namussuz
corruption *n* yozlaşma
cosmetic *n* kozmetik
cosmic *adj* kozmik
cosmonaut *n* kozmonot
cost *iv* mal etmek
cost *n* masraf
costly *adj* pahalı
costume *n* kostüm
cottage *n* kulübe
cotton *n* pamuk
couch *n* kanepe
cough *n* öksürük
cough *v* öksürmek
council *n* konsey; meclis
counsel *v* öğüt vermek
counsel *n* tavsiye; avukat
counselor *n* danışman; avukat
count *v* saymak
count *n* madde; sayma
countdown *n* geriye sayım
countenance *n* çehre
counter *n* sayaç; tezgah
counter *v* uymamak
counteract *v* karşı koymak
counterfeit *v* taklit etmek
counterfeit *adj* taklit; sahte
counterpart *n* mukabil
countess *n* kontes
countless *adj* sayısız
country *n* ülke
countryman *n* taşralı
countryside *n* kırsal bölge
county *n* ilçe
coup *n* darbe
couple *n* çift; iki tane
coupon *n* kupon
courage *n* cesaret
courageous *adj* cesaretli
courier *n* kurye
course *n* ders; süreç
court *n* avlu; saray
court *v* fayda sağlamak
courteous *adj* nazik
courtesy *n* kibarlık
courthouse *n* adliye sarayı
courtship *n* iltifat

C

courtyard *n* iç bahçe
cousin *n* kuzen; yeğen
cove *n* körfez
covenant *n* mukavele
cover *n* kapsam; örtü
cover *v* kapsamak
cover up *v* üstünü örtmek
coverage *n* kapsam
covert *adj* gizli
coverup *n* gizleme
covet *v* imrenmek
cow *n* inek
coward *n* korkak
cowardice *n* korkaklık
cowardly *adv* korkakça
cowboy *n* kovboy
cozy *adj* rahat
crab *n* yengeç
crack *n* çatlak
crack *v* çatlamak
cradle *n* beşik
craft *n* zanaat; hile
craftsman *n* zanaatkar
cram *v* tıkıştırmak
cramp *n* kramp
cramped *adj* kramp girmiş
crane *n* vinç
crank *n* manivela; krank
cranky *adj* tuhaf
crap *n* bok; değersiz eşya
crappy *adj* boktan; zırva
crash *n* şangırtı
crash *v* kaza yapmak
crass *adj* kaba
crater *n* krater
crave *v* arzulamak
craving *n* arzu
crawl *v* sürünmek
crayon *n* krayon
craziness *n* çılgınlık
crazy *adj* çılgın
creak *v* gıcırdamak
creak *n* gıcırtı
cream *n* krem
creamy *adj* kremalı
crease *n* kırma; buruşuk
crease *v* buruştırmak
create *v* yaratmak
creation *n* yaratım
creative *adj* yaratıcı
creativity *n* yaratıcılık
creator *n* yaratıcı
creature *n* yaratık
credibility *n* güvenilirlik
credible *adj* güvenilir
credit *n* kredi

creditor *n* alacaklı
creed *n* iman
creek *n* dere
creep *v* emeklemek
creepy *adj* korkunç
cremate *v* kremasyon
crest *n* tepelik
crevice *n* yarık
crew *n* ekip
crib *n* yemlik
cricket *n* kriket
crime *n* suç
criminal *adj* suçlu
cripple *adj* sakat
cripple *v* sakat etmek
crisis *n* kriz
crisp *adj* çıtır
criss-cross *v* çaprazlama
crispy *adj* çıtır
criterion *n* kriter
critical *adj* kritik; eleştirel
criticism *n* eleştiri; tenkit
criticize *v* eleştirmek
critique *n* eleştiri
crockery *n* çanak çömlek
crocodile *n* timsah
crony *n* kafadar
crook *n* dönemeç
crooked *adj* virajlı
crop *n* ekin
cross *n* çarpı
cross *adj* çarpılı
cross *v* karşıya geçmek
cross out *v* üstünü çizmek
crossfire *n* çapraz ateş
crossing *n* geçit
crossroads *n* dörtyol; kavşak
crosswalk *n* yaya geçidi
crossword *n* çapraz bulmaca
crouch *v* çömelmek
crow *n* karga
crow *v* horoz ötüşü
crowbar *n* kaldıraç
crowd *n* kalabalık
crowd *v* doluşmak
crowded *adj* kalabalık
crown *n* taç; hükümdarlık
crown *v* taç giymek
crucial *adj* can alıcı
crucifix *n* çarmıh
crucifixion *n* çarmıha germe
crucify *v* çarmıha germek
crude *adj* ham; kaba
cruel *adj* acımasız
cruelty *n* acımasızlık
cruise *v* gemi yolculuğu

C

crumb *n* kırıntı
crumble *v* ufalamak
crunchy *adj* çıtır
crusade *n* haçlı seferi
crusader *n* Haçlı
crush *v* ezmek
crushing *adj* izdiham
crust *n* kabuk
crusty *adj* kabuklu
crutch *n* destek
cry *n* feryat
cry *v* ağlamak
cry out *v* haykırmak
crying *n* çığlık
crystal *n* kristal
cub *n* acemi
cube *n* küp
cubic *adj* kübik
cubicle *n* küçük bölme
cucumber *n* salatalık; hıyar
cuddle *v* kucaklamak
cuff *n* kolluk; manşet
cuisine *n* mutfak
culminate *v* son bulmak
culpability *n* kabahatli
culprit *n* suçlu
cult *n* kült; mezhep
cultivate *v* yetiştirmek
cultivation *n* ekip biçme
cultural *adj* kültürel
culture *n* kültür
cumbersome *adj* elverişsiz
cunning *adj* kurnaz
cup *n* fincan
cupboard *n* dolap
curable *adj* tedavisi mümkün
curator *n* küratör
curb *v* engellemek
curb *n* engel
curdle *v* pıhtılaşmak
cure *v* tedavi etmek
cure *n* tedavi etmek
curiosity *n* merak
curious *adj* meraklı
curl *v* dolamak; sarmak
curl *n* büklüm; lüle
curly *adj* bukle
currency *n* döviz
current *adj* şu anki
currently *adv* şu anda
curse *v* lanetlemek
curtail *v* kısa kesmek
curtain *n* perde
curve *n* kıvrım
curve *v* kıvırmak
cushion *n* minder

cushion *v* hafifletmek
cuss *v* küfür
custard *n* muhallebi
custodian *n* muhafız
custody *n* muhafaza
custom *n* gelenek
customary *adj* geleneksel
customer *n* müşteri
custom-made *adj* ısmarlama
customs *n* gümrük
cut *n* kesik
cut *iv* kesmek
cut back *v* kısaltmak
cut down *v* azaltmak
cut off *v* kesmek
cut out *v* kesmek; biçmek
cute *adj* sevimli
cutlery *n* çatal bıçak
cutter *n* kesici; filika
cyanide *n* siyanür
cycle *n* dönüş; devir
cyclist *n* bisikletçi
cyclone *n* siklon; kasırga
cylinder *n* silindir
cynic *adj* kinik
cynicism *n* kinizm
cypress *n* servi
cyst *n* kist
czar *n* çar

D

dad *n* baba
dagger *n* hançer
daily *adv* günlük
dairy farm *n* mandıra
daisy *n* papatya
dam *n* baraj
damage *n* zarar
damage *v* zarar vermek
damaging *adj* zarar veren
damn *v* kahretmek
damnation *n* lanet
damp *adj* nem
dampen *v* nemlendirmek
dance *n* dans
dance *v* dans etmek
dancing *n* dans
dandruff *n* saç kepeği
danger *n* tehlike
dangerous *adj* tehlikeli
dangle *v* sarkmak
dare *v* cesaret etmek
dare *n* cüret
daring *adj* yiğit

dark *adj* koyu renk
darken *v* karartmak
darkness *n* karanlık
darling *adj* sevgili
darn *v* yamamak
dart *n* dart
dash *v* hızlı koşmak
dashing *adj* atılgan
data *n* veri
database *n* veritabanı
date *n* tarih; buluşma
date *v* tarih koymak
daughter *n* kız çocuk
daughter-in-law *n* gelin
daunt *v* yıldırmak
daunting *adj* gözüpek
dawn *n* seher
day *n* gün
daydream *v* hayal kurmak
daze *v* sersemletmek
dazed *adj* sersem
dazzle *v* göz kamaştırmak
dazzling *adj* göz kamaştıran
de luxe *adj* lüks
deacon *n* diyakoz
dead *adj* ölü
dead end *n* çıkmaz sokak
deaden *v* hafifletmek
deadline *n* son tarih
deadlock *adj* çıkmaz
deadly *adj* ölümcül
deaf *adj* sağır
deafen *v* sağır etmek
deafening *adj* sağır edici
deafness *n* sağırlık
deal *iv* anlaşmak
deal *n* anlaşma
dealer *n* dağıtımcı
dealings *n* muamele
dean *n* dekan
dear *adj* sevgili
dearly *adv* pahalıya
death *n* ölüm
death toll *n* ölü sayısı
death trap *n* ölüm tuzağı
deathbed *n* ölüm yatağı
debase *v* değerini düşürmek
debatable *adj* tartışılabilir
debate *v* tartışmak
debate *n* tartışma
debit *n* borç
debrief *v* sorguya çekmek
debris *n* döküntü
debt *n* borç
debtor *n* borçlu
debunk *v* çürütmek

D

debut *n* başlangıç
decade *n* on yıl
decadence *n* zeval
decaff *adj* kafeinsiz
decapitate *v* başını kesmek
decay *v* çürümek
decay *n* çürük
deceased *adj* mehrum
deceit *n* hile
deceitful *adj* hilekar
deceive *v* kandırmak
December *n* Aralık
decency *n* edep
decent *adj* edepli
deception *n* aldatma
deceptive *adj* yanıltıcı
decide *v* karar vermek
deciding *adj* kesin
decimal *adj* ondalık sayı
decimate *v* kırıp geçirmek
decipher *v* şifre çözmek
decision *n* karar
decisive *adj* kararlı
deck *n* deste
declaration *n* bildiri
declare *v* bildirmek
declension *n* ad çekimi
decline *v* reddetmek
decline *n* meyil; düşüş
decompose *v* ayrıştırmak
décor *n* dekor
decorate *v* dekore etmek
decorative *adj* dekoratif
decorum *n* uygun davranış
decrease *v* azalmak
decrease *n* düşüş
decree *n* kararname
decree *v* buyurmak
decrepit *adj* yıpranmış
dedicate *v* adamak
dedication *n* adak
deduce *v* ithaf
deduct *v* hesaptan düşmek
deductible *adj* indirimli
deduction *n* indirim
deed *n* iş; eylem
deem *v* saymak; farzetmek
deep *adj* derin
deepen *v* derinleştirmek
deer *n* geyik
deface *v* çirkinleştirmek
defame *v* kara çalmak
defeat *v* yenmek
defeat *n* yenilgi
defect *n* kusur
defect *v* iltica etmek

defection *n* kusur
defective *adj* kusurlu
defend *v* savunmak
defendant *n* savalı; sanık
defender *n* savunucu
defense *n* savunma
defenseless *adj* savunmasız
defer *v* ertelemek
defiance *n* muhalefet
defiant *adj* muhalif
deficiency *n* eksiklik
deficient *adj* eksik
deficit *n* zarar
defile *v* bozmak
define *v* tanımlamak
definite *adj* kesin
definition *n* tanım
definitive *adj* kati
deflate *v* söndürmek
deform *v* biçimsizleştirmek
deformity *n* biçimsizlik
defraud *v* dolandırmak
defray *v* ödemek
defrost *v* buzlarını çözmek
deft *adj* becerikl
defy *v* kafa tutmak
degenerate *v* yozlaşmak
degenerate *adj* dejenere
degeneration *n* dejenerasyon
degradation *n* itibarsızlık
degrade *v* rütbesini indirmek
degrading *adj* alçaltıcı
degree *n* derece
dehydrate *v* su kaybetmek
deign *v* tenezzül etmek
deity *n* tanrı
dejected *adj* kederli
delay *v* ertelemek
delay *n* gecikme
delegate *v* yetki aktarmak
delegate *n* delege
delegation *n* delegasyon
delete *v* silmek
deliberate *adj* temkinli
delicacy *n* kibarlık
delicate *adj* narin
delicious *adj* lezzetli
delight *n* hoş
delight *v* sevindirmek
delightful *adj* hoş
delinquency *n* suçluluk
delinquent *adj* suçlu
deliver *v* doğurmak
delivery *n* teslim; doğum
delude *v* aldatmak
deluge *n* tufan

D

delusion *n* hayal; hile
demand *v* talep etmek
demand *n* talep
demanding *adj* ısrarcı
demean *v* alçaltmak
demeanor *n* tavır
demented *adj* kaçık
demise *n* vefat
democracy *n* demokrasi
democratic *adj* demokratik
demolish *v* yıkmak
demolition *n* yıkım
demon *n* şeytan
demonstrate *v* ispat etmek
demonstrative *adj* kanıtlayan
demote *v* indirgemek
den *n* mağara
denial *n* inkar
denigrate *v* iftira etmek
Denmak *n* Danimarka
denominator *n* payda
denote *v* belirtmek
denounce *v* ihbar etmek
dense *adj* yoğun
density *n* yoğunluk
dent *v* yamultmak
dent *n* girinti
dental *adj* dişsel
dentist *n* diş doktoru
dentures *n* takma diş
deny *v* inkar etmek
deodorant *n* deodorant
depart *v* sapmak
department *n* departman
departure *n* ayrılış
dependable *adj* güvenilir
dependence *n* bağlılık
dependent *adj* muhtaç
depict *v* betimlemek
deplete *v* tüketmek
deplore *v* acı duymak
deploy *v* konuşlanmak
deployment *n* konuşlandırma
deport *v* sınırdışı etmek
deportation *n* sınırdışı
depose *v* görevden almak
deposit *n* emanet; depozit
depot *n* depo
deprave *adj* ayartıcı
depravity *n* ahlak bozukluğu
depreciate *v* ucuzlatmak
depreciation *n* yıpranma payı
depress *v* canını sıkmak
depressing *adj* can sıkıcı
depression *n* depresyon
deprive *v* yoksun bırakmak

deprived *adj* yoksun
deprivation *n* mahrumiyet
depth *n* derinlik
derail *v* raydan çıkmak
derailment *n* raydan çıkma
deranged *adj* deli
derelict *adj* sahipsiz
deride *v* alay etmek
derivative *adj* türev
derive *v* türetmek
derogatory *adj* onur kırıcı
descend *v* inmek
descendant *n* torun
descent *n* iniş
describe *v* tarif etmek
description *n* tarif
descriptive *adj* tanımlayıcı
desecrate *v* saygısızlık etmek
desert *n* çöl
desert *v* sahra; terkedilmiş
deserted *adj* ıssız
deserter *n* kaçak
deserve *v* hak etmek
deserving *adj* layık
design *n* tasarım; amaç
designate *v* işaret etmek
desirable *adj* çekici
desire *n* arzu
desire *v* arzulamak
desist *v* vazgeçmek
desk *n* masa; resepsiyon
desolate *adj* kimsesiz
desolation *n* haraplık
despair *n* umutsuzluk
desperate *adj* umutsuz
despicable *adj* adi
despise *v* hor görmek
despite *c* rağmen
despondent *adj* meyus
despot *n* despot
despotic *adj* despot
dessert *n* tatlı
destination *n* hedef
destiny *n* kader
destitute *adj* yoksul
destroy *v* harap etmek
destroyer *n* yok edici
destruction *n* yıkım
destructive *adj* yıkıcı
detach *v* ayırmak
detachable *adj* ayrılabilir
detail *n* detay
detail *v* ayrıntıya inmek
detain *v* alıkoymak
detect *v* meydana çıkarmak
detective *n* detektif

D

detector *n* detektör
detention *n* alıkoyma
deter *v* caydırmak
detergent *n* deterjan
deteriorate *v* kötüleştirmek
deterioration *n* kötüleşme
determination *n* kararlılık
determine *v* karar vermek
deterrence *n* caydırma
detest *v* nefret etmek
detonate *v* patlatmak
detonation *n* patlama
detonator *n* patlatıcı
detour *n* dolambaçlı yol
detriment *n* ziyan
detrimental *adj* zararlı
devaluation *n* devaluasyon
devalue *v* devalüe etmek
devastate *v* harap etmek
devastating *adj* harap edici
devastation *n* tahribat
develop *v* geliştirmek
development *n* kalkınma
deviation *n* sapma
device *n* aygıt
devil *n* şeytan
devious *adj* şeytanca
devise *v* tasarlamak
devoid *adj* mahrum
devote *v* adamak
devotion *n* sadakat
devour *v* yiyip yutmak
devout *adj* dindar
dew *n* çiy
diabetes *n* diyabet
diabetic *adj* diyabetik
diabolical *adj* zalim
diagnose *v* teşhis koymak
diagnosis *n* teşhis
diagonal *adj* köşegen
diagram *n* diyagram
dial *n* kadran
dial *v* çevirmek
dial tone *n* çevir sesi
dialect *n* lehçe
dialogue *n* diyalog
diameter *n* çap
diamond *n* elmas
diaper *n* bez
diarrhea *n* ishal
diary *n* günce
dice *n* oyun zarları
dictate *v* yazdırmak
dictator *n* diktatör
dictatorial *adj* diktatörce
dictatorship *n* diktatörlük

dictionary *n* sözlük
die *v* ölmek
die out *v* nesli tükenmek
diet *n* diyet
differ *v* başka olmak
difference *n* fark
different *adj* farklı
difficult *adj* zor
difficulty *n* zorluk
diffuse *v* dağıtmak
dig *iv* kazmak
digest *v* sindirmek
digestion *n* sindirim
digestive *adj* dijestif
digit *n* basamak
dignify *v* ondurlandırmak
dignitary *n* rütbe
dignity *n* asalet
digress *v* konudan ayrılmak
dilapidated *adj* harap
dilemma *n* ikilem
diligence *n* özen
diligent *adj* gayretli
dilute *v* sulandırmak
dim *adj* loş
dim *v* azaltmak
dime *n* on sent
dimension *n* boyut
diminish *v* azaltmak
dine *v* akşam yemeği yemek
diner *n* restoran
dining room *n* yemek odası
dinner *n* akşam yemeği
dinosaur *n* dinazor
diphthong *n* diftong
diploma *n* diploma
diplomacy *n* diplomasi
diplomat *n* diplomat
diplomatic *adj* diplomatik
dire *adj* korkunç
direct *adj* doğrudan
direct *v* emretmek
direction *n* yön
director *n* yönetici
directory *n* dizin
dirt *n* kir
dirty *adj* kirli
disability *n* özür
disabled *adj* sakatlık
disadvantage *n* dezavantaj
disagree *v* anlaşmamak
disagreeable *adj* nahoş
disagreement *n* anlaşmazlık
disappointing *adj* umut kırıcı
disappointment *n* hayal kırıklığı
disapproval *n* onaylamama

D

disapprove *v* onaylamamak
disarm *v* silahsızlandırmak
disaster *n* felaket
disastrous *adj* feci
disband *v* terhis etmek
disbelief *n* inanmama
disburse *v* para harcamak
discard *v* atmak
discern *v* ayırtetmek
discharge *v* ödemek; boşaltmak
discharge *n* ödeme; boşaltma
disciple *n* havari; çömez
discipline *n* disiplin
disclaim *v* yadsımak
disclose *v* açığa vurmak
discomfort *n* rahatsızlık
disconnect *v* bağlantıyı kesmek
discontent *adj* hoşnutsuzluk
discontinue *v* durdurmak
discord *n* uyuşmazlık
discordant *adj* uyumsuz
discount *n* indirim
discount *v* indirim yapmak
discourage *v* cesaretini kırmak
discouragement *n* cesaretsizlik
discouraging *adj* şevk kırıcı
discourtesy *n* nezaketsizlik
discover *v* keşfetmek
discovery *n* keşif
discreet *adj* tedbirli
discrepancy *n* uyuşmazlık
discretion *n* sağduyu
discriminate *v* fark gözetmek
discrimination *n* ayrım
discuss *v* tartışmak
discussion *n* tartışma
disdain *n* tepeden bakma
disease *n* hastalık
disembark *v* karaya çıkarmak
disenchanted *adj* inancını yitirmiş
disentangle *v* çözmek
disfigure *v* biçimsizleştirmek
disgrace *n* yüzkarası
disgrace *v* gözden düşmek
disgraceful *adj* utanç verici
disgruntled *adj* küskün
disguise *v* kılık değiştirmek
disguise *n* kılık değiştirmiş
disgust *n* iğrenmek
disgusting *adj* iğrenç
dish *n* yemek; tabak çatal
dishearten *v* umudunu kırmak
dishonest *adj* sahtekar
dishonesty *n* sahtekarlık
dishonor *n* alçaklık
dishonorable *adj* alçak

dishwasher *n* bulaşık makinası
disillusion *n* hayal kırıklığı
disinfect *v* dezenfekte etmek
disinfectant *n* dezenfektan
disintegrate *v* parçalamak
disintegration *n* bölünme
disinterested *adj* tarafsızlık
disk *n* disk
dislike *v* hoşlanmamak
dislike *n* hoşlanmama
dislocate *v* yerinden çıkarmak
dislodge *v* yerinden oynatmak
disloyal *adj* vefasız
disloyalty *n* vefasızlık
dismal *adj* keferli
dismantle *v* parçalara ayırmak
dismay *n* umutsuzluk
dismay *v* dehşete düşürmek
dismiss *v* kovmak
dismissal *n* işten çıkarma
dismount *v* kaldırmak; indirmek
disobedience *n* itaatsizlik
disobedient *adj* itaatsiz
disobey *v* itaat etmemek
disorder *n* kargaşa
disorganized *adj* düzensiz
disoriented *adj* kafası karışmış
disown *v* yadsımak
disparity *n* farklı
dispatch *v* dağıtmak
dispel *v* defetmek
dispensation *n* dağıtma
dispense *v* dağıtmak
dispersal *n* dağılım
disperse *v* dağıtmak
displace *v* yerini değiştirmek
display *n* görüntü; sergi
display *v* görüntülemek
displease *v* sinirlendirmek
displeasing *adj* nahoş
disposable *adj* bir kullanımlık
disposal *n* elden çıkarma
dispose *v* elden çıkarmak
disprove *v* aksini kanıtlamak
dispute *n* münakaşa
dispute *v* anlaşmazlık
disqualify *v* diskalifiye etmek
disregard *v* önemsememek
disrepair *n* bakımsızlık
disrespect *n* saygısızlık
disrespectful *adj* saygısız
disrupt *v* bozmak
disruption *n* bozma
dissatisfied *adj* tatmin olmamış
disseminate *v* saçmak
dissent *v* kabul etmemek

D

dissident *adj* muhalif
dissimilar *adj* farklı
dissipate *v* dağıtmak
dissolute *adj* çapkın; rezil
dissolution *n* erime
dissolve *v* eritmek
dissonant *adj* ahenksiz
dissuade *v* caydırmak
distance *n* uzaklık
distant *adj* uzak
distaste *n* beğenmeme
distasteful *adj* tatsız
distill *v* damıtmak
distinct *adj* farklı
distinction *n* üstün
distinctive *adj* kendine özgü
distinguish *v* ayırtetmek
distort *v* biçimini bozmak
distortion *n* çarpıtma
distract *v* dikkatini dağıtmak
distraction *n* dikkat dağınıklığı
distraught *adj* çılgına dönmüş
distress *n* üzüntü
distress *v* endişelenmek
distressing *adj* endişe verici
distribute *v* dağıtmak
distribution *n* dağıtım
district *n* mahalle
distrust *n* itaatsizlik
distrust *v* itimat etmemek
distrustful *adj* itimatsız
disturb *v* rahatsız etmek
disturbance *n* rahatsızlık
disturbing *adj* rahatsız edici
disunity *n* koukluk
disuse *n* kullanılmazlık
ditch *n* hendek; çukur
dive *v* dalmak
diver *n* dalgıç
diverse *adj* çeşit
diversify *v* çeşitlendirmek
diversion *n* eğlence
diversity *n* çeşitlilik
divert *v* yönlendirmek
divide *v* bölmek
dividend *n* bölünen; pay
divine *adj* ilahi
diving *n* dalış
divinity *n* ilahilik
divisible *adj* bölünebilir
division *n* bölüm
divorce *n* boşanma
divorce *v* boşanmak
divorcee *n* boşanan
divulge *v* ifşa etmek
dizziness *n* başı dönen

dizzy *adj* sersem
do *iv* yapmak
docile *adj* uysal
docility *n* uysallık
dock *n* tersane; rıhtım
dock *v* yanaşmak
doctor *n* doktor
doctrine *n* öğreti
document *n* doküman
documentary *n* belgesel
dog *n* köpek
dogmatic *adj* dogmatik
dole out *v* sadaka vermek
doll *n* oyuncak bebek
dollar *n* dolar
dolphin *n* yunus
dome *n* kubbe
domestic *adj* aile içi; yerel
domesticate *v* evcilleştirmek
dominate *v* egemen olmak
domination *n* hakimiyet
domineering *adj* mütehakkim
dominion *n* egemenlik
donate *v* bağış yapmak
donation *n* bağış
donkey *n* eşek
donor *n* bağışçı
doom *n* korkunç son
doomed *adj* mahkumiyet
door *n* kapı
doorbell *n* kapı zili
doorstep *n* kapı girişi
doorway *n* kapı aralığı
dope *n* malumat
dope *v* uyuşturucu vermek
dormitory *n* yatakhane
dosage *n* dozaj
dossier *n* dosya
dot *n* nokta
double *adj* çift
double *v* iki katına çıkarmak
double-check *v* kontrol etmek
double-cross *v* kazık atmak
doubt *n* şüphe
doubt *v* şüphelenmek
doubtful *adl* şüpheli
dough *n* hamur
dove *n* güvercin
down *adv* aşağıda
down payment *n* peşinat
downcast *adj* morali bozuk
downfall *n* yıkılış
downhill *adv* yokuş aşağı
downpour *n* sağanak
downsize *v* işgücünü azaltmak
downstairs *adv* aşağıda

D

down-to-earth *adj* gerçekçi
downtown *n* çarşı
downtrodden *adj* mazlum
downturn *n* sıkıntılı dönem
dowry *n* çeyiz
doze *n* hafif uyku
doze *v* şekerleme yapmak
dozen *n* düzine
draft *n* taslak; askere alma
draft *v* taslak çizmek
draftsman *n* teknik ressam
drag *v* sürüklemek
dragon *n* dragon
drain *v* akıtmak
drainage *n* kanalizasyon
dramatic *adj* dramatik
dramatize *v* dramatize etmek
drape *n* kumaşla örtmek
drastic *adj* şiddetli
draw *n* kura
draw *iv* çizmek; çekiliş yapmak
drawback *n* sakınca
drawer *n* çekmece
drawing *n* çizim
dread *v* çok korkmak
dreaded *adj* dehşet
dreadful *adj* ürkütücü
dream *iv* hayal kurmak
dream *n* hayal; rüya
dress *n* giysi
dress *v* giyinmek
dresser *n* şifoniyer
dressing *n* sargı
dried *adj* kuru
drift *v* sürüklemek
drift apart *v* kendini koyvermek
drifter *n* avare
drill *v* matkaplamak
drill *n* matkap; talim
drink *iv* içmek
drink *n* içecek
drinkable *adj* içilir
drinker *n* içkici
drip *v* damlatmak
drip *n* damla
drive *n* araba gezintisi
drive *iv* araç sürmek
drive at *v* demek istemek
drive away *v* kovmak
driver *n* sürücü
driveway *n* özel araba yolu
drizzle *v* çiselemek
drizzle *n* çisenti
drop *n* damla; düşüş
drop *v* damlamak
drop in *v* uğramak

drop off *v* uyuyakalmak
drop out *v* okulu terk etmek
drought *n* kuraklık
drown *v* boğulmak
drowsy *adj* uykulu
drug *n* ilaç
drug *v* ilaç vermek
drugstore *n* eczane
drum *n* davul; şarjör
drunk *adj* sarhoş
drunkenness *n* sarhoşluk
dry *v* kurutmak
dry *adj* kuru
dryclean *v* kuru temizlemek
dryer *n* kurutucu
dual *adj* ikili
dubious *adj* kuşkulu
duchess *n* düşes
duck *n* ördek
duck *v* suya daldırmak
duct *n* oluk
due *adj* gereken; kalan
duel *n* düello
dues *n* aidat
duke *n* dük
dull *adj* kalın kafalı
duly *adv* usulüne uygun
dumb *adj* dilsiz; budala
dummy *n* maket
dummy *adj* sözde
dump *v* terketmek
dump *n* dökmek
dung *n* gübre
dungeon *n* zindan
dupe *v* dolandırmak
duplicate *v* kopyalamak
duplication *n* sureti
durable *adj* dayanıklı
duration *n* müddet
during *pre* sırasında
dusk *n* alacakaranlık
dust *n* toz
dusty *adj* tozlu
Dutch *adj* Hollandalı
duty *n* görev
dwarf *n* cüce
dwell *iv* ikamet etmek
dwelling *n* ikametgah
dwindle *v* gittikçe küçülmek
dye *v* boyamak
dye *n* boya
dying *adj* ölmekte olan
dynamic *adj* dinamik
dynamite *n* dinamit
dynasty *n* hanedan

E

each *adj* her
each other *adj* her bir
eager *adj* hevesli
eagerness *n* heveslilik
eagle *n* kartal
ear *n* kulak; başak
earache *n* kulak ağrısı
eardrum *n* kulak zarı
early *adv* erken
earmark *v* tayin etmek
earn *v* kazanmak
earnestly *adv* ciddiyetle
earnings *n* kazanç
earphones *n* kulaklık
earring *n* küpe
earth *n* toprak; dünya
earthquake *n* deprem
earwax *n* kulak mumu
ease *v* kolaylaştırmak
ease *n* kolaylık, rahatlık
easily *adv* kolayca
east *n* doğu
eastbound *adj* doğuya giden
Easter *n* Paskalya
eastern *adj* doğusal
easterner *n* doğulu
eastward *adv* doğuya doğru
easy *adj* kolay; rahat
eat *iv* yemek
eat away *v* aşındırmak
ebb *v* cezir
eccentric *adj* acayip
echo *n* yankı
eclipse *n* gök tutulması
ecology *n* ekoloji
economical *adj* ekonomik
economize *v* tasarruf etmek
economy *n* ekonomi
ecstasy *n* mutluluk
ecstatic *adj* çok mutlu
edge *n* uç
edgy *adj* sinirli
edible *adj* yenilebilir
edifice *n* büyük yapı
edit *v* düzenlemek
edition *n* sürüm
educate *v* eğitmek
educational *adj* eğitimsel
eerie *adj* ürkütücü
effect *n* etki
effective *adj* etkili
effectiveness *n* tesirlilik
efficiency *n* etkenlik

efficient *adj* verimli
effigy *n* büst
effort *n* çaba
effusive *adj* coşkun
egg *n* yumurta
egg white *n* yumurta akı
egoism *n* bencillik
egoist *n* egoist
eight *adj* sekiz
eighteen *adj* on sekiz
eighth *adj* sekizinci
eighty *adj* seksen
either *adj* ikisinden biri
either *adv* ikisinden biri
eject *v* fışkırtmak
elapse *v* akıp gitmek
elastic *adj* elastik
elated *adj* sevinçli
elbow *n* dirsek
elder *n* yaşlı
elderly *adj* yaşlıca
elect *v* seçmek
election *n* seçim
electric *adj* elektrik
electrician *n* elektrikçi
electricity *n* elektrik
electronic *adj* elektronik
elegance *n* zerafet
elegant *adj* zarif
element *n* eleman
elementary *adj* temel; kolay
elephant *n* fil
elevate *v* yükseltmek
elevation *n* yükselti
elevator *n* asansör
eleven *adj* on bir
eleventh *adj* on birinci
eligible *adj* seçilebilir
eliminate *v* gidermek
elm *n* karaağaç
eloquence *n* belagat
else *adv* başka
elsewhere *adv* başka bir yere
elude *v* atlatmak
elusive *adj* ele geçmez
emaciated *adj* çok zayıf
emanate *v* yayılmak
emancipate *v* azat etmek
embalm *v* mumyalamak
embark *v* binmek
embarrass *v* utandırmak
embassy *n* elçilik
embellish *v* süslemek
embers *n* köz
embitter *v* gücendirmek
emblem *n* amblem

embody *v* kapsamak
emboss *v* kabartmak
embrace *v* kucaklaşmak
embrace *n* kucak
embroider *v* süslemek
embroidery *n* süs
embroil *v* karıştırmak
embryo *n* embriyon
emerald *n* zümrüt
emerge *v* meydana çıkmak
emergency *n* acil
emigrant *n* göçmen
emigrate *v* göçmek
emission *n* salım
emit *v* salmak
emotion *n* duygu
emotional *adj* duygusal
emperor *n* imparator
emphasis *n* vurgu
emphasize *v* vurgulamak
empire *n* imparator
employ *v* kullanmak
employee *n* çalışan
employer *n* işveren
employment *n* iş
empress *n* imparatoriçe
emptiness *n* boşluk
empty *adj* boş
empty *v* boşaltmak
enable *v* etkinleştirmek
enchant *v* büyülemek
enchanting *adj* büyüleyici
encircle *v* kuşatmak
enclave *n* yerleşim bölgesi
enclose *v* kapsamak
enclosure *n* kapsam
encompass *v* ihtiva etmek
encounter *n* karşılaşma
encourage *v* cesaret vermek
encroach *v* saldırmak
encyclopedia *n* ansiklopedi
end *n* son
end *v* sonlandırmak
end up *v* olup çıkmak
endanger *v* tehlikeye sokmak
endeavor *v* gayret etmek
endeavor *n* gayret
ending *n* son
endless *adj* sonsuz
endorse *v* telkin etmek
endorsement *n* ciro
endure *v* dayanmak
enemy *n* düşman
energetic *adj* enerji dolu
energy *n* enerji
enforce *v* uygulamak

engage *v* meşgul etmek
engaged *adj* meşgul
engagement *n* nişanlı
engine *n* makina
engineer *n* mühendis
England *n* İngiltere
English *adj* İngiliz
engrave *v* kazımak
engraving *n* kazı
engrossed *adj* meşgul
engulf *v* içine çekmek
enhance *v* geliştirmek
enjoy *v* keyfini çıkarmak
enjoyable *adj* keyifli
enjoyment *n* keyif
enlarge *v* büyütmek
enlargement *n* büyütme
enlighten *v* aydınlatmak
enlist *v* askere kaydolmak
enormous *adj* kocaman
enough *adv* yeteri kadar
enrage *v* öfkelendirmek
enrich *v* zenginleştirmek
enroll *v* askere kaydolmak
enrollment *n* sicile kaydetmek
ensure *v* garanti etmek
entail *v* icap ettirmek
enter *v* girmek
enterprise *n* girişim; kuruluş
entertain *v* eğlendirmek
entertaining *adj* eğlenceli
entertainment *n* eğlence
enthrall *v* büyülemek
enthralling *adj* büyüleyici
enthuse *v* göklere çıkarmak
enthusiasm *n* şevk
entice *v* ayartmak
enticement *n* cazibe
enticing *adj* cezbedici
entire *adj* hepsi
entirely *adv* tamamıyla
entrance *n* giriş
entreat *v* yalvarmak
entree *n* esas yemek
entrenched *adj* sağlam
entrepreneur *n* girişimci
entrust *v* emanet etmek
entry *n* giriş
enumerate *v* saymak
envelop *v* kuşatmak
envelope *n* zarf
envious *adj* kıskanç
environment *n* çevre
envisage *v* tasavvur etmek
envoy *n* delege; son söz
envy *n* haset

envy *v* haset etmek
epidemic *n* salgın
epilepsy *n* sara
episode *n* bölüm; fasıl
epistle *n* risale; mektup
epitaph *n* mezar kitabesi
epitomize *v* özetlemek
epoch *n* devir
equal *adj* eşit
equality *n* eşitlik
equate *v* eşitlemek
equation *n* denklem
equator *n* ekvator
equilibrium *n* denge
equip *v* donatmak
equipment *n* donatım; gereç
equivalent *adj* eşdeğer
era *n* çağ
eradicate *v* yok etmek
erase *v* silmek
eraser *n* silgi
erect *v* kalkmak
erect *adj* kalkık
err *v* yanılmak
errand *n* ayak işi
erroneous *adj* hatalı
error *n* hata
erupt *v* püskürmek
eruption *n* patlak verme
escalate *v* yükseltmek
escalator *n* asansör
escapade *n* macera
escape *v* kaçmak
escort *n* refakatçı
esophagus *n* yemek borusu
especially *adv* özellikle
espionage *n* casusluk
essay *n* rapor; deneme
essence *n* öz varlık
essential *adj* temel
establish *v* kurmak
estate *n* arazi
esteem *v* itibar
estimate *v* kestirmek
estimation *n* tahmin
estuary *n* haliç
eternity *n* ebediyet
ethical *adj* ahlaki
ethics *n* ahlak
etiquette *n* görgü kuralları
euphoria *n* coşku
Europe *n* Avrupa
European *adj* Avrupalı
evacuate *v* boşaltmak
evade *v* kurtulmak
evaluate *v* değerlendirmek

evaporate *v* buharlaştırmak
evasion *n* kaçamak
evasive *adj* baştansavma
eve *n* arife
even *adj* bile
even if *c* osla bile
even more *c* daha da
evening *n* akşam
event *n* olay
eventuality *n* ihtimal
eventually *adv* nihayet
ever *adv* hiç; hep
everlasting *adj* sonsuz
every *adj* her
everybody *pro* herkes
everyday *adj* her gün
everyone *pro* herkes
everything *pro* her şey
evict *v* tahliye ettirmek
evidence *n* delil
evil *n* kötülük
evil *adj* uğursuz
evoke *v* uyandırmak
evolution *n* evrim
evolve *v* evrim geçirmek
exact *adj* tamamıyla
exaggerate *v* abartmak
exalt *v* yüceltmek
examination *n* sınav
examine *v* sınamak
example *n* örnek
exasperate *v* çileden çıkarmak
excavate *v* kazı yapmak
exceed *v* aşmak
exceedingly *adv* aşırı
excel *v* üstün olmak
excellence *n* üstünlük
excellent *adj* mükemmek
except *pre* haricinde
exception *n* istisna
exceptional *adj* istisnai
excerpt *n* alıntı
excess *n* fazlalık
excessive *adj* aşırı
exchange *v* takas etmek
excitement *n* heyecan
exciting *adj* heyecan verici
exclaim *v* çığlık atmak
exclude *v* dışlamak
excruciating *adj* dayanılmaz
excursion *n* gezinti
excuse *v* mazur görmek
excuse *n* mazeret
execute *v* yürütmek
executive *n* yönetim
exemplary *adj* örnek olarak

E

exemplify *v* örnek vermek
exempt *adj* muaf
exemption *n* muafiyet
exercise *n* egzersiz
exercise *v* alıştırma yapmak
exert *v* güç kullanmak
exertion *n* gayret
exhaust *v* tüketmek
exhausting *adj* yorucu
exhaustion *n* yorgunluk
exhibit *v* sergilemek
exhibition *n* sergi
exhilarating *adj* neşelendirici
exhort *v* teşvik etmek
exile *n* sürgün
exist *v* var olmak
existence *n* varlık
exit *n* çıkış
exodus *n* akın
exonerate *v* aklamak
exorbitant *adj* aşırı yüksek
exorcist *n* üfürükçü
exotic *adj* egzotik
expand *v* genleşmek
expansion *n* genleşme
expect *v* tahmin etmek
expectancy *n* umut
expectation *n* beklenti
expediency *n* menfaat
expedient *adj* uygun
expedition *n* keşif gezisi
expel *v* kovmak
expenditure *n* masraf
expense *n* masraf
expensive *adj* pahalı
experience *n* deneyim
experiment *n* deney
expert *adj* uzman
expiate *v* kefaret
expiation *n* kefaret
expiration *n* bitiş
expire *v* süresi bitmek
explain *v* açıklamak
explicit *adj* net
explode *v* patlamak
exploit *v* sömürmek
exploit *n* istismar
explore *v* keşfetmek
explorer *n* kaşif
explosion *n* patlama
explosive *adj* patlayıcı
export *v* ihracat
expose *v* maruz bırakmak
exposed *adj* maruz
express *adj* hızlı; kesin
express *v* beyan etmek

expression *n* anlatım
expressly *adv* hızlıca
expropriate *v* kamulaştırmak
expulsion *n* ihraç
exquisite *adj* üstün
extend *v* uzatmak
extension *n* uzatma
extent *n* kapsam
extenuating *adj* hafiflemiş
exterior *adj* harici
exterminate *v* yok etmek
external *adj* dış
extinct *adj* nesli tükenmiş
extinguish *v* söndürmek
extort *v* sızdırmak
extortion *n* haraç
extra *adv* ekstra
extract *v* çıkartmak
extradite *v* iade etmek
extradition *n* iade
extraneous *adj* yabancı
extravagance *n* israf
extravagant *adj* savurgan
extreme *adj* aşırı
extremist *adj* radikal
extremities *n* uç nokta
extricate *v* kurtarmak
extroverted *adj* dışadönük
exude *v* sızmak
exult *v* bayram etmek
eye *n* göz
eyebrow *n* kaş
eye-catching *adj* göz alan
eyeglasses *n* gözlük
eyelash *n* kirpik
eyelid *n* göz kapağı
eyesight *n* görüş yeteneği; gücü
eyewitness *n* görgü tanığı

F

fable *n* masal
fabric *n* kumaş
fabricate *v* uydurmak
fabulous *adj* harika
face *n* yüz
facet *n* yüzey; faseta
facilitate *v* kolaylaştırmak
facing *pre* yüz
fact *n* gerçek
factor *n* etken
factory *n* fabrika
factual *adj* gerçekçi

F

faculty *n* fakülte
fad *n* geçici heves
fade *v* sönmek
faded *adj* sönük
fail *v* başaramamak
failure *n* başarısızlık
faint *v* bayılmak
faint *n* donuk
faint *adj* zayıf
fair *n* fuar
fair *adj* dürüst
fairness *n* adaletlilik
fairy *n* peri
faith *n* inanç; güven
faithful *adj* inançlı; dürüst
fake *v* uydurmak
fake *adj* sahte
fall *n* düşüş; Sonbahar
fall *iv* düşmek
fall back *v* geri çekilmek
fall behind *v* geride kalmak
fall down *v* düşmek
fall through *v* gerçekleşmemek
fallacy *n* yanıltmaca
fallout *n* radyoaktif serpinti
falsehood *n* yalan
falsify *v* çarpıtmak
falter *v* tereddüt etmek
fame *n* ün
familiar *adj* tanıdık
family *n* aile
famine *n* kıtlık
famous *adj* ünlü
fan *n* yelpaze; hayran
fanatic *adj* fanatik
fancy *adj* özel
fang *n* köpekdişi
fantastic *adj* enfes
fantasy *n* fantazi
far *adv* uzakta
faraway *adj* uzakta
farce *n* fars
fare *n* yol parası
farewell *n* elveda
farm *n* çiftlik
farmer *n* çiftçi
farming *n* tarım
farmyard *n* çiftlik
farther *adv* daha uzak
fascinate *v* etkilemek
fashion *n* moda
fast *adj* hızlı
fasten *v* bağlamak
fat *n* yağ
fat *adj* şişman
fatal *adj* ölümcül

fate *n* kader
fateful *adj* vahim
father *n* baba
fatherhood *n* babalık
father-in-law *n* kayınpeder
fatherly *adj* babacan
fathom out *v* çözmek
fatigue *n* yorgunluk
fatten *v* şişmanlamak
fatty *adj* yağlı
faucet *n* musluk
fault *n* hata
faulty *adj* hatalı
favor *n* iyilik
favorable *adj* hoşa giden
favorite *adj* favori
fear *n* korku
fearful *adj* korkunç
feasible *adj* mümkün
feast *n* ziyafet
feat *n* marifet
feather *n* tüy
feature *n* özellik
February *n* Şubat
fed up *adj* sıkkın
federal *adj* federal
fee *n* ücret
feeble *adj* kuvvetsiz
feed *iv* beslemek
feedback *n* geribildirim
feel *iv* hissetmek
feeling *n* duygu
feelings *n* his
feet *n* ayaklar
feign *v* numara yapmak
fellow *n* arkadaş
fellowship *n* grup
felon *n* suçlu
felony *n* ağır suç
female *n* kadın; dişi
feminine *adj* kadınsı
fence *n* çit
fencing *n* eskrim
fend *v* savunmak
fend off *v* kovmak
fender *n* çamurluk
ferment *v* mayalamak
ferment *n* maya
ferocious *adj* vahşi
ferocity *n* vahişilik
ferry *n* feribot
fertile *adj* verimli
fertility *n* verimlilik
fertilize *v* gübrelemek
fervent *adj* hararetli
fester *v* iltihaplanmak

festive *adj* şen
festivity *n* şenlik
fetid *adj* kokuşmuş
fetus *n* cenin
feud *n* kan davası
fever *n* humma
feverish *adj* hummalı
few *adj* az
fewer *adj* daha az
fiancé *n* nişanlı
fiber *n* fiber
fickle *adj* vefasız
fiction *n* masal
fictitious *adj* hayali
fiddle *n* keman
fidelity *n* sadakat
field *n* alan
fierce *adj* şiddetli
fiery *adj* kızgın
fifteen *adj* onbeş
fifth *adj* beşinci
fifty *adj* elli
fifty-fifty *adv* yarı yarıya
fig *n* incir
fight *iv* kavga etmek
fight *n* kavga
fighter *n* kavgacı
figure *n* şekil; rakam
figure out *v* anlamak
file *v* dosyalamak
file *n* dosya; törpü
fill *v* doldurmak
filling *n* dolgu
film *n* film
filter *n* filtre
filter *v* filtrelemek
filth *n* pislik
filthy *adj* pis
fin *n* yüzgeç
final *adj* son
finalize *v* bitirmek
finance *v* finans
financial *adj* finansal
find *iv* bulmak
find out *v* keşfetmek
fine *n* iyi; para cezası
fine *v* para cezası vermek
fine *adv* iyi
fine *adj* iyi
finger *n* parmak
fingernail *n* tırnak
fingerprint *n* parmak izi
fingertip *n* parmak ucu
finish *v* bitirmek
Finland *n* Finlandiya
Finnish *adj* Fince

fire *v* ateşlemek; kovmak
fire *n* ateş
firearm *n* ateşli silah
firecracker *n* kestanefişeği
firefighter *n* itfaiyeci
fireman *n* itfaiyeci
fireplace *n* şömine
firewood *n* yakacak
fireworks *n* havai fişek
firm *adj* sıkı
firm *n* firma
firmness *n* sıkılık
first *adj* birinci; ilk
fish *n* balık
fisherman *n* balıkçı
fishy *adj* şüphe uyandıran
fist *n* yumruk
fit *n* sağlıklı; nöbet
fit *v* uymak
fitness *n* sağlık; spor
fitting *adj* uygun
five *adj* beş
fix *v* onarmak
fjord *n* fiyort
flag *n* bayrak
flagpole *n* gönder
flamboyant *adj* frapan
flame *n* alev
flammable *adj* yanıcı
flank *n* böğür
flare *n* parıltı
flare-up *v* hiddetlenmek
flash *n* flaş
flashlight *n* el feneri
flashy *adj* parıltılı
flat *n* apartman dairesi
flat *adj* düz
flatten *v* düzleştirmek
flatter *v* yağ çekmek
flattery *n* kompliman
flaunt *v* sergilemek
flavor *n* çeşni
flaw *n* kusur
flawless *adj* kusursuz
flea *n* pire
flee *iv* firar etmek
fleece *n* yün
fleet *n* filo
fleeting *adj* donanma
flesh *n* et
flex *v* bükmek
flexible *adj* esnek
flicker *v* titreşmek
flier *n* pilot; uçak
flight *n* uçuş; firar
flimsy *adj* dayanıksız

flip *v* çevirmek
flirt *v* flört etmek
float *v* su üstünde durmak
flock *n* sürü
flog *v* dövmek
flood *v* sel
floodgate *n* bent kapağı
flooding *n* sel basma
floodlight *n* projektör
floor *n* zemin
flop *n* fiyasko; şlap
floss *n* diş ipliği
flour *n* un
flourish *v* serpilmek
flow *v* akmak
flow *n* akış
flower *n* çiçek
flowerpot *n* saksı
flu *n* grip
fluctuate *v* yükselip alçalmak
fluently *adv* akıcı bir şekilde
fluid *n* sıvı
flunk *v* sınavda çakmak
flush *v* birden akmak
flute *n* flüt
flutter *v* çırpınmak
fly *iv* uçmak
fly *n* uçuş
foam *n* köpük
focus *n* odak
focus on *v* focus on
foe *n* düşman
fog *n* sis
foggy *adj* sisli
foil *v* set çekmek
fold *v* katlamak
folder *n* klasör
folks *n* millet
folksy *adj* arkadaşça
follow *v* takip etmek
follower *n* yandaş
folly *n* delilik
fond *adj* sevgi dolu; meraklı
fondle *v* okşamak
fondness *n* düşkünlük
food *n* yemek
foodstuff *n* yiyecek
fool *v* aldatmak
fool *adj* budala
foot *n* ayak
football *n* futbol
footnote *n* dipnot
footprint *n* ayak izi
footstep *n* adım
footwear *n* ayakkabılar
for *pre* için

forbid *iv* yasaklamak
force *n* güç
force *v* zorlamak
forceful *adj* kuvvetli
forcibly *adv* zorla
forecast *iv* tahmin
forefront *n* ön plan
foreground *n* ön plan
forehead *n* alın
foreign *adj* yabancı; harici
foreigner *n* yabancı
foreman *n* ustabaşı
foremost *adj* başta gelen
foresee *iv* ileriyi görmek
foreshadow *v* habercisi olmak
foresight *n* tedbir
forest *n* orman
foretell *v* kehanette bulunmak
forever *adv* ebediyen
forewarn *v* uyarmak
foreword *n* önsöz
forge *v* sahtesini yapmak
forgery *n* sahte
forget *v* unutmak
forgivable *adj* affedilir
forgive *v* affetmek
forgiveness *n* bağışlama
fork *n* çatal
form *n* şekil
formal *adj* resmi
formality *n* resmiyet
formalize *v* resmileştirmek
formally *adv* resmi olarak
format *n* biçim
formation *n* düzen
former *adj* önceki
formerly *adv* eskiden
formidable *adj* korkunç
formula *n* formül
forsake *iv* vazgeçmek
fort *n* kale
forthcoming *adj* mevcut
forthright *adj* açıksözlü
fortify *v* kuvvetlendirmek
fortitude *n* metanetli
fortress *n* büyük kale
fortunate *adj* şanslı
fortune *n* kısmet
forty *adj* kırk
forward *adv* ileride
fossil *n* fosil
foster *v* beslemek
foul *adj* kirli
foundation *n* tesis; fondöten
founder *n* kurucu
foundry *n* dökümhane

fountain *n* çeşme
four *adj* dört
fourteen *adj* ondört
fourth *adj* dördüncü
fox *n* tilki
foxy *adj* kurnaz
fraction *n* kesir
fracture *n* kırık
fragile *adj* kırılgan
fragment *n* parça
fragrance *n* koku
fragrant *adj* kokulu
frail *adj* narin
frailty *n* zaaf
frame *n* çerçeve; iskelet
frame *v* ifade etmek
framework *n* taslak
France *n* Fransa
franchise *n* imtiyaz
frank *adj* dürüst
frankly *adv* dürüstçe
frankness *n* dürüstlük
frantic *adj* dellenmiş
fraternal *adj* kardeşçe
fraternity *n* kardeşlik
fraud *n* hile
fraudulent *adj* hileli
freckle *n* çil
freckled *adj* çilli
free *v* özgür bırakmak
free *adj* özgür; bedava
freedom *n* özgürlük
freeway *n* otoyol
freeze *iv* dondurmak
freezer *n* buzluk
freezing *adj* soğuk
freight *n* nakliye
French *adj* Fransız
frenetic *adj* telaşlı
frenzied *adj* çılgın
frenzy *n* çılgın
frequency *n* sıklık
frequent *adj* sık; yaygın
frequent *v* dadanmak
fresh *adj* taze
freshen *v* tazelemek
freshness *n* tazelik
friar *n* papaz
friction *n* sürtünme
Friday *n* Cuma
fried *adj* kızarmış
friend *n* arkadaş
friendship *n* arkadaşlık
fries *n* cips
frigate *n* fırkateyn
fright *n* korku

frighten *v* korkutmak
frightening *adj* korkunç
frigid *adj* duygusuz
fringe *n* kahkül; özenti
frivolous *adj* önemsiz
frog *n* kurbağa
from *pre* den; dan
front *n* ön; cephe
front *adj* ön
frontage *n* bina cephesi
frontier *n* hudut
frost *n* ayaz
frostbite *n* soğuk ısırması
frostbitten *adj* donmuş
frosty *adj* kırağılı
frown *v* kaşlarını çatmak
frozen *adj* donmuş
frugal *adj* tutumlu
frugality *n* tutumluluk
fruit *n* meyve
fruitful *adj* verimli
fruity *adj* meyveli
frustrate *v* engellemek
frustration *n* hüsran
fry *v* kızartmak
frying pan *n* tava
fuel *n* yakıt
fuel *v* yakıt almak
fugitive *n* kaçak
fulfill *v* tamamlamak
fulfillment *n* tamamlama
full *adj* dolu
fully *adv* tamamen
fumes *n* duman
fumigate *v* dezenfekte etmek
fun *n* eğlenceli
function *n* işlev
fund *n* bütçe
fund *v* sermaye bulmak
fundamental *adj* temel
funds *n* sermaye
funeral *n* cenaze
fungus *n* küf mantar
funny *adj* komik
fur *n* kürk
furious *adj* sinirli
furiously *adv* sinirli bir şekilde
furnace *n* ocak
furnish *v* döşemek
furnishings *n* donatmak
furniture *n* mobilya
furor *n* kızgınlık
furrow *n* kırışık
furry *adj* tüyleri kabarık
further *adv* ötede
furthermore *adv* dahası

fury *n* gazap
fuse *n* sigorta
fusion *n* kaynaşma
fuss *n* yaygara
fussy *adj* yaygaracı
futile *adj* nafile
futility *n* faydasızlık
future *n* gelecek
fuzzy *adj* tüylü

G

gadget *n* alet
gag *n* şaka
gag *v* susturmak
gage *v* bahse girmek
gain *v* elde etmek
gain *n* kazanç
gal *n* kız
galaxy *n* galaksi
gale *n* sert rüzgar
gall bladder *n* safra kesesi
gallant *adj* efendi
gallery *n* galeri
gallon *n* galon
gallop *v* dörtnala gitmek
gallows *n* darağacı
galvanize *v* galvanizlemek
gamble *v* kumar oynamak
game *n* oyun
gang *n* çete
gangrene *n* kangren
gangster *n* gangster
gap *n* boşluk; fiyat aralığı
garage *n* garaj
garbage *n* çöplük
garden *n* bahçe
gardener *n* bahçıvan
gargle *v* gargara yapmak
garland *n* çelenk
garlic *n* sarımsak
garment *n* giysi
garnish *v* donatmak
garnish *n* garnitür
garrison *n* garnizon
garrulous *adj* geveze
garter *n* jartiyer
gas *n* gaz
gash *n* derin yara
gasoline *n* benzin
gasp *v* solumak
gastric *adj* midesel
gate *n* geçit

gather *v* toplamak
gathering *n* toplantı
gauge *v* kalibrasyon
gauze *n* gazlı bez
gaze *v* gözünü dikmek
gear *n* alet; vites
geese *n* kaz
gem *n* mücevher
gender *n* cinsiyet
gene *n* gen
general *n* genel
generalize *v* genellemek
generate *v* üretmek
generation *n* nesil
generator *n* jeneratör
generic *adj* soysal
generosity *n* cömertlik
genetic *adj* genetik
genial *adj* cana yakın
genius *n* deha
genocide *n* soykırım
genteel *adj* efendi
gentle *adj* kibar
gentleman *n* efendi
gentleness *n* kibarlık
genuflect *v* diz çökmek
genuine *adj* hakiki
geography *n* coğrafya
geology *n* jeoloji
geometry *n* geometri
germ *n* mikrop
German *adj* Alman
Germany *n* Almanya
germinate *v* çimlenmek
gerund *n* ulaç
gestation *n* gebelik
gesticulate *v* jestler yapmak
gesture *n* jest
get *iv* almak
get along *v* anlaşmak
get away *v* kaçmak
get back *v* öç almak
get by *v* geçmek
get down *v* indirmek
get down to *v* başlamak
get in *v* içeri girmek
get off *v* inmek
get out *v* çıkarmak
get over *v* unutmak
get together *v* buluşmak
get up *v* kalkmak
geyser *n* kaynaç
ghastly *adj* korkunç
ghost *n* hayalet
giant *n* dev
gift *n* hediye

gifted *adj* yetenekli
gigantic *adj* kocaman
giggle *v* kıkırdamak
gimmick *n* hile
ginger *n* zencefil; kızıl
gingerly *adv* ihtiyatla
giraffe *n* zürafa
girl *n* kız
girlfriend *n* kız arkadaş
give *iv* vermek
give away *v* hediye etmek
give back *v* iade etmek
give in *v* razı olmak
give out *v* duyurmak
give up *v* vazgeçmek
glacier *n* buzul
glad *adj* memnun
gladiator *n* gladyatör
glamorous *adj* çekici
glance *v* göz atmak
glance *n* bakış
gland *n* salgı bezi
glare *n* parıltı
glass *n* cam
glasses *n* gözlük
glassware *n* züccaciye
gleam *n* pırıltı
gleam *v* parıldamak
glide *v* süzülmek
glimmer *n* ışık
glimpse *n* gözüne ilişme
glimpse *v* gözüne ilişmek
glitter *v* pırıldamak
globe *n* küre
globule *n* kürecik
gloom *n* sıkıntı
gloomy *adj* kasvetli
glorify *v* yüceltmek
glorious *adj* şerefli
glory *n* şan
gloss *n* parlaklık
glossary *n* sözlük
glossy *adj* parlak
glove *n* eldiven
glow *v* parlamak
glucose *n* glikoz
glue *n* zamk
glue *v* zamklamak
glut *n* aşırı
glutton *n* obur
gnaw *v* kemirmek
go *iv* gitmek
go ahead *v* ilerlemek
go away *v* ayrılmak
go back *v* dönmek
go down *v* düşmek

go in *v* girmek
go on *v* devam etmek
go out *v* dışarı çıkmak
go over *v* incelemek
go through *v* gözden geçirmek
go under *v* batmak
go up *v* yükselmek
goad *v* dürtmek
goal *n* gol; amaç
goalkeeper *n* kaleci
goat *n* keçi
gobble *v* hızlı yemek
God *n* Tanrı
goddess *n* tanrıça
godless *adj* tanrıtanımaz
goggles *n* koruyucu gözlük
gold *n* anltın
golden *adj* altından
good *adj* iyi
good-looking *adj* yakışıklı
goodness *n* iyilik
goods *n* mallar
goodwill *n* iyi niyet
goof *v* hata yapmak
goof *n* aptal
goose *n* kaz
gorge *n* geçit
gorgeous *adj* güzel
gorilla *n* goril
gory *adj* kanlı
gospel *n* incil
gossip *v* dedikodu yapmak
gossip *n* dedikodu
gout *n* gut
govern *v* yönetmek
government *n* hükümet
governor *n* vali
gown *n* gecelik
grab *v* kavramak
grace *n* zarafet
graceful *adj* zarif
gracious *adj* kibar
grade *n* derece
gradual *adj* kademeli
graduate *v* mezun olmak
graduation *n* mezuniyet
graft *v* yamalamak
graft *n* yama
grain *n* tahıl
gram *n* gram
grammar *n* gramer
grand *adj* görkemli
grandchild *n* torun
granddad *n* dede
grandfather *n* büyükbaba
grandmother *n* büyükanne

G

grandparents *n* büyükbaba ve büyükbaba
grandson *n* erkek torun
grandstand *n* tribün
granite *n* granit
granny *n* nine
grant *v* kabul etmek
grant *n* ödenek
grape *n* üzüm
grapefruit *n* greypfrut
grapevine *n* asma
graphic *adj* grafik
grasp *n* yakalama
grasp *v* kavramak; anlamak
grass *n* çimen
grassroots *adj* ortadirek
grateful *adj* minnettar
gratify *v* hoşnut etmek
gratifying *adj* tatminkar
gratitude *n* minnettarlık
gratuity *n* teberru
grave *adj* ciddi
grave *n* mezar
gravel *n* çakıl
gravely *adv* ciddi şekilde
gravestone *n* mezar taşı
graveyard *n* mezarlık
gravitate *v* yönelmek
gravity *n* yerçekimi
gravy *n* sos
gray *adj* gri
grayish *adj* grimsi
graze *v* otlamak
graze *n* otlama; sıyrık
grease *v* yağlamak
grease *n* et yağı
greasy *adj* yağlı; kaygan
great *adj* büyük
greatness *n* fevkalade
Greece *n* Yunanistan
greed *n* hırs
greedy *adj* hırslı
Greek *adj* Yunan
green *adj* yeşil
green bean *n* taze fasulye
greenhouse *n* sera
Greenland *n* grönland
greet *v* selamlamak
greetings *n* selamlama
gregarious *adj* girişken
grenade *n* el bombası
greyhound *n* tazı
grief *n* keder
grievance *n* yakınma
grieve *v* kederlen
grill *v* ızgara yapmak

grill *n* ızgara
grim *adj* korkunç
grimace *n* yüz ekşitme
grime *n* kir
grind *iv* öğütmek
grip *v* sımsıkı tutmak
grip *n* sap
gripe *n* sancı
grisly *adj* ürkütücü
groan *v* inlemek
groceries *n* bakkaliye
groin *n* kasık
groom *n* güvey
groove *n* oluk
gross *adj* iğrenç; brüt
grossly *adv* fena halde
grotesque *adj* gülünç
grotto *n* mağara
grouch *v* söylenmek
grouchy *adj* dırdırcı
ground *n* zemin
ground floor *n* zemin kat
groundless *adj* asılsız
groundwork *n* groundwork
group *n* grup
grow *iv* yetiştirmek
grow up *v* büyümek
growl *v* hırlamak
grown-up *n* yetişkin
growth *n* büyüme
grudge *n* garez
grudgingly *adv* istemeyerek
gruelling *adj* yorucu
gruesome *adj* iğrenç
grumble *v* homurdanma
grumpy *adj* huysuz
guarantee *v* garanti etmek
guarantee *n* garanti
guarantor *n* garantör
guard *n* nöbet
guardian *n* koruyucu
guerrilla *n* gerilla
guess *v* tahmin etmek
guess *n* tahmin
guest *n* misafir
guidance *n* kılavuzluk
guide *v* kılavuzluk etmek
guide *n* kılavuz
guidebook *n* rehber
guidelines *n* ana noktalar
guild *n* lonca
guile *n* kurnazlık
guillotine *n* giyotin
guilt *n* suç
guilty *adj* suçlu
guise *n* kılık

guitar *n* gitar
gulf *n* körfez
gull *n* martı
gullible *adj* saf
gulp *v* dedikodu
gulp *n* yudum
gulp down *v* yutmak
gum *n* sakız; damak
gun *n* silah
gun down *v* öldürmek
gunfire *n* ateş etme
gunman *n* tüfekçi
gunpowder *n* barut
gunshot *n* atış menzili
gust *n* bora
gusto *n* zevk
gusty *adj* fırtınalı
gut *n* mide
guts *n* yürek; metanet
gutter *n* oluk; sefalet
guy *n* adam
guzzle *v* hızlı içmek
gymnasium *n* spor salonu
gynecology *n* jinekoloji
gypsy *n* çingene

H

habit *n* alışkanlık
habitable *adj* oturulur
habitual *adj* alışılmış
hack *v* yarmak
haggle *v* pazarlık etmek
hail *n* selam
hail *v* selamlamak
hair *n* saç
hairbrush *n* saç fırçası
haircut *n* saç kesimi
hairdo *n* saç şekli
hairdresser *n* kuaför
hairpiece *n* peruk
hairy *adj* kıllı
half *n* yarım
half *adj* yarı
hall *n* koridor
hallway *n* hol
halt *v* durdurmak
halve *v* yarıya bölmek
ham *n* domuz eti
hamburger *n* hamburger
hamlet *n* mezra
hammer *n* çekiç
hammock *n* hamak

hand *n* el
hand down *v* devretmek
hand in *v* teslim etmek
hand out *v* dağıtmak
hand over *v* havale etmek
handbag *n* el çantası
handbook *n* el kitabı
handcuff *v* kelepçelemek
handcuffs *n* kelepçe
handful *n* avuç dolusu
handgun *n* tabanca
handicap *n* engel
handkerchief *n* mendil
handle *v* işlemek
handle *n* el sürmek
handmade *adj* el yapımı
handout *n* sadaka
handrail *n* handrail
handshake *n* el sıkışma
handsome *adj* yakışıklı
handwritting *n* el yazısı
handy *adj* kullanışlı
hang *iv* asmak
hang around *v* etrafta takılmak
hang on *v* sıkı tutunmak
hanger *n* askı
hangup *n* güçlük
happen *v* olmak
happening *n* vaka
happiness *n* mutluluk
happy *adj* mutlu
harass *v* rahatsız etmek
harassment *n* usanç
harbor *n* liman; barınak
hard *adj* zor
harden *v* sertleştirmek
hardly *adv* zorla
hardness *n* sertlik
hardship *n* sıkıntı
hardware *n* donanım
hardwood *n* kereste
hardy *adj* dayanıklı
hare *n* tavşan
harm *v* zarar vermek
harm *n* zarar
harmful *adj* zararlı
harmless *adj* zararsız
harmony *n* uyum
harp *n* harp
harpoon *n* zıpkın
harrowing *adj* acıklı
harsh *adj* hırçın
harshly *adv* insafsızca
harshness *n* hırçınlık
harvest *n* hasat
harvest *v* hasat etmek

hashish *n* haşhaş
hassle *v* tartışmak
hassle *n* zorluk
haste *n* acele
hasten *v* hız vermek
hastily *adv* acele şekilde
hasty *adj* düşüncesiz
hat *n* şapka
hatchet *n* nacak
hate *v* nefret etmek
hateful *adj* nefret dolu
hatred *n* nefret
haughty *adj* kibirli
haul *v* çekmek
haunt *v* sık uğramak
have *iv* sahip olmak
haven *n* sığınak
havoc *n* hasar
hawk *n* atmaca
hay *n* saman
haystack *n* saman sapı
hazard *n* tehlike
hazardous *adj* tehlikeli
haze *n* sis
hazelnut *n* fındık
hazy *adj* dumanlı
he *pro* o erkek
head *n* baş
head for *v* yol almak
headache *n* baş ağrısı
heading *n* reis
head-on *adv* gerçekten
headphones *n* kulaklık
headquarters *n* garnizon
headway *n* ilerleme
heal *v* iyileştirmek
healer *n* iyileştirici
health *n* sağlık
healthy *adj* sağlıklı
heap *n* yığın
heap *v* kümelemek
hear *iv* işitmek
hearing *n* duruşma
hearsay *n* söylenti
hearse *n* cenaze arabası
heart *n* kalp
heartbeat *n* kalp atışı
heartburn *n* mide ekşimesi
hearten *v* yüreklendirmek
heartfelt *adj* candan
hearth *n* şömine
heartless *adj* kalpsiz
hearty *adj* yürekten
heat *v* ısıtmak
heat *n* ısı
heater *n* ısıtıcı

heathen *n* kafir
heating *n* kalorifer
heatwave *n* sıcak dalgası
heaven *n* cennet
heavenly *adj* cennet gibi
heaviness *n* ağırlık
heavy *adj* ağır
heckle *v* sözünü kesmek
hectic *adj* heyecanlı
heed *v* önemsemek
heel *n* topuk
height *n* boy
heighten *v* yükseltmek
heinous *adj* tiksindirici
heir *n* mirasçı
heiress *n* kadın mirasçı
heist *n* soygun
helicopter *n* helikopter
hell *n* cehennem
hello *e* selam
helm *n* dümen
helmet *n* miğfer
help *v* yardım etmek
help *n* yardım
helper *n* yardımcı
helpful *adj* yardımsever
helpless *adj* savunmasız
hem *n* baskı
hemisphere *n* yarıküre
hemorrhage *n* kanama
hen *n* tavuk
hence *adv* dolayısıyla
henchman *n* dalkavuk
her *adj* o kıza; o kızın
herald *v* müjdecisi olmak
herald *n* müjdeci
herb *n* baharat
here *adv* burada
hereafter *adv* ileride
hereby *adv* bu vesileyle
hereditary *adj* ırsi
heresy *n* dalalet
heretic *adj* kafir
heritage *n* miras
hermetic *adj* havageçirmez
hermit *n* keşiş
hernia *n* fıtık
hero *n* kahraman
heroic *adj* şanlı
heroin *n* eroin
heroism *n* kahramanlık
hers *pro* o kızın
herself *pro* kendisine
hesitant *adj* tereddütlü
hesitate *v* tereddüt etmek
hesitation *n* tereddüt

heyday *n* altın çağ
hiccup *n* hıçkırık
hidden *adj* gizli
hide *iv* gizlenmek
hideaway *n* gizleme yeri,
hideous *adj* korkunç
hierarchy *n* hiyerarşi
high *adj* yüksek
highlight *n* highlight
highly *adv* pek çok
Highness *n* Ekselanslar
highway *n* anayol
hijack *v* uçak kaçırmak
hijack *n* kaçırma
hijacker *n* korsan
hike *v* yürüyüş yapmak
hike *n* yürüyüş
hilarious *adj* komik
hill *n* tepe
hillside *n* yamaç
hilltop *n* tepe üstü
hilly *adj* tepelik
hilt *n* kabza
hinder *v* engellemek
hindrance *n* engel
hindsight *n* tüfeğin gezi
hinge *v* mentese takmak
hinge *n* menteşe

hint *n* ipucu
hint *v* ipucu vermek
hip *n* kalça
hire *v* kiralamak
his *adj* o erkek
his *pro* o erkeğin
Hispanic *adj* İspanyol
hiss *v* tıslamak
historian *n* tarihçi
history *n* tarih
hit *n* isabet; başarı
hit *iv* vurmak
hit back *v* misilleme yapmak
hitch *n* engel
hitch up *v* koşmak
hitchhike *n* otostop yapmak
hitherto *adv* şimdiye kadar
hive *n* arı kovanı
hoard *v* biriktirmek
hoarse *adj* boğuk
hoax *n* şaka
hobby *n* hobi
hog *n* domuz
hoist *v* yukarı çekmek
hoist *n* vinç
hold *iv* tutmak
hold back *v* kendini tutmak
hold on to *v* tutunmak

hold out *v* sabırla beklemek
hold up *v* yukarı kaldırmak.
holdup *n* durdurma
hole *n* delik
holiday *n* tatil
holiness *n* kutsallık
Holland *n* Hollanda
hollow *adj* boş
holocaust *n* facia
holy *adj* ilahi
homage *n* hürmet
home *n* ev
homeland *n* yurt
homeless *adj* evsiz
homely *adj* sade
homemade *adj* ev yapımı
homesick *adj* evini özlemiş
hometown *n* memleket
homework *n* ev ödevi
homicide *n* cinayet
homily *n* hitabe
honest *adj* dürüst
honesty *n* dürüstlük
honey *n* bal
honeymoon *n* balayı
honk *v* korna çalmak
honor *n* onur
hood *n* kukuleta
hoodlum *n* kabadayı
hoof *n* toynak
hook *n* kanca; orak
hooligan *n* holigan
hop *v* zıplamak
hope *n* umut
hopeful *adj* umutlu
hopefully *adv* ümitle
hopeless *adj* ümitsiz
horizon *n* ufuk
horizontal *adj* yatay
hormone *n* hormon
horn *n* boynuz
horrendous *adj* tüyler ürpertici
horrible *adj* korkunç
horrify *v* korkutmak
horror *n* korku
horse *n* at
hose *n* su hortumu
hospital *n* hastane
hospitality *n* konukseverlik
host *n* ev sahibi
hostage *n* rehine
hostess *n* sahibe
hostile *adj* düşmanca
hostility *n* düşmanlık
hot *adj* sıcak
hotel *n* otel

hound *n* tazı
hour *n* saat
hourly *adv* saatlik
house *n* ev
household *n* ev halkı
housekeeper *n* kahya
housewife *n* ev hanımı
housework *n* ev işi
hover *v* dolaşmak
how *adv* neden; nasıl
however *c* ancak
howl *v* ulumak
howl *n* uluma
hub *n* göbek
huddle *v* sıkışmak
hug *v* kucaklamak
hug *n* kucak
huge *adj* kocaman
hull *n* kavuz
hum *v* mırıldanmak
human *adj* insancıl
human being *n* insanoğlu
humanities *n* insanlık
humankind *n* insanoğlu
humble *adj* alçakgönüllü
humbly *adv* mütevazı şekilde
humid *adj* nemli
humidity *n* rutubet
humiliate *v* küçük düşürmek
humility *n* alçakgönüllülük
humor *n* mizah
humorous *adj* güldürücü
hump *n* kambur
hunch *n* önsezi
hunchback *n* kambur
hunched *adj* kambur
hundred *adj* yüz
hundredth *adj* yüzüncü
hunger *n* açlık
hungry *adj* aç
hunt *v* avlanmak
hunter *n* avcı
hunting *n* elek
hurdle *n* engel
hurl *v* fırlatmak
hurricane *n* kasırga
hurriedly *adv* aceleyle
hurry *v* acele ettirmek
hurry up *v* acele etmek
hurt *iv* yaralamak
hurt *adj* yaralı
hurtful *adj* kırıcı
husband *n* koca
hush *n* huşu
hush up *v* örtbas etmek
husky *adj* kısık

hustle *n* koşuşturma
hut *n* baraka
hydraulic *adj* hidrolik
hydrogen *n* hidrojen
hyena *n* sırtlan
hygiene *n* hijyen
hymn *n* ilahi
hyphen *n* kısa çizgi
hypnosis *n* hipnoz
hypnotize *v* hipnotize etmek
hypocrisy *n* ikiyüzlülük
hypocrite *adj* ikiyüzlü
hypothesis *n* varsayım
hysteria *n* histeri
hysterical *adj* isteri

I

I *pro* ben
ice *n* buz
ice cream *n* dondurma
ice cube *n* buz kalıbı
ice skate *v* buz pateni
iceberg *n* buzdağı
icebox *n* buzluk
ice-cold *adj* buz gibi
icon *n* ikon
icy *adj* buzlu
idea *n* fikir
ideal *adj* ideal
identical *adj* tıpkısı; özdeş
identify *v* tespit etmek
identity *n* kimlik
ideology *n* ideoloji
idiom *n* deyim
idiot *n* gerizekalı
idiotic *adj* aptalca
idle *adj* aylak
idol *n* idol
idolatry *n* putperestlik
if *c* eğer
ignite *v* aydınlatmak
ignorance *n* cehalet

ignorant *adj* cahil
ignore *v* gözardı etmek
ill *adj* hasta
illegal *adj* yasadışı
illegible *adj* okunaksız
illegitimate *adj* gayri meşru
illicit *adj* yasadışı
illiterate *adj* okumamış
illness *n* hastalık
illogical *adj* mantıksız
illuminate *v* aydınlatmak
illusion *n* sanrı
illustrate *v* örneklemek
illustration *n* resim; örnek
illustrious *adj* ünlü
image *n* görüntü
imagination *n* hayalgücü
imagine *v* hayal etmek
imbalance *n* dengesizlik
imitate *v* taklit etmek
imitation *n* taklit
immaculate *adj* tertemiz
immaturity *n* hamlık
immediately *adv* hemen
immense *adj* bucaksız
immerse *v* batırmak
immersion *n* batma
immigrant *n* göçmen
immigrate *v* göç etmek
immigration *n* göç
imminent *adj* yakın
immobile *adj* hareketsiz
immoral *adj* ahlaksız
immorality *n* ahlaksızlık
immortal *adj* ölümsüz
immortality *n* ölümsüzlük
immune *adj* bağışık
immunity *n* bağışıklık
immutable *adj* sabit
impact *n* vuruş; etki
impact *v* vurmak
impair *v* bozmak
impartial *adj* tarafsız
impatience *n* sabırsızlık
impatient *adj* sabırsız
impeccable *adj* hatasız
impediment *n* engel
impending *adj* yakın
imperfection *n* kusur
imperial *adj* şahane
imperialism *n* imparatorluk
impersonal *adj* gayri şahsi
impertinence *n* küstahlık
impertinent *adj* terbiyesiz
impetuous *adj* aceleci
implacable *adj* yatıştırılmaz

implicate *v* karıştırmak
implication *n* ima
implicit *adj* dahili
implore *v* dilemek
imply *v* ima etmek
impolite *adj* kaba
import *v* ithal etmek
importance *n* önem
importation *n* ithalat
impose *v* aldatmak
imposing *adj* heybetli
imposition *n* hile; ceza
impossibility *n* imkansızlık
impossible *adj* imkansız
impotent *adj* iktidarsız
impound *v* el koymak
impoverished *adj* yoksul
imprecise *adj* dikkatsiz
impress *v* etkilemek
impressive *adj* çarpıcı
imprison *v* hapse atmak
improbable *adj* beklenmedik
impromptu *adv* doğaçlama
improper *adj* münasebetsiz
improve *v* geliştirmek
improvement *n* gelişme
impulse *n* dürtü
impulsive *adj* atılgan
impunity *n* muaf olma
impure *adj* ahlaksız
in *pre* içinde
in depth *adv* derinlemesine
inability *n* acizlik
inaccurate *adj* yanlış
inadequate *adj* yetersiz
inadmissible *adj* kabul edilemez
inappropriate *adj* uygunsuz
inasmuch as *c* madem ki
inaugurate *v* açılış yapmak
inauguration *n* açılış
incalculable *adj* değişken
incapable *adj* kabiliyetsiz
incapacitate *v* aciz bırakmak
incarcerate *v* hapsedilme
incense *n* tütsü; günlük
incentive *n* dürtü; neden
inception *n* başlangıç
incessant *adj* aralıksız
inch *n* inç
incident *n* hadise
incidentally *adv* tesadüfen
incision *n* açım; insizyon
incite *v* kışkırtmak
incitement *n* fitnecilik; tahrik
inclination *n* eğilim
incline *v* eğilmek

include *v* içermek
inclusive *adv* dahil
incoherent *adj* abuk sabuk
income *n* gelir
incoming *adj* gelen; yeni
incompatible *adj* uyuşmaz
incompetence *n* beceriksizlik
incompetent *adj* beceriksiz
incomplete *adj* bitmemiş
inconsistent *adj* tutarsız
inconvenient *adj* zahmetli
incorporate *v* anonim
incorrect *adj* yanlış
incorrigible *adj* akıllanmaz
increase *v* artmak
increase *n* artış
increasing *adj* artan
incredible *adj* inanılmaz
increment *n* artış; kazanç
incriminate *v* suçlamak
incur *v* maruz kalmak
incurable *adj* devasız
indecency *n* ahlaksızlık
indecision *n* kararsızlık
indecisive *adj* kararsız
indeed *adv* gerçekten
indefinite *adj* belirsiz
indemnity *n* tazminat
independence *n* bağımsızlık
independent *adj* bağımsız
index *n* içindekiler
indicate *v* göstermek
indication *n* belirti
indict *v* itham etmek
indifference *n* ilgisizlik
indifferent *adj* ilgisiz
indigent *adj* yoksul
indigestion *n* hazımsızlık
indirect *adj* dolaylı
indiscreet *adj* patavatsız
indispensable *adj* zorunlu
indisposed *adj* isteksiz
indisputable *adj* su götürmez
indivisible *adj* bölünmez
indoor *adv* yapı içi
induce *v* neden olmak
indulge *v* teslim olmak
indulgent *adj* yüz veren
industrious *adj* endüstriyel
industry *n* endüstri
ineffective *adj* etkisiz
inefficient *adj* etkisiz
inept *adj* uygunsuz
inequality *n* eşitsizlik
inevitable *adj* kaçınılmaz
inexcusable *adj* bağışlanamaz

inexpensive *adj* ucuz
inexperienced *adj* deneyimsiz
inexplicable *adj* açıklanamaz
infallible *adj* yanılmaz
infamous *adj* adı çıkmış
infancy *n* bebeklik
infant *n* bebek
infantry *n* piyadeler
infect *v* bulaştırmak
infection *n* enfeksiyon
infectious *adj* bulaşıcı
infer *v* çıkarmak
inferior *adj* aşağılık
infertile *adj* çorak
infested *adj* istila et
infidelity *n* sadakatsizlik
infiltrate *v* sızmak
infinite *adj* sonsuz
infirmary *n* revir
inflate *v* şişirmek
inflation *n* enflasyon
inflexible *adj* eğilmez
inflict *v* acı çektirmek
influence *n* etki
influential *adj* nüfuzlu
influenza *n* nezle
influx *n* istila
inform *v* haber vermek
informal *adj* resmi olmayan
informality *n* teklifsiz
information *n* bilgi
informer *n* ihbarcı; haberci
infraction *n* ihlal
infrequent *adj* seyrek
infusion *n* içine dökme
ingenuity *n* ustalık
ingest *v* yemek
ingot *n* külçe
ingrained *adj* kökleşmiş
ingratiate *v* sevdirmek
ingratitude *n* nankörlük
ingredient *n* malzeme
inhabit *v* yerleşmek
inhabitant *n* oturan kimse
inhale *v* içine çekmek
inherit *v* miras kalmak
inheritance *n* kalıt
inhibit *v* ket vurmak
inhuman *adj* acımasız
initial *adj* başlangıç
initially *adv* baştaki
initiate *v* başlatmak
initiative *n* inisiyatif
injection *n* enjeksiyon
injure *v* zarar vermek
injurious *adj* zararlı

injury *n* hasar
injustice *n* haksızlık
ink *n* mürekkep
inkling *n* ipucu
inlaid *adj* işlemeli
inland *adv* içerilerde
inland *adj* ülkenin iç kısmı
in-laws *n* akraba
inmate *n* oturan kimse
inn *n* han
innate *adj* temelinde
inner *adj* iç
innocence *n* masumiyet
innocent *adj* masum
innovation *n* yenilik
innuendo *n* kinaye
innumerable *adj* hesapsız
input *n* girdi
inquest *n* soruşturma
inquire *v* araştırmak
inquiry *n* araştırma
inquisition *n* soruşturma
insane *adj* deli
insanity *n* delilik
insatiable *adj* doymaz
inscription *n* kitabe
insect *n* böcek
insecurity *n* endişeli
insensitive *adj* düşüncesiz
inseparable *adj* ayrılmaz
insert *v* takmak
insertion *n* ekleme
inside *adj* içinde
inside *pre* içinde
inside out *adv* tersyüz
insignificant *adj* önemsiz
insinuation *n* üstü kapalı
insipid *adj* sönük
insist *v* ısrar etmek
insistence *n* ısrar
insolent *adj* küstah
insoluble *adj* çözülmez
insomnia *n* uykusuzluk
inspect *v* denetlemek
inspection *n* teftiş
inspector *n* müfettiş
inspiration *n* esin kaynağı
inspire *v* esinlemek
instability *n* istikrarsızlık
install *v* kurmak
installation *n* kuruluş
installment *n* taksit
instance *n* an; örnek
instant *n* ani
instantly *adv* anında
instead *adv* yerine

instigate *v* kışkırtmak
instil *v* işlemek
instinct *n* içgüdü
institute *v* tesis etmek
institution *n* müessese
instruct *v* okutmak
instructor *n* öğretmen
insufficient *adj* yetersiz
insulate *v* yalıtmak
insulation *n* yalıtım
insult *v* hakaret etmek
insult *n* hakaret
insurance *n* sigorta
insure *v* sigorta olmak
insurgency *n* isyan
insurrection *n* isyan
intact *adj* bozulmamış
intake *n* yeme
integrate *v* bütünleştirmek
integration *n* birleştirme
integrity *n* bütünlük
intelligent *adj* zeki
intend *v* kastetmek
intense *adj* şiddetli
intensity *n* yoğunluk
intensive *adj* yoğun
intention *n* amaç
intercept *v* kesişmek
intercession *n* araya girme
interchange *v* değiştirmek
interchange *n* değişim
interest *n* çıkar; ilgi
interested *adj* ilgili
interesting *adj* ilginç
interfere *v* karışmak
interference *n* engel
interior *adj* içinde
interlude *n* ara dönem
intermediary *n* arada bulunan
intern *v* staj yapmak
interpret *v* tercüme etmek
interpretation *n* tercüme
interpreter *n* tercüman
interrupt *v* yarıda kesmek
interruption *n* arasını kesme
intersect *v* kesişmek
interval *n* aralık
intervene *v* araya girmek
intervention *n* aracılık
interview *n* mülakat
intestine *n* bağırsak
intimacy *n* samimilik
intimate *adj* samimi
intimidate *v* korkutmak
intolerable *adj* çekilmez
intolerance *n* toleranssızlık

intoxicated *adj* alkollü
intravenous *adj* damariçi
intrepid *adj* yılmaz
intricate *adj* karışık
intrigue *n* entrika
intriguing *adj* ilgi çekici
intrinsic *adj* esas
introduce *v* tanıştırmak
introduction *n* giriş
introvert *adj* içedönük
intrude *v* zorla girmek
intruder *n* davetsiz
intrusion *n* zorla girme
intuition *n* sezgi
inundate *v* su basmak
invade *v* istila etmek
invader *n* istilacı
invalid *n* geçersiz
invaluable *adj* çok değerli
invasion *n* istila
invent *v* icat etmek
invention *n* buluş
inventory *n* stok
invest *v* yatırım yapmak
investigation *n* soruşturma
investment *n* yatırım
investor *n* yatırımcı
invincible *adj* yenilmez
invisible *adj* görünmez
invitation *n* davet
invite *v* davet etmek
invoice *n* fatura
invoke *v* yardım istemek
involve *v* içermek
involved *v* sarmak
involvement *n* kuşatma
inward *adj* dahili
inwards *adv* ruhsal
iodine *n* iyot
irate *adj* öfkeli
Ireland *n* İrlanda
Irish *adj* İrlandalı
iron *n* demir
iron *v* ütülemek
ironic *adj* alaycı
irony *n* ironi
irrational *adj* mantıksız
irrefutable *adj* çürütülemez
irregular *adj* düzensiz
irrelevant *adj* alakasız
irreparable *adj* onarılamaz
irresistible *adj* dayanılmaz
irrespective *adj* bakmaksızın
irrevocable *adj* değişmez
irrigate *v* sulamak
irrigation *n* lavaj

irritate *v* can sıkmak
irritating *adj* can sıkıcı
Islamic *adj* islami
island *n* ada
isle *n* adacık
isolate *v* izole etmek
isolation *n* izolasyon
issue *n* olay; sayı
Italian *adj* İtalyan
italics *adj* italik
Italy *n* İtalya
itch *v* kaşınmak
itchiness *n* kaşıntı
item *n* öğe
itinerary *n* yolcu rehberi
ivory *n* fildişi

J

jackal *n* çakal
jacket *n* ceket
jackpot *n* bingo
jaguar *n* jaguar
jail *n* hapis
jail *v* hapse atmak
jailer *n* gardiyan
jam *n* karışıklık; reçel
janitor *n* kapıcı
January *n* Ocak
Japan *n* Japonya
Japanese *adj* Japon
jar *n* kavanoz
jasmine *n* yasemin
jaw *n* çene
jealous *adj* kıskanç
jealousy *n* kıskançlık
jeans *n* jean pantolon
jeopardize *v* risk
jerk *v* ani çekiş
jerk *n* ahmak
jersey *n* kazak
Jew *n* Musevilik
jewel *n* cevher
jeweler *n* kuyumcu

jewelry store *n* kuyumcu
Jewish *adj* Musevi
jigsaw *n* bozyap
job *n* iş
jobless *adj* işsiz
join *v* katılmak
joint *n* eklem; esrar
jointly *adv* ortak olarak
joke *n* şaka; fıkra
joke *v* şaka yapmak
jokingly *adv* şakayla
jolly *adj* keyifli
jolt *v* dürtmek
jolt *n* darbe; etki
journal *n* gazete
journalist *n* gazeteci
journey *n* yolculuk
jovial *adj* keyifli
joy *n* neşe
joyful *adj* neşeli
joyfully *adv* neşeyle
jubilant *adj* çok sevinçli
Judaism *n* Musevi alemi
judge *n* hakim
judgment *n* karar
judicious *adj* adaletli
jug *n* sürahi
juggler *n* hilebaz
juice *n* meyve suyu
juicy *adj* sulu
July *n* Temmuz
jump *v* zıplamak
jump *n* sıçrayış
jumpy *adj* gergin
junction *n* kavşak
June *n* Haziran
jungle *n* orman
junior *adj* ast
junk *n* çöp
jury *n* jüri
just *adj* sadece
justice *n* adalet
justify *v* doğrulamak
justly *adv* adil bir şekilde
juvenile *n* çocuk

K

kangaroo *n* kanguru
karate *n* karate
keep *iv* saklamak
keep on *v* devam etmek
keep up *v* ayak uydurmak
keg *n* fıçı
kennel *n* köpek evi
kettle *n* çaydanlık
key *n* anahtar
key ring *n* anahtarlık
keyboard *n* klavye
kick *v* tekmelemek
kickback *n* rüşvet
kickoff *n* başlangıç
kid *n* çocuk
kidnap *v* adam kaçırmak
kidnapping *n* adam kaçırma
kidney *n* böbrek
kidney bean *n* barbunya
kill *v* öldürmek
killer *n* katil
killing *n* vurgun
kilogram *n* kilogram
kilometer *n* kilometre
kilowatt *n* kilovat
kind *adj* kibar
kindle *v* alevlendirmek
kindly *adv* kibarca
kindness *n* kibarlık
king *n* kral
kingdom *n* kraliyet
kinship *n* akrabalık
kiosk *n* büfe
kiss *v* öpmek
kiss *n* öpücük
kitchen *n* mutfak
kite *n* uçurtma
kitten *n* kedi
knee *n* diz
kneecap *n* diz kapağı
kneel *iv* dizlenmek
knife *n* bıçak
knight *n* şovalye
knit *v* örmek
knob *n* budak
knock *n* darbe
knock *v* kapı çalmak
knot *n* düğüm
know *iv* bilmek
know-how *n* beceri
knowingly *adv* bilerek
knowledge *n* bilgi

L

lab *n* laboratuar
label *n* etiket
labor *n* iş gücü
laborer *n* işçi
labyrinth *n* labirent
lace *n* dantel; şerit
lack *v* eksilmek
lack *n* eksik
lad *n* delikanlı
ladder *n* portatif merdiven
laden *adj* dükkan
lady *n* hanım
ladylike *adj* hanım gibi
lagoon *n* gölcük
lake *n* göl
lamb *n* kuzu
lame *adj* aksak; kusurlu
lament *v* ağıt yakmak
lament *n* ağıt
lamp *n* lamba
lamppost *n* elektrik direği
lampshade *n* abajur
land *n* arazi
land *v* uçağın konması
landfill *n* arazi doldurma
landing *n* karaya çıkarma
landlady *n* ev sahibesi
landlocked *adj* kara ile çevrili
landlord *n* ev sahibi
landscape *n* manzara
lane *n* yol şeridi
language *n* dil
languish *v* cansızlaşmak
lantern *n* fanus
lap *n* kucak; etap
lapse *n* geçme
lapse *v* intikal etmek
larceny *n* hırsızlık
lard *n* domuz yağı
large *adj* geniş
larynx *n* boğaz
laser *n* lazer
lash *n* acı söz; kamçı
lash *v* ayıplamak
lash out *v* saldırmak
last *v* sona ermek
last *adj* son
last name *n* soyisim
last night *adv* dün gece
lasting *adj* tükenmeyen
lastly *adv* nihayet
latch *n* mandal
late *adv* geç

lately *adv* son zamanlarda
later *adv* sonraları
later *adj* daha sonra
lateral *adj* büyüme
latest *adj* en sonuncu
lather *n* köpük; tornacı
latitude *n* enlem
laugh *v* gülmek
laugh *n* kahkaha
laughable *adj* gülünç
laughing stock *n* maskara
laughter *n* kahkaha
launch *n* başlangıç
launch *v* fırlatmak
laundry *n* çamaşırhane
lavatory *n* lavabo
lavish *adj* bol
lavish *v* israf etmek
law *n* kanun
lawful *adj* adil; meşru
lawmaker *n* kanuni
lawn *n* çimen
lawsuit *n* dava
lawyer *n* avukat
lax *adj* belirsiz
laxative *adj* yumuşatıcı
lay *n* örnek
lay *iv* sermek; yaymak
lay off *v* ara vermek
layer *n* katman
layman *n* mesleği olmayan
lay-out *n* düzenlemek
laziness *n* tembellik
lazy *adj* tembel
lead *iv* başı çekmek
lead *n* kurşun; ara kablosu
leaded *adj* kurşun kaplı
leader *n* lider
leadership *n* liderlik
leading *adj* ana
leaf *n* yaprak
leaflet *n* bildiri
league *n* lig
leak *v* sızmak
leak *n* akıntı
leakage *n* sızdırmazlık
lean *adj* cılız; eğik
lean *iv* dayanmak
lean back *v* geri yaslanmak
lean on *v* yaslanmak
leaning *n* meyil
leap *iv* zıplamak
leap *n* sıçrama
leap year *n* artıkyıl
learn *iv* öğrenmek
learned *adj* okumuş

L

learner *n* öğrenci
learning *n* öğrenme
lease *v* kiralamak
lease *n* kira sözleşmesi
leash *n* tasma
least *adj* en ufak
leather *n* deri
leave *iv* geride bırakmak
leave out *v* ihmal etmek
lectern *n* kürsü
lecture *n* ders
ledger *n* hesap defteri
leech *n* sülük
leftovers *n* artıklar
leg *n* bacak
legacy *n* miras
legal *adj* yasal
legality *n* yasallık
legalize *v* yasallaştırmak
legend *n* efsane
legible *adj* okunur
legion *n* ordu; tümen
legislate *v* kanun yapmak
legislation *n* yasama
legislature *n* yasama meclisi
legitimate *adj* yasal
leisure *n* serbestlik
lemon *n* limon
lemonade *n* limonata
lend *iv* ödünç vermek
length *n* uzunluk
lengthen *v* uzatmak
lengthy *adj* fazlasıyla uzun
leniency *n* yumuşaklık
lenient *adj* hoşgörülü
lense *n* mercek
lentil *n* mercimek
leopard *n* leopar
leper *n* cüzzamlı
leprosy *n* cüzam
less *adj* daha az
lessee *n* kiracı
lessen *v* azalmak
lesser *adj* daha az
lesson *n* ders
lessor *n* kiralayan
let *iv* bırakmak
let down *v* boşa çıkarmak
let go *v* vazgeçmek
let in *v* içeri almak
let out *v* azad etmek
lethal *adj* öldürücü
letter *n* yazı; mektup
lettuce *n* marul
leukemia *n* lösemi
level *n* düzey; kademe

lever *n* manivela
leverage *n* piston
lewd *adj* müstehcen
liability *n* mesuliyet
liable *adj* sorumlu
liaison *n* irtibat
liar *adj* yalancı
libel *n* iftira
liberate *v* azat etmek
liberation *n* azat
liberty *n* özgürlük
library *n* kütüphane
lice *n* bitler
licence *n* lisans
license *v* lisanslamak
lick *v* yalamak
lid *n* kapak
lie *iv* yalan söylemek
lie *v* uzanmak
lie *n* yalan
lieu *n* mahal
lieutenant *n* teğmen
life *n* yaşam
lifeguard *n* cankurtaran
lifeless *adj* cansız
lifestyle *n* yaşam stili
lifetime *adj* yaşam süreci
lift *v* kaldırmak
lift off *v* havalanmak
lift-off *n* kalkış
ligament *n* bağ; köprü
light *iv* aydınlatmak
light *adj* hafif; ışıklı
light *n* ışık
lighter *n* çakmak
lighthouse *n* deniz feneri
lighting *n* aydınlatma
lightly *adv* umursamazca
lightning *n* şimşek
lightweight *n* hafif sıklet
likable *adj* cana yakın
like *pre* gibi; benzer
like *v* hoşlanmak
likelihood *n* ihtimal
likely *adv* muhtemelen
likeness *n* benzerlik
likewise *adv* benzer şekilde
liking *n* alaka
limb *n* bacak
lime *n* kireç
limestone *n* kireçtaşı
limit *n* hudut; kenar
limit *v* sınırlandırmak
limitation *n* limit
limp *v* topallamak
limp *n* gevşek

L

linchpin *n* dingil çivisi
line *n* çizgi
line up *v* sıraya girmek
linen *n* keten
linger *v* ayrılamamak
lingerie *n* kadın iç çamaşırı
lingering *adj* çok yavaş
lining *n* dizgin
link *v* bağlamak
link *n* bağlantı; halka
lion *n* aslan
lioness *n* dişi aslan
lip *n* dudak
liqueur *n* likör
liquid *n* sıvı
liquidate *v* sıvılaştırmak
liquidation *n* sıvılaştırma
liquor *n* içki; et suyu
list *v* liste yapmak
list *n* liste
listen *v* dinlemek
listener *n* dinleyici
litany *n* ayin
liter *n* litre
literal *adj* değişmez
literally *adv* gerçekten
literate *adj* okuryazar
literature *n* edebiyat
litigation *n* dava açmak
litre *n* litre
litter *n* çöp
little *adj* küçük
little bit *n* birazcık
little by little *adv* azar azar
liturgy *n* ayin
live *adj* canlı hayvan
live *v* yaşamak
live off *v* geçimini sağlamak
live up *v* hayatta kalmak
livelihood *n* geçim yolu
lively *adj* canlı
liver *n* ciğer
livestock *n* canlı hayvan
livid *adj* çok öfkeli
living room *n* oturma odası
lizard *n* kertenkele
load *v* yüklemek
load *n* yük
loaded *adj* doldurulmuş
loaf *n* somun
loan *v* ödünç vermek
loan *n* ödünç
loathe *v* tiksinmek
loathing *n* nefret
lobby *n* lobi; geçiş
lobby *v* kulis yapmak

L

lobster *n* ıstakoz
local *adj* yerel
localize *v* lokalize etmek
locate *v* yerini belirlemek
located *adj* yerleştirilmiş
location *n* konum
lock *v* kilitlemek
lock *n* kilit
lock up *v* hapsetmek
locker room *n* soyunma odası
locksmith *n* çilingir
locust *n* ağustosböceği
lodge *v* konaklamak
lodging *n* ufak ev
lofty *adj* yüksek
log *n* kütük
log *v* ağaç kesmek
log in *v* oturum açmak
log off *v* oturum kapatmak
logic *n* mantık
logical *adj* mantıklı
loin *n* mantıksal
loneliness *n* yalnızlık
lonely *adv* yalnız başına
loner *n* yalnız
lonesome *adj* yapayalnız
long *adj* uzun
long for *v* özlemek
longing *n* arzu
longitude *n* boylam
long-term *adj* uzun süreli
look *n* bakış; faal
look *v* bakmak
look after *v* gözetmek
look at *v* gözden geçirmek
look down *v* tepeden bakmak
look for *v* aramak; beklemek
look forward *v* beklemek
look into *v* incelemek
look out *v* dikkat etmek
look over *v* gözden geçirmek
look through *v* incelemek
looking glass *n* ayna
looks *n* görünüş
loom *n* dokuma tezgahı
loom *v* büyümek
loophole *n* gözetleme deliği
loose *v* ateşlemek
loose *adj* bol
loosen *v* gevşetmek
loot *v* ganimetlemek
loot *n* ganimet
lord *n* lord
lordship *n* lordluk
lose *iv* kaybetmek
loser *n* zavallı; mağlup

L

loss *n* kayıp
lot *adv* hepsi
lotion *n* losyon
lots *adj* birçok
lottery *n* piyango
loud *adj* gürültülü
loudly *adv* kaba
loudspeaker *n* hoparlör
lounge *n* lonca
louse *n* bit
lousy *adj* berbat; bitli
lovable *adj* sevimli
love *v* sevmek
love *n* sevgi
lovely *adj* güzel
lover *n* sevgili
loving *adj* sevecen
low *adj* alçak
lower *adj* daha alçak
lowkey *adj* uyumlu
lowly *adj* alçakgönüllü
loyal *adj* sadık
loyalty *n* sadakat
lubricate *v* yağlamak
lubrication *n* gresleme
lucid *adj* açık seçik
luck *n* şans
lucky *adj* şanslı
lucrative *adj* kazançlı
ludicrous *adj* aptalca
luggage *n* bagaj
lukewarm *adj* ılık
lull *n* durgunluk
lumber *n* kereste
luminous *adj* aydınlık
lump *n* küme; şişkinlik
lump sum *n* götürü
lunacy *n* cinnet
lunatic *adj* ruh hastası
lunch *n* öğle yemeği
lung *n* akciğer
lure *v* ayartmak
lurid *adj* korkunç
lurk *v* pusuda beklemek
lush *adj* ayyaş
lust *v* arzulamak
lust *n* arzu
lustful *adj* azgın
luxurious *adj* konforlu
luxury *n* lüks
lynch *v* linç etmek
lynx *n* karakulak
lyrics *n* şarkı sözü

M

machine *n* makina
mad *adj* sinirli
madam *n* hanımefendi
madden *v* delirtmek
madly *adv* delice
madman *n* deli
madness *n* delilik
magazine *n* magazin
magic *n* sihir
magical *adj* sihirli
magician *n* sihirbaz
magistrate *n* yargıç
magnet *n* mıknatıs
magnetic *adj* manyetik
magnetism *n* manyetizma
magnificent *adj* görkemli
magnify *v* büyütmek
magnitude *n* boyut
maid *n* bayan hizmetçi
maiden *n* bakire
mail *v* postalamak
mail *n* posta
mailbox *n* posta kutusu
mailman *n* postacı
maim *v* sakatlamak
main *adj* ana
mainland *n* ana kara
mainly *adv* başlıca
maintain *v* devam ettirmek
maintenance *n* bakım
majestic *adj* görkemli
majesty *n* majeste
major *n* binbaşı
major *adj* önemli; ana
majority *n* çoğunluk
make *n* yapım
make *iv* yapmak
make up *v* barışmak
make up for *v* telafi etmek
maker *n* fail; imalatçı
makeup *n* makyaj
malaria *n* sıtma
male *n* erkek
malevolent *adj* art niyetli
malfunction *v* arızalı çalışmak
malfunction *n* arızalı çalışma
malice *n* fesat
malign *v* çamur atmak
malignancy *n* habislik
malignant *adj* kötü niyetli
mall *n* kapalı çarşı
mammal *n* memeli
mammoth *n* mamud

man *n* adam
manage *v* yönetmek
manageable *adj* yönetilir
management *n* yönetim
manager *n* müdür
mandate *n* ferman
mandatory *adj* zorunlu
maneuver *n* manevra
manger *n* yemlik
mangle *v* parçalamak
manhandle *v* tartaklamak
manhunt *n* insan avı
maniac *adj* manyak
manifest *v* manifesto
mankind *n* insan soyu
manliness *n* erkeklik
manly *adj* erkeksi
manner *n* tavır
mannerism *n* kişisel özellik
manners *n* adap
manpower *n* insan gücü
mansion *n* konak
manslaughter *n* adam öldürme
manual *n* el kitabı
manual *adj* elle yapılan
manufacture *v* imal etmek
manure *n* gübre
manuscript *n* el yazısı
many *adj* birçok
map *n* harita
marble *n* bilye
march *n* askeri yürüyüş
March *n* Mart
mare *n* kısrak
margin *n* hudut; fazlalık
marginal *adj* marjinal
marinate *v* marine etmek
marine *adj* bahriyeli
marital *adj* evlilikle ilgili
mark *n* işaret
mark *v* işaretlemek
mark down *v* fiyat düşürmek
marker *n* belirteç
market *n* market
marksman *n* nişancı
marmalade *n* marmelat
marriage *n* evlilik
married *adj* evli
marrow *n* ilik
marry *v* evlenmek
Mars *n* Mars
marshal *n* mareşal; polis şefi
martyr *n* şehit
martyrdom *n* şehitlik
marvel *n* harika
marvelous *adj* fevkalade

marxist *adj* Marksçı
masculine *adj* maskülen
mash *v* ezmek
mask *n* maske
masochism *n* mazoşizm
mason *n* mason; duvarcı
masquerade *v* kılık değiştirmek
mass *n* kütle; kilise ayini
massacre *n* kırım
massage *n* masaj
massage *v* masaj yapmak
masseur *n* masör
masseuse *n* masöz
massive *adj* kocaman
mast *n* bayrak direği
master *n* usta
master *v* baş eğdirmek
mastermind *n* beyin
mastermind *v* yönetmek
masterpiece *n* başyapıt
mastery *n* egemenlik
mat *n* hasır
match *n* yarışma; akran
match *v* eşlemek;
mate *n* arkadaş
material *n* madde; kumaş
materialism *n* maddecilik
maternal *adj* anaç
maternity *n* annelik
math *n* matematik
matriculate *v* kaydetmek
matrimony *n* evlenme
matter *n* cisim; konu
mattress *n* şilte
mature *adj* olgun
maturity *n* olgunluk
maul *v* ağaç tokmak
maxim *n* atasözü
maximum *adj* maksimum
May *n* Mayıs
may *iv* olabilir
may-be *adv* belki
mayhem *n* kargaşa
mayor *n* belediye başkanı
maze *n* hayret
meadow *n* çayır
meager *adj* bereketsiz
meal *n* yemek
mean *iv* demek istemek
mean *adj* kötü kalpli
meaning *n* anlam
meaningful *adj* anlamlı
meaningless *adj* anlamsız
meanness *n* kötülük
means *n* araç
meantime *adv* bu arada

meanwhile *adv* bu sırada
measles *n* kızamık
measure *v* ölçmek
measurement *n* ölçüm
meat *n* et
meatball *n* köfte
mechanic *n* mekanik
mechanism *n* mekanizma
medal *n* madalya
medallion *n* madalyon
meddle *v* burnunu sokmak
mediate *v* ara bulmak
mediator *n* ara bulucu
medication *n* ilaç tedavisi
medicinal *adj* gezgin
medicine *n* ilaç
medieval *adj* ortaçağ
mediocre *adj* alelade
mediocrity *n* aleladelik
meditation *n* meditasyon
medium *adj* orta
meek *adj* alçakgönüllü
meet *iv* buluşmak
meeting *n* toplantı
melancholy *n* melankoli
mellow *adj* cana yakın
mellow *v* olgunlaştırmak
melodic *adj* melodik
melody *n* melodi
melon *n* kavun
melt *v* erimek
member *n* üye
membership *n* üyelik
membrane *n* membran
memento *n* hatıra
memo *n* kısa not
memoirs *n* anılar
memorable *adj* unutulmaz
memorize *v* ezberlemek
memory *n* hafıza
men *n* erkekler
menace *n* göz dağı
mend *v* onarmak
meningitis *n* menenjit
menopause *n* menapoz
menstruation *n* aybaşı
mental *adj* kaçık
mentality *n* zihniyet
mentally *adv* aklen
mention *v* bahsetmek
mention *n* ima
menu *n* menü
merchandise *n* alıp satmak
merchant *n* tüccar
merciful *adj* insaflı
merciless *adj* insafsız

mercury *n* cıva
mercy *n* insaf
merely *adv* adeta
merge *v* birleşmek
merger *n* birleşme
merit *n* değer
merit *v* layık olmak
mermaid *n* deniz kızı
merry *adj* mutlu
mesh *n* ağ; elek
mesmerize *v* büyülemek
mess *n* dağınıklık
mess up *v* altüst etmek
message *n* mesaj
messenger *n* haberci
Messiah *n* Mesih
messy *adj* dağınık
metal *n* metal
metallic *adj* metalik
metaphor *n* istiare
meteor *n* meteor
meter *n* metre
method *n* metod
methodical *adj* düzenli
meticulous *adj* titiz
metric *adj* ölçülü
metropolis *n* anakent
Mexican *adj* Meksikalı
mice *n* fareler
microbe *n* mikrop
microphone *n* mikrofon
microscope *n* mikroskop
microwave *n* microwave
midday *n* gün ortası
middle *n* orta
middleman *n* aracı
midget *n* cüce
midnight *n* geceyarısı
midsummer *n* yaz ortası
midwife *n* ebe
mighty *adj* güçlü
migraine *n* migren
migrant *n* göçmen
migrate *v* göçmek
mild *adj* hafif
mildew *n* küf
mile *n* mil
mileage *n* dönem
militant *adj* azimli
milk *n* süt
milky *adj* sütlü
mill *n* değirmen
millennium *n* milenyum
milligram *n* miligram
millimeter *n* milimetre
million *n* milyon

millionaire *n* milyoner
mime *v* mimik yapmak
mince *v* doğramak
mincemeat *n* kıyma
mind *v* dikkat etmek
mind *n* zeka; hafıza
mindful *adj* dikkatli
mindless *adj* akılsız
mine *n* kaynak; mayın
mine *v* mayın döşemek
mine *pro* benimki
minefield *n* mayın tarlası
miner *n* mayıncı
mineral *n* mineral
miniature *n* minyatür
minimum *n* minimum
miniskirt *n* mini etek
minister *n* bakan; papaz
minister *v* hizmet etmek
ministry *n* bakanlık
minor *adj* önemsiz
minority *n* azınlık
mint *n* nane
mint *v* para basmak
minus *adj* eksi
minute *n* dakika
miracle *n* mucize
miraculous *adj* mucizevi
mirage *n* serap
mirror *n* ayna
miscarriage *n* yanlışlık yapmak
miscarry *v* düşük yapmak
mischief *n* fenalık
mischievous *adj* afacan
misconduct *n* kabahat
misdemeanor *n* kabahat
miser *n* hasis
miserable *adj* zavallı
misery *n* acı
misfit *adj* uyumsuz
misfortune *n* aksilik
misgiving *n* endişe
misguided *adj* yanlış
mislead *v* aldatmak
misleading *adj* aldatıcı
misplace *v* kaybetmek
misprint *n* baskı hatası
miss *v* özlemek
miss *n* bayan
missile *n* misil
missing *adj* kayıp
mission *n* görev
missionary *n* misyoner
mist *n* buğu
mistake *iv* hata yapmak
mistake *n* hata

M

mistaken *adj* yanlış
mister *n* bay
mistreat *v* hor kullanmak
mistreatment *n* kıyım
mistress *n* bayan; dost
mistrust *n* kuşku
mistrust *v* güvenmemek
misty *adj* belirsiz
misunderstand *v* yanlış anlamak
misuse *n* hatalı kullanım
mitigate *v* azaltmak
mix *v* karıştırmak
mixed-up *adj* arapsaçı gibi
mixer *n* mikser
mixture *n* karışım
mix-up *n* anlaşmazlık
moan *v* inlemek
moan *n* inilti
mob *v* üşüşmek
mob *n* ayak takımı
mobile *adj* hareketli
mobster *n* gangster
mock *v* alay etmek
mockery *n* alay
mode *n* mod
model *n* örnek; model
moderate *adj* ılımlı
moderation *n* azalma
modern *adj* modern
modest *adj* alçakgönüllü
modify *v* azaltmak
module *n* modül
moisten *v* nemlendirmek
moisture *n* nem
molar *n* kütlesel
mold *v* kalıp dökmek
mold *n* kalıp; küf
moldy *adj* küflü
mole *n* ben; köstebek
molecule *n* molekül
molest *v* uğraşmak
mom *n* anne
moment *n* an
momentarily *adv* bir an için
momentous *adj* ciddi
monarch *n* hükümdar
monarchy *n* monarşi
monastery *n* manastır
monastic *adj* keşiş
Monday *n* Pazartesi
money *n* para
money order *n* havale
monitor *v* izlemek
monk *n* papaz
monkey *n* maymun
monogamy *n* tek eşlilik

monologue *n* monolog
monopoly *n* monopol
monotonous *adj* monoton
monotony *n* monoton
monster *n* canavar
monstrous *adj* azman
month *n* ay
monthly *adv* aylık
monument *n* anıt
monumental *adj* devasa
mood *n* ruh hali
moody *adj* huysuz
moon *n* ay
moor *v* demiı atmak
mop *v* paspas yapmak
moral *adj* ahlaki
moral *n* ahlak
morality *n* etik
more *adj* daha
moreover *adv* dahası
morning *n* sabah
moron *adj* gerizekalı
morphine *n* morfin
morsel *n* lokma
mortal *adj* ölümlü
mortality *n* fanilik
mortar *n* havan topu
mortgage *n* ipotek
mortification *n* aşağılama
mortify *v* çürütmek
mortuary *n* morg
mosaic *n* mozaik
mosque *n* cami
mosquito *n* sivrisinek
moss *n* yosun
most *adj* en çok
mostly *adv* başlıca
motel *n* motel
moth *n* güve; pervane
mother *n* anne
motherhood *n* annelik
mother-in-law *n* kaynana
motion *n* hareket
motionless *adj* hareketsiz
motivate *v* motive etmek
motive *n* dürtü; sebep
motor *n* motor
motorcycle *n* motosiklet
motto *n* ilke
mouldy *adj* küflü
mount *n* binek
mount *v* tırmanmak
mountain *n* dağ
mountainous *adj* dağlık
mourn *v* yas tutmak
mourning *n* yas

mouse *n* fare
mouth *n* ağız
move *n* hareket; adım
move *v* hareket etmek
move back *v* geri çekilmek
move forward *v* ilerlemek
move out *v* çıkmak
move up *v* yukarı taşımak
movement *n* hareket
movie *n* film
mow *v* biçmek
much *adv* çok
mucus *n* mukus
mud *n* çamur
muddle *n* dağınıklık
muddy *adj* çamurlu
muffle *v* susturmak
muffler *n* boyun atkısı
mug *n* bardak
mug *v* saldırıp soymak
mugging *n* saldırı
mule *n* katır
multiple *adj* çoklu
multiplication *n* çoğalma
multiply *v* çoğalmak
multitude *n* izdiham
mummy *n* anne
mumps *n* kabakulak
munitions *n* cephane
murder *n* cinayet
murderer *n* katil
murky *adj* anlaşılması güç
murmur *v* homurdanma
murmur *n* hırıltı
muscle *n* kas
museum *n* müze
mushroom *n* mantar
music *n* müzik
musician *n* müzisyen
Muslim *adj* Müslüman
must *iv* gerekmek
mustache *n* bıyık
mustard *n* hardal
muster *v* içtima yapmak
mutate *v* değişmek
mute *adj* dilsiz
mutilate *v* değiştirmek
mutiny *n* ayaklanma
mutually *adv* karşılıklı olarak
muzzle *v* silahı doğrultmak
muzzle *n* namlu ağzı
my *adj* benim
myopic *adj* miyop
myself *pro* kendim
mysterious *adj* gizemli
mystery *n* gizem

mystic *adj* esrarengiz
mystify *v* aklını karıştırmak
myth *n* efsane

N

nag *v* dırdır etmek
nagging *adj* dırdır
nail *n* tırnak; çivi
naive *adj* saf
naked *adj* çıplak
name *n* isim
namely *adv* yani
nanny *n* bakıcı
nap *n* kısa uyku
napkin *n* mendil
narcotic *n* narkotik
narrate *v* betimlemek
narrow *adj* dar
narrowly *adv* anca
nasty *adj* edepsiz
nation *n* ulus
national *adj* ulusal
nationality *n* vatandaşlık
nationalize *v* millileştirmek
native *adj* yerli
natural *adj* doğal
naturally *adv* doğal olarak
nature *n* doğa
naughty *adj* yaramaz
nausea *n* mide bulantısı
nave *n* dingil başlığı
navel *n* merkez
navigate *v* seyretmek
navigation *n* seyir
navy *n* bahriye
navy blue *adj* deniz mavisi
near *pre* yakın
nearby *adj* yakınlarda
nearly *adv* neredeyse
nearsighted *adj* miyop
neat *adj* düzenli
necessary *adj* gerekli
necessitate *v* gerekli kılmak
necessity *n* gereklilik
neck *n* boyun
necklace *n* kolye
necktie *n* kravat
need *v* gerekmek
need *n* yardım; gerek
needle *n* iğne
needless *adj* gereksiz
needy *adj* yardıma muhtaç

negative *adj* negatif
neglect *v* ihmal etmek
neglect *n* ihmal
negligence *n* dikkatsizlik
negligent *adj* ihmalkar
negotiate *v* pazarlık etmek
negotiation *n* pazarlık
neighbor *n* komşu
neighborhood *n* komşuluk
neither *adj* hiçbiri
neither *adv* hiçbiri
nephew *n* yeğen
nerve *n* sinir
nervous *adj* sinirli; endişeli
nest *n* yuva
net *n* ağ
Netherlands *n* Hollanda
network *n* çevrim
neurotic *adj* evhamlı
neutral *adj* nötr
never *adv* asla
nevertheless *adv* yine de
new *adj* yeni
newborn *n* yeni doğmuş
newcomer *n* yeni gelen
newly *adv* yeni
newlywed *adj* yeni evli
news *n* haberler
newscast *n* haber bülteni
newsletter *n* bülten
newspaper *n* gazete
newsstand *n* gazete bayii
next *adj* sıradaki
next door *adj* yan kapı
nibble *v* kemirmek
nice *adj* güzel
nicely *adv* güzelce
nickel *n* nikel
nickname *n* lakap
nicotine *n* nikotin
niece *n* kuzen
night *n* gece
nightfall *n* alacakaranlık
nightgown *n* gecelik
nightingale *n* bülbül
nightmare *n* karabasan
nine *adj* dokuz
nineteen *adj* ondokuz
ninety *adj* doksan
ninth *adj* dokuzuncu
nip *n* ayaz; çimdik
nip *v* çimdik atmak
nipple *n* meme ucu
nitpicking *adj* eften püften
nitrogen *n* nitrojen
no one *pro* kimse

nobility *n* asalet
noble *adj* asil
nobleman *n* asilzade
nobody *pro* kimse
nocturnal *adj* geceleyin
nod *v* baş işareti
noise *n* gürültü
noisy *adj* gürültücü
none *pre* hiçbiri
nonetheless *c* yine de
nonsense *n* saçma
nonsmoker *n* sigara içmeyen
nonstop *adv* durmadan
noon *n* öğlen
noose *n* ilişki; tuzak
nor *c* ne de
norm *n* kural
normal *adj* normal
normally *adv* normalde
north *n* kuzey
northeast *n* kuzeydoğu
northern *adj* kuzeye ait
northerner *adj* kuzeyli
Norway *n* Norveç
Norwegian *adj* Norveçli
nose *n* burun
nosedive *v* pike yapmak
nostalgia *n* nostalji
nostril *n* burun deliği
nosy *adj* meraklı
not *adv* değil
notable *adj* önemli
notably *adv* kayda değer
notary *n* noter
notation *n* formül
note *v* not
notebook *n* not defteri
noteworthy *adj* kayda değer
nothing *n* hiçbir şey
notice *v* farketmek
notice *n* bildiri; ihtar
noticeable *adj* önemli
notification *n* bildiri
notify *v* bildirmek
notion *n* düşünce
notorious *adj* adı çıkmış
noun *n* isim
nourish *v* beslemek
nourishment *n* beslenme
novel *n* hikaye
novelist *n* yazar
novelty *n* acayiplik
November *n* Kasım
novice *n* çaylak
now *adv* şimdi
nowadays *adv* bugünlerde

nowhere *adv* hiçbir yerde
noxious *adj* ahlakı bozan
nozzle *n* ağızlık
nuance *n* ayrıntı
nuclear *adj* nükleer
nude *adj* çıplak
nudist *n* nüdist
nudity *n* çıplaklık
nuisance *n* baş ağrısı
null *adj* sıfır
nullify *v* sıfırlamak
numb *adj* uyuşuk
number *n* sayı
numbness *n* uyuşukluk
numerous *adj* sayısız
nun *n* rahibe
nurse *n* hemşire
nurse *v* bakıcılık yapmak
nursery *n* kreş; fidanlık
nurture *v* büyütmek
nut *n* fındık; çatlak
nutrition *n* beslenme
nutritious *adj* besleyici
nut-shell *n* fındık kabuğu
nutty *adj* çatlak; lezzetli

O

oak *n* meşe ağacı
oar *n* işçi
oasis *n* vaha
oath *n* yemin
oatmeal *n* yulaf ezmesi
obedience *n* itaat
obedient *adj* itaatkar
obese *adj* obez
obey *v* uymak
object *v* karşı çıkmak
object *n* obje
objection *n* itiraz
objective *n* amaç
obligate *v* mecbur etmek
obligation *n* mecburiyet
obligatory *adj* zorunlu
obliged *adj* borçlu olmak
oblique *adj* dolambaçlı
obliterate *v* aşındırmak
oblivious *adj* dikkatsiz
obnoxious *adj* çirkin
obscene *adj* açık saçık
obscenity *n* açık saçık laf
obscure *adj* anlaşılması güç
obscurity *n* anlaşılmazlık

observation *n* gözlem
observatory *n* gözlemevi
observe *v* gözlemlemek
obsess *v* aklına takılmak
obsession *n* saplantı
obsolete *adj* eski
obstacle *n* engel
obstinacy *n* inat
obstinate *adj* dik başlı
obstruct *v* engellemek
obstruction *n* arıza
obtain *v* elde etmek
obvious *adj* belli
obviously *adv* belli ki
occasion *n* fırsat
occasionally *adv* ara sıra
occult *adj* anlaşılmaz
occupant *n* oturan
occupation *n* uğraş
occupy *v* işgal etmek
occur *v* vuku bulmak
ocean *n* okyanus
October *n* Ekim
octopus *n* ahtapot
ocurrence *n* oluş
odd *adj* garip
oddity *n* gariplik
odds *n* eşitsizlik
odious *adj* iğrenç
odometer *n* yol sayacı
odor *n* koku
odyssey *n* odise
of *pre* onun
off *adv* açıkta
offend *v* utandırmak
offense *n* gücenme
offensive *adj* hakaret edici
offer *v* teklif etmek
offer *n* teklif
offering *n* adak
office *n* ofis
officer *n* memur
official *adj* resmi
officiate *v* görev yapmak
offset *v* daldırma
offspring *n* akran
off-the-record *adj* gizli
often *adv* sıklıkla
oil *n* yağ
ointment *n* merhem
okay *adv* tamam
old *adj* yaşlı
old age *n* yaşlılık
old-fashioned *adj* eski moda
olive *n* zeytin
olympics *n* olimpiyat

omelette *n* omlet
omen *n* alamet
omission *n* ihmal
omit *v* dahil etmemek
on *pre* üstünde
once *adv* bir kerede
once *c* bir kere
one *adj* bir
oneself *pre* biri
ongoing *adj* süren
onion *n* soğan
onlooker *n* izleyici
only *adv* yalnız
onset *n* başlangıç
onslaught *n* hamle
onwards *adv* beri
opaque *adj* opak
open *v* açmak
open *adj* açık
open up *v* açılmak
opening *n* açılış
open-minded *adj* açık fikirli
openness *n* açıklık
opera *n* opera
operate *v* işletmek
operation *n* operasyon
opinion *n* fikir
opinionated *adj* dik kafalı
opium *n* afyon
opponent *n* muhalif
opportune *adj* elverişli
opportunity *n* fırsat
oppose *v* karşı koymak
opposite *adj* karşıt
opposite *adv* karşıda
opposite *n* karşı
opposition *n* direniş
oppression *n* baskı
opt for *v* tercih etmek
optical *adj* optik
optician *n* göz doktoru
optimism *n* iyimserlik
optimistic *adj* iyimser
option *n* seçenek
optional *adj* isteğe bağlı
opulence *n* bolluk
or *c* veya
oracle *n* ayrıcalık
orally *adv* ağızdan
orange *n* portakal
orangutan *n* orangutan
orbit *n* yörünge
orchard *n* bostan
orchestra *n* orkestra
ordain *v* atamak
ordeal *n* çile

order *n* buyruk; sıra
ordinarily *adv* genelde
ordinary *adj* basit; sıradan
ordination *n* buyurma
ore *n* maden
organ *n* organ
organism *n* organizma
organist *n* orgcu
organization *n* kuruluş
orient *n* doğu
oriental *adj* doğuya özgü
orientation *n* alışma
oriented *adj* yönlü
origin *n* köken
original *adj* orjinal
originally *adv* orjinal olarak
originate *v* başlamak
ornament *n* aksesuar
ornamental *adj* bezemeli
orphan *n* kimsesiz
orphanage *n* öksüzler yurdu
orthodox *adj* göreneksel
ostentatious *adj* azametli
ostrich *n* devekuşu
other *adj* başka
otherwise *adv* aksi takdirde
otter *n* su samuru
ought to *iv* meli malı eki
ounce *n* ons
our *adj* bizim
ours *pro* bizimki
ourselves *pro* bizler
oust *v* defetmek
out *adv* dışarıda
outbreak *n* baş gösterme
outburst *n* feveran
outcast *adj* kimsesiz
outcome *n* akıbet
outcry *n* bağırış
outdated *adj* çağdışı
outdo *v* bastırmak
outdoor *adv* ev dışında
outdoors *adv* açık havada
outer *adj* dış
outfit *n* donatım
outgoing *adj* açık yürekli
outgrow *v* büyümek
outing *n* gezinti
outlaw *v* feshetmek
outlet *n* satış yeri
outline *n* ana çizgiler
outlook *n* bakış açısı
outmoded *adj* demode
outperform *v* aşmak
outpouring *n* taşma
output *n* çıktı

outrage *n* büyük ayıp
outrageous *adj* acımasız
outright *adj* açık sözlü
outrun *v* aşmak
outset *n* başlangıç
outside *adv* dışarıda
outsider *n* dışlanmış
outskirts *n* civar
outspoken *adj* açık sözlü
outstanding *adj* göze çarpan
outstretched *adj* uzanmış
outward *adj* dışa doğru
outweigh *v* ağır basmak
oval *adj* oval
ovary *n* yumurtalık
ovation *n* tezahürat
oven *n* fırın
over *pre* üstünde
overall *adv* toplamda
overbearing *adj* ağır basan
overcast *adj* basık
overcharge *v* abartmak
overcoat *n* manto
overcome *v* alt etmek
overdo *v* abartmak
overdone *adj* abartılı
overdose *n* dozaşımı
overdue *adj* gecikmiş
overflow *v* akmak
overhaul *v* elden geçirmek
overlap *v* üstüste binmek
overlook *v* aldırmamak
overnight *adv* bir gecede
overpower *v* boyun eğdirmek
overrate *v* büyütmek
override *v* ağır basmak
overrule *v* geçersiz kılmak
overrun *v* aşmak
overseas *adv* deniz aşırı
oversee *v* denetlemek
oversight *n* dikkatsizlik
overstate *v* abartmak
overstep *v* çok ileri gitmek
overthrow *v* çökertmek
overthrow *n* alaşağı edilme
overturn *v* alabora etmek
overview *n* genel bakış
overweight *adj* fazla kilolu
overwhelm *v* alt etmek
owe *v* borçlu olmak
owing to *adv* nedeniyle
owl *n* baykuş
own *v* sahibi olmak
own *adj* kendi
owner *n* mal sahibi
ownership *n* mülkiyet

ox *n* öküz
oxen *n* öküz
oxygen *n* oksijen
oyster *n* istiridye

P

pace *v* yürümek
pace *n* adım
pacify *v* yatıştırmak
pack *v* paketlemek
package *n* paket
pact *n* pakt
pad *v* doldurmak
padding *n* yastık
padlock *n* kilit
pagan *adj* putperest
page *n* sayfa; uşak
pail *n* kova
pain *n* eziyet
painful *adj* acı veren
painkiller *n* ağrı kesici
painless *adj* zahmetsiz
paint *v* boyamak
paint *n* boya
paintbrush *n* boya fırçası
painter *n* ressam
painting *n* tablo; levha
pair *n* çift
pajamas *n* pijama
pal *n* ahbap
palace *n* saray
palate *n* damak
pale *adj* soluk
paleness *n* solukluk
palm *n* avuç
palpable *adj* hissedilebilir
paltry *adj* değersiz
pamper *v* şımartmak
pamphlet *n* broşür
pan *n* tava
pancreas *n* pankreas
pander *v* yaltaklanmak
pang *n* ıstırap
panic *n* panik
panorama *n* panorama
panther *n* panter
pantry *n* kiler
pants *n* pantolon; don
pantyhose *n* tayt
papacy *n* papalık
paper *n* kağıt
paperclip *n* kağıt raptiyesi

paperwork *n* formalite
parable *n* kıssa
parachute *n* paraşüt
parade *n* gösteriş
paradise *n* cennet
paradox *n* paradoks
paragraph *n* paragraf
parakeet *n* papağan
parallel *n* paralel
paralysis *n* felç
paralyze *v* felç olmak
parameters *n* parametre
paramount *adj* fevkalade
paranoid *adj* paranoyak
parasite *n* parazit
parcel *n* paket
parcel post *n* paket postası
parch *v* kavurmak
parchment *n* parşömen
pardon *v* özür dilemek
pardon *n* özür
parenthesis *n* parantez
parents *n* ebeveyn
parish *n* mahalle
parity *n* parite
park *v* park etmek
park *n* park
parking *n* park yeri
parliament *n* parlamento
parochial *adj* yerel
parrot *n* papağan
parsley *n* maydonoz
parsnip *n* behmen
part *v* parçalanmak
part *n* parça
partial *adj* kısmi
partially *adv* kısmen
participate *v* katılmak
participation *n* katılma
participle *n* sıfat
particle *n* tanecik
particular *adj* belirli
particularly *adv* özellikle
parting *n* bölünme çizgisi
partisan *n* partizan
partition *n* bölümlemek
partly *adv* kısmi
partner *n* ortak
partnership *n* ortaklık
partridge *n* keklik
party *n* parti; toplantı
pass *n* geçiş
pass *v* geçmek
pass away *v* ölmek
pass out *v* bayılmak
passage *n* geçit

passenger *n* yolcu
passer-by *n* yoldan geçen
passion *n* tutku
passionate *adj* tutkulu
passive *adj* pasif
passport *n* pasaport
password *n* şifre
past *adj* geçmiş
paste *v* yapıştırmak
paste *n* zamk; çiriş
pastime *n* eğlence
pastor *n* rahip
pastoral *adj* kırsal
pastry *n* hamur işi
pasture *n* çayır
pat *n* okşamak
patch *v* yamalamak
patch *n* yama
patent *n* patent
patent *adj* patentli
paternity *n* babalık
path *n* yol
pathetic *adj* acınası
patience *n* sabır
patient *adj* sabırlı
patio *n* avlu
patriarch *n* ata
patriot *n* vatansever
patriotic *adj* yurtsever
patrol *n* karakol
patron *n* patron; efendi
patronage *n* hamilik
pattern *n* desen
pavement *n* kaldırım
pavilion *n* pavyon
paw *n* pençe
pawn *v* rehine koyma
pawnbroker *n* tefeci
pay *n* ödeme
pay *iv* ödemek
pay back *v* geri ödemek
pay off *v* tazminat vermek
payable *adj* ödenecek
paycheck *n* maaş çeki
payee *n* ödenen kişi
payment *n* ödeme
payroll *n* maaş bordrosu
payslip *n* maaş makbuzu
pea *n* bezelye
peace *n* huzur; barış
peaceful *adj* huzurlu
peach *n* şeftali
peacock *n* tavuskuşu
peak *n* doruk
peanut *n* yerfıstığı
pear *n* armut

P

pearl *n* inci
peasant *n* köylü
pebble *n* çakıl
peck *v* yemlemek
peck *n* sürü
peculiar *adj* özgün
pedagogy *n* pedagoji
pedal *n* pedal
pedantic *adj* mektepli
pedestrian *n* yaya
peel *v* soymak
peel *n* kabuk
peep *v* dikizlemek
peer *n* eş
pelican *n* pelikan
pellet *n* tane
pen *n* mürekkepli kalem
penalty *n* ceza
penance *n* kefaret
penchant *n* eğilim
pencil *n* kalem
pendant *n* asılı şey
pending *adj* beklemede
pendulum *n* sarkaç
penetrate *v* içine işlemek
penguin *n* penguen
penicillin *n* penisilin
peninsula *n* yarımada
penitent *n* tövbekar
penniless *adj* parasız
penny *n* peni
pension *n* emekli aylığı
pentagon *n* beşgen
pent-up *adj* hapsedilmiş
people *n* halk
pepper *n* biber
per *pre* kişi başına
perceive *v* anlamak
percent *adv* yüzde
percentage *n* yüzdelik
perception *n* algılama
perennial *adj* yıl boyu süren
perfect *adj* mükemmel
perfection *n* mükemmeliyet
perforate *v* içine işlemek
perforation *n* delik
perform *v* işlemek
performance *n* performans
perfume *n* parfüm
perhaps *adv* belki de
peril *n* tehlike
perilous *adj* tehlikeli
perimeter *n* çevre
period *n* müddet
perish *v* ölmek
perishable *adj* dayanıksız

permanent *adj* kalıcı
permeate *v* içine işlemek
permission *n* izin
permit *v* izin vermek
pernicious *adj* zararlı
perpetrate *v* icra etmek
persecute *v* zulmetmek
persevere *v* ısrar etmek
persist *v* üstelemek
persistence *n* direnme
persistent *adj* inatçı
person *n* şahıs
personal *adj* şahsi
personality *n* kişilik
personnel *n* personel
perspective *n* bakış açısı
perspiration *n* ter
perspire *v* terlemek
persuade *v* ikna etmek
persuasion *n* ikna
persuasive *adj* ikna edici
pertain *v* ait olmak
pertinent *adj* uygun
perturb *v* bozmak
perverse *adj* sapık
pervert *adj* sapık
pessimism *n* karamsarlık
pessimistic *adj* karamsar
pest *n* böcek
pester *v* kafa ütülemek
pesticide *n* tarım ilacı
pet *n* evcil hayvan
petal *n* petal
petite *adj* zarif
petition *n* dilekçe
petrified *adj* donakalmış
petroleum *n* petrol
pettiness *n* küçüklük
petty *adj* önemsiz; adi
pew *n* uzun bank
phantom *n* hayalet
pharmacist *n* eczacı
pharmacy *n* eczane
phase *n* evre
pheasant *n* sülün
phenomenon *n* görüngü
philosopher *n* filozof
philosophy *n* felsefe
phobia *n* fobi
phone *n* telefon
phone *v* telefon etmek
phoney *adj* sahte
phosphorus *n* fosfor
photo *n* fotoğraf
photocopy *n* fotokopi
photograph *v* fotoğraf çekmek

P

photographer *n* fotoğrafçı
photography *n* fotoğraf
phrase *n* deyim
physically *adv* fiziksel olarak
physician *n* hekim
physics *n* fizik
pianist *n* piyanist
piano *n* piyano
pick *v* almak; koparmak
pick up *v* kaldırmak
pickpocket *n* yankesicilik
pickup *n* kamyonet
picture *n* resim
picture *v* resimlemek
picturesque *adj* güzel
pie *n* tart
piece *n* parça
piecemeal *adv* yavaş yavaş
pier *n* rıhtım
pierce *v* içine işlemek
piercing *n* delme
piety *n* dindarlık
pig *n* domuz
pigeon *n* güvercin
piggy bank *n* kumbara
pile *v* yığmak
pile *n* yığın
pile up *v* yığmak
pilfer *v* çalmak
pilgrim *n* hacı
pilgrimage *n* hac
pill *n* ilaç
pillage *v* soymak
pillar *n* direk
pillow *n* yastık
pillowcase *n* yastık kılıfı
pilot *n* pilot
pimple *n* sivilce
pin *n* iğne
pincers *n* kerpeten
pinch *v* çimdiklemek
pinch *n* çimdik; tutam
pine *n* çam ağacı
pineapple *n* ananas
pink *adj* pembe
pint *n* pinta
pioneer *n* öncü
pious *adj* dindar
pipe *n* düdük; boru
pipeline *n* boru hattı
piracy *n* korsanlık
pirate *n* korsan
pistol *n* tabanca
pit *n* çukur
pitch-black *adj* kapkara
pitchfork *n* saman tırmığı

pitfall *n* tuzak; tehlike
pitiful *adj* hazin
pity *n* şefkat
placard *n* pankart
placate *v* yatıştırmak
place *n* yer
placid *adj* sessiz
plague *n* uğraşmak
plain *n* sade
plain *adj* sade; düz
plainly *adv* anlaşılıyor ki
plaintiff *n* davacı
plan *v* planlamak
plan *n* plan
plane *n* uçak
planet *n* gezegen
plant *v* ekmek
plant *n* bitki
plaster *n* sıva
plaster *v* sıva vurmak
plastic *n* plastik
plate *n* tabak
plateau *n* yayla
platform *n* düzlem
platinum *n* platin
platoon *n* takım
plausible *adj* akla yatkın
play *v* eğlenmek
play *n* oyun; faaliyet
player *n* oyuncu
playful *adj* oyunbaz
playground *n* oyun alanı
plea *n* iddia
plead *v* yalvarmak
please *v* memnun etmek
pleasing *adj* hoş
pleasure *n* sevinç
pleat *n* kıvrım
pleated *adj* kırmalı
pledge *v* rehine koymak
pledge *n* rehin
plentiful *adj* çok
plenty *n* bolca
pliable *adj* katlanabilir
pliers *n* kerpeten
plot *n* arsa; suikast
plow *v* çift sürmek
ploy *n* manevra
pluck *v* koparmak
plug *v* çalışmak
plug *n* fiş; piston
plum *n* erik
plumber *n* tesisatçı
plumbing *n* boru tesisatı
plummet *v* dibe vurmak
plump *adj* tıknaz

plunder *v* talan etmek
plunge *v* saplamak
plunge *n* dalış; atılma
plural *n* çoğul
plus *adj* artı
plush *adj* pelüş; lüks
plutonium *n* plütonyum
pneumonia *n* zatürree
pocket *n* cep
poem *n* şiir
poet *n* şair
poetry *n* şiir
poignant *adj* keskin
point *n* nokta; maksat
point *v* yöneltmek
pointed *adj* sivri
pointless *adj* mantıksız
poise *n* dengelemek
poison *v* zehirlemek
poison *n* zehir
poisoning *n* zehirleyen
poisonous *adj* zehirli
Poland *n* Polonya
polar *adj* kutupsal
pole *n* kutup
police *n* polis
policeman *n* polis
policy *n* poliçe
Polish *adj* Polonyalı
polish *n* cila
polish *v* cilalamak
polite *adj* kibar
politeness *n* kibarlık
politician *n* siyasetçi
politics *n* politika
poll *n* oylama
pollen *n* polen
pollute *v* kirletmek
pollution *n* kirlilik
polygamist *adj* çokeşli
polygamy *n* çokeşlilik
pomegranate *n* nar
pomposity *n* tafra
pond *n* gölet
ponder *v* zihninde tartmak
pontiff *n* piskopos
pool *n* havuz; ekip
pool *v* birleştirmek
poor *n* fakir
poorly *adv* başarısızlıkla
popcorn *n* patlamış mısır
Pope *n* Papa
poppy *n* gelincik
popular *adj* popüler
population *n* nüfus
porcelain *n* porselen

P

porch *n* veranda
porcupine *n* oklu kirpi
pore *n* gözenek
pork *n* domuz eti
porous *adj* geçirgen
port *n* liman; kapı
portable *adj* taşınabilir
portent *n* belirtisi
porter *n* kapıcı
portion *n* porsiyon
portrait *n* portre
portray *v* betimlemek
Portugal *n* Portekiz
Portuguese *adj* Portekizli
pose *v* poz vermek
pose *n* poz
posh *adj* lüks
position *n* pozisyon
positive *adj* pozitif
possess *v* sahip olmak
possession *n* mülk
possibility *n* olanak
possible *adj* mümkün
post *n* posta
post office *n* postahane
postage *n* posta ücreti
postcard *n* kart
poster *n* poster
posterity *n* zürriyet
postman *n* postacı
postmark *n* posta damgası
postpone *v* ertelemek
postponement *n* erteleme
pot *n* kap; ödül
potato *n* patates
potent *adj* güçlü
potential *adj* potansiyel
pothole *n* derin çukur
pound *v* vurmak
pound *n* darbe; libre
pour *v* dökmek
poverty *n* yoksulluk
powder *n* pudra; toz
power *n* güç
powerful *adj* güçlü
powerless *adj* güçsüz
practical *adj* pratik
practice *n* talim
practise *v* alıştırma yapmak
practising *adj* avukatlık yapan
pragmatist *adj* çıkarcı
prairie *n* yayla
praise *v* övmek
praise *n* övgü
praiseworthy *adj* övgüye değer
prank *n* muziplik

P

prawn *n* karides
pray *v* dua etmek
prayer *n* dua
preach *v* vaaz vermek
preacher *n* vaiz
preaching *n* vaaz
preamble *n* giriş
precarious *adj* güvenilmez
precaution *n* önlem
precedent *n* emsal
preceding *adj* sabık
precept *n* emir
precious *adj* değerli
precipice *n* uçurum
precise *adj* tam; doğru
precision *n* isabet
precocious *adj* turfanda
precursor *n* öncü
predecessor *n* ata
predicament *n* hal
predict *v* öngörmek
prediction *n* öngörü
predilection *n* hoşlanma
predisposed *adj* eğilimli
predominate *v* üstün olmak
preempt *v* önlemek
prefabricate *v* kurmak
preface *n* önsöz
prefer *v* tercih etmek
preference *n* tercih
prefix *n* önek
pregnancy *n* hamilelik
pregnant *adj* hamile
prejudice *n* önyargı
preliminary *adj* hazırlayıcı
prelude *n* giriş
premature *adj* erken
premeditate *v* tasarlamak
premeditation *n* kasıt
premier *adj* birinci
premise *n* arazi
premises *n* arazi
premonition *n* önsezi
preoccupation *n* tasa
preoccupy *v* işgal etmek
preparation *n* hazırlık
prepare *v* hazırlamak
preposition *n* ilgeç
prerequisite *n* önkoşul
prerogative *n* ayrıcalık
prescribe *v* emretmek
prescription *n* talimat
presence *n* varlık
present *adj* şimdiki
present *v* sunmak
presentation *n* sunum

preserve *v* saklamak
preside *v* nezaret etmek
presidency *n* başkanlık
president *n* başkan
press *n* basın; basımevi
press *v* baskı yapmak
pressing *adj* acil; sıkışık
pressure *v* sıkıştırmak
pressure *n* basınç
prestige *n* prestij
presume *v* zannetmek
presumption *n* zan
presuppose *v* varsaymak
presupposition *n* varsayılan
pretend *v* yapar görünmek
pretense *n* hile
pretension *n* iddia
pretty *adj* güzel
prevail *v* yenmek
prevalent *adj* yaygın
prevent *v* önlemek
prevention *n* önleme
preventive *adj* önleyici
preview *n* önizleme
previous *adj* önceki
previously *adv* önceden
prey *n* av
price *n* fiyat
pricey *adj* pahalı
prick *v* delmek
pride *n* gurur
priest *n* rahip
priestess *n* rahibe
priesthood *n* papazlık
primacy *n* üstünlük
primarily *adv* başlıca
prime *adj* asıl
primitive *adj* ilkel
prince *n* prens
princess *n* prenses
principal *adj* başlıca
principle *n* ilke
print *v* çıktı almak
print *n* çıktı
printer *n* yazıcı
printing *n* basma
prior *adj* evvel
priority *n* öncelik
prism *n* prizma
prison *n* hapis
prisoner *n* tutsak
privacy *n* gizlilik
private *adj* özel
privilege *n* imtiyaz
prize *n* ödül
probability *n* ihtimal

probable *adj* olası
probe *v* araştırmak
probing *n* sınama
problem *n* sorun
problematic *adj* sorunlu
procedure *n* prosedür
proceed *v* ileri gitmek
proceedings *n* takibat
proceeds *n* hasılat
process *n* süreç
procession *n* kafile
proclaim *v* beyan etmek
proclamation *n* ilan
procrastinate *v* ertelemek
procreate *v* doğurmak
procure *v* edinmek
prod *v* dürtmek
prodigious *adj* olağanüstü
prodigy *n* harika
produce *v* üretmek
produce *n* ürün
product *n* ürün
production *n* üretim
productive *adj* üretken
profane *adj* kafir
profess *v* itiraf etmek
profession *n* uğraş
professional *adj* profesyonel
professor *n* profesör
proficiency *n* ehliyet
proficient *adj* mahir
profile *n* belgi
profit *v* kar etmek
profit *n* kar
profitable *adj* kar getiren
profound *adj* önemli
program *n* program
programmer *n* programcı
progress *v* ilerlemek
progress *n* ilerleme
progressive *adj* aşamalı
prohibit *v* menetmek
prohibition *n* yasak
project *v* proje yapmak
project *n* proje
projectile *n* itici
prologue *n* öndeyiş
prolong *v* uzatmak
promenade *n* gezinti
prominent *adj* ileri gelen
promiscuous *adj* karmakarışık
promise *n* vaat
promote *v* terfi ettirmek
promotion *n* terfi
prompt *adj* çabuk
prone *adj* eğilimli

pronoun *n* zamir
pronounce *v* telaffuz etmek
proof *n* kanıt
propaganda *n* propaganda
propagate *v* yaymak
propel *v* sürmek
propensity *n* eğilim
proper *adj* düzgün; uygun
properly *adv* uygun şekilde
property *n* mal
prophecy *n* kehanet
prophet *n* peygamber
proportion *n* oran
proposal *n* teklif
propose *v* teklif etmek
proposition *n* teşebbüs
prose *n* düzyazı
prosecute *v* dava açmak
prosecutor *n* savcı
prospect *n* umut
prosper *v* gelişmek
prosperity *n* refah
prosperous *adj* başarılı
prostate *n* prostat
prostrate *adj* bitkin
protect *v* korumak
protection *n* koruma
protein *n* protein
protest *v* protesto etmek
protest *n* protesto
protocol *n* protokol
prototype *n* ön ürün
protract *v* uzatmak
protracted *adj* uzatılmış
protrude *v* pırtlamak
proud *adj* gururlu
proudly *adv* gurulu biçimde
prove *v* kanıtlamak
proven *adj* kanıtlanmış
proverb *n* atasözü
provide *v* sağlamak
providence *n* basiret
providing that *c* şartıyla
province *n* vilayet
provision *n* karşılık
provisional *adj* geçici
provocation *n* korkutma
provoke *v* kışkırtmak
prow *n* pruva
prowler *n* serseri
proximity *n* yakınlık
proxy *n* vekaletname
prudence *n* sağgörü
prudent *adj* akıllı
prune *v* budamak
prune *n* kuru erik

pseudonym *n* rumuz
psychiatrist *n* psikiyatrist
psychiatry *n* psikiyatri
psychic *adj* psişik
psychology *n* psikoloji
psychopath *n* psikopat
puberty *n* buluğ
public *adj* genel
publication *n* yayın
publicity *n* reklam
publicly *adv* alenen
publish *v* basmak
publisher *n* yayımcı
pudding *n* muhallebi
puerile *adj* çocukça
puff *n* üfürük
puffy *adj* kabarık
pull *v* çekmek
pull ahead *v* önüne geçmek
pull down *v* yıkmak
pull out *v* uzaklaşmak
pulley *n* makara
pulp *n* ezme
pulpit *n* kürsü
pulsate *v* sıçramak
pulse *n* nabız
pulverize *v* yenmek
pump *v* emmek
pump *n* pompa
pumpkin *n* helvacı kabağı
punch *v* yumruklamak
punch *n* zımba; kuvvet
punctual *adj* dakik
puncture *n* delik; patlama
punishment *n* ceza
pupil *n* öğrenci
puppet *n* kukla
puppy *n* köpek yavrusu
purchase *v* kazanmak
purchase *n* iştira; alınım
pure *adj* saf
puree *n* püre
purgatory *n* araf
purge *n* tasfiye
purge *v* temizlemek
purification *n* arındırma
purify *v* durulamak
purity *n* saflık
purple *adj* mor
purpose *n* amaç
purposely *adv* kasten
purse *n* cüzdan
pursue *v* kovalamak
pursuit *n* kovalama
pus *n* iltihap
push *v* itmek

put *iv* koymak
put aside *v* saklamak
put off *v* ertelemek
put out *v* söndürmek
put up *v* misafir etmek
put up with *v* dayanmak
putrid *adj* kokmuş
puzzle *n* bilmece
puzzling *adj* şaşırtıcı
pyramid *n* piramid
python *n* piton

Q

quagmire *n* batak
quail *n* sinmek
quake *v* sallanmak
qualify *v* hak kazanmak
quality *n* nitelik
qualm *n* umutsuzluk
quandery *n* tereddüt
quantity *n* nicelik
quarrel *v* kavga etmek
quarrel *n* kavga
quarrelsome *adj* kavgacı
quarry *n* taşocağı
quarter *n* çeyrek
quarterly *adj* üç ayda bir
quarters *n* kışla
quash *v* iptal etmek
queen *n* kraliçe
queer *adj* garip
quell *v* bastırmak
quench *v* tatmin etmek
quest *n* araştırma
question *v* sorgulamak
question *n* soru
questionnaire *n* anket
queue *n* sıra
quick *adj* çabuk
quickly *adv* acele
quicksand *n* bataklık
quiet *adj* sessiz
quietness *n* sessizlik
quilt *n* yorgan
quit *iv* çıkmak;
quite *adv* oldukça
quiver *v* ürpermek
quiz *v* sınav
quotation *n* alıntı
quote *v* alıntı yapmak
quotient *n* bölüm

R

rabbi *n* haham
rabbit *n* tavşan
rabies *n* kuduz
raccoon *n* rakun
race *v* yarışmak
race *n* yarış; ırk
racism *n* ırkçılık
racist *adj* ırkçı
racket *n* raket; gürültü
radar *n* radar
radiation *n* radyasyon
radiator *n* radyatör
radical *adj* radikal
radio *n* radyo
radish *n* turp
radius *n* yarıçap
raffle *n* piyango
raft *n* sal
rag *n* bez
rage *n* öfke
ragged *adj* yırtık pırtık
raid *n* baskın; akın
raid *v* baskın yapmak
raider *n* baskıncı
rail *n* demiryolu
railroad *n* demiryolu
rain *n* yağmur
rain *v* yağmur yağmak
rainbow *n* gökkuşağı
raincoat *n* yağmurluk
rainfall *n* sağanak
rainy *adj* yağmurlu
raise *n* artış
raise *v* arttırmak
raisin *n* kuru üzüm
rake *n* tarak; tırmık
rally *n* ralli; miting
ram *n* koç; çekiç
ram *v* dövmek
ramification *n* dallanma
ramp *n* rampa
rampage *v* öfkelenmek
rampant *adj* şahlanmış
ramson *n* sarımsak
ranch *n* hayvan çiftliği
rancor *n* garez
randomly *adv* rastgele
range *n* saha
rank *n* rütbe
rank *v* düzenlemek
ransack *v* yoklamak
rape *v* tecavüz etmek
rape *n* şalgam

rapid *adj* hızlı
rapist *n* tecavüzcü
rapport *n* ahenk; yakınlık
rare *adj* nadir
rarely *adv* nadiren
rascal *n* yaramaz kimse
rash *v* çekip almak
rash *n* atak
raspberry *n* ahududu
rat *n* sıçan
rate *n* hız; oran
rather *adv* oldukça
ratification *n* onaylama
ratify *v* onaylamak
ratio *n* oran
ration *n* hisse
rational *adj* rasyonel
rattle *v* tıkırdamak
ravage *v* harap etmek
ravage *n* yıkım
rave *v* çıldırmak
raven *n* kuzgun
ravine *n* geçit
raw *adj* çiğ
ray *n* ışın
raze *v* tahrip etmek
razor *n* jilet
reach *v* uzatmak
reach *n* görüş sahası
react *v* tepki vermek
reaction *n* tepki
read *iv* okumak
reader *n* okuyucu
readiness *n* gönüllülük
reading *n* okuma; anlam
ready *adj* hazır
real *adj* gerçek
realism *n* gerçekçilik
reality *n* hakikat
realize *v* farkına varmak
really *adv* gerçekten
realm *n* memleket
realty *n* emlak
reap *v* biçmek
rear *v* yetiştirmek
rear *n* geri
rear *adj* art
reason *v* sonuç çıkarmak
reason *n* sebep
reasonable *adj* makul
reasoning *n* muhakeme
rebate *n* indirim
rebel *v* isyan etmek
rebel *n* isyancı
rebellion *n* isyan
rebirth *n* yeniden doğuş

rebound *v* yansımak
rebuff *v* reddetmek
rebuff *n* azarlama
rebuke *v* azarlamak
rebuke *n* azar
rebut *v* çürütmek
recall *v* anımsamak
recant *v* caymak
recede *v* çekilmek
receipt *n* fatura
receive *v* almak
recent *adj* geçmiş
reception *n* resepsiyon
receptionist *n* resepsiyoncu
receptive *adj* kavrayışlı
recess *n* çekilmek
recession *n* geri çekilme
recharge *v* şarj etmek
recipe *n* yemek tarifi
reciprocal *adj* karşılıklı
recital *n* ifade
recite *v* nakletmek
reckless *adj* umursamaz
reckon *v* farz etmek
recline *v* dayanmak
recluse *n* münzevi
recognition *n* tanıma; kabul
recognize *v* tanımak
recollect *v* anımsamak
recollection *n* anılar
recommend *v* önermek
recompense *n* mükafat
record *v* kaydetmek
record *n* plak; belge
recording *n* kayıt
recount *n* nakletmek
recoup *v* telafi etmek
recourse *v* başvurmak
recourse *n* başvuru
recover *v* kurtarmak
recovery *n* iyileşme
recreate *v* ihya etmek
recreation *n* rekreasyon
recruit *v* işe almak
recruit *n* acemi asker
recruitment *n* personel alma
rectangle *n* dikdörtgen
rectangular *adj* dikdörtgen
rectify *v* ıslah etmek
rector *n* rektör
rectum *n* rektum
recur *v* nüksetmek
recurrence *n* tekerrür
red *adj* kırmızı
red tape *n* bürokrasi
redden *v* kırmızılaşmak

redeem *v* kefaret vermek
redemption *n* itfa
red-hot *adj* çok hevesli
redo *v* tekrar yapmak
redouble *v* yoğunlaştırmak
redress *v* doğrultmak
reduce *v* azaltmak
redundant *adj* ağdalı
reed *n* saz
reef *n* resif
reel *n* makara; tura
reelect *v* yeniden seçmek
reentry *n* yeniden girme
refer to *v* tekabül etmek
referee *n* hakem
reference *n* referans
referendum *n* referandum
refine *v* rafine etmek
refinery *n* rafineri
reflect *v* yansıtmak
reflection *n* yansıtma
reflexive *adj* dönüşlü
reform *v* ıslahat; reform
reform *n* reform
refrain *v* kaçınmak
refresh *v* yenilemek
refreshing *adj* tazeleyici
refreshment *n* soğuk içecek
refrigerate *v* soğutmak
refuel *v* yakıt almak
refuge *n* sığınak
refugee *n* mülteci
refund *v* geri ödemek
refund *n* geri ödeme
refusal *n* geri çevirme
refuse *v* reddetmek
refuse *n* ret
refute *v* yalanlamak
regal *adj* krala ait
regard *v* saymak
regarding *pre* hakkında
regardless *adv* bakmaksızın
regards *n* saygılar
regeneration *n* rejenerasyon
regent *n* kral naibi
regime *n* rejim
regiment *n* alay
region *n* bölge
regional *adj* bölgesel
register *v* kaydolmak
registration *n* kayıt
regret *v* pişman olmak
regret *n* pişmanlık
regrettable *adj* üzücü
regularity *n* düzen
regularly *adv* düzenli şekilde

regulate *v* düzenlemek
regulation *n* düzenleme
rehabilitate *v* tamir etmek
rehearsal *n* prova
rehearse *v* prova etmek
reign *n* saltanat
reimburse *v* iade etmek
reimbursement *n* iade
rein *v* dizginlemek
rein *n* dizgin
reindeer *n* rengeyiği
reinforce *v* takviye etmek
reinforcements *n* takviye
reiterate *v* yinelemek
reject *v* reddetmek
rejection *n* ret
rejoice *v* çok sevinmek
rejuvenate *v* gençleştirmek
related *adj* ilişkili
relationship *n* ilişki
relative *adj* göreli
relative *n* akraba
relax *v* rahatlamak
relaxation *n* rahatlama
relaxing *adj* rahatlatıcı
relay *v* anahtarlamak
release *v* yayımlamak
relegate *v* göndermek
relent *v* yumuşamak
relentless *adj* amansız
relevant *adj* yerinde
reliable *adj* güvenilir
reliance *n* itimat
relic *n* kalıntı
relief *n* ferahlama
relieve *v* ferahlamak
religion *n* din
religious *adj* dindar
relinquish *v* feragat etmek
relish *v* lezzet vermek
relive *v* tekrar yaşamak
relocate *v* yer değiştirmek
relocation *n* yerleşme
reluctant *adj* gönülsüz
reluctantly *adv* gönülsüzlükle
rely on *v* itimat etmek
remain *v* kalmak
remainder *n* kalıntı
remaining *adj* geri kalan
remains *n* ceset
remark *v* açıklamak
remark *n* açıklama
remarkable *adj* dikkate değer
remedy *v* deva olmak
remedy *n* deva
remember *v* hatırlamak

remembrance *n* anma
remind *v* hatırlatmak
reminder *n* hatırlatma
remission *n* hafifletme
remit *v* vazgeçmek
remittance *n* havale
remnant *n* kalıntı
remodel *v* tadilat yapmak
remorse *n* vicdan azabı
remorseful *adj* çok pişman
remote *adj* uzak
removal *n* kaldırma
remove *v* çıkarmak
renew *v* yenileştirmek
renewal *n* yenileme
renounce *v* vazgeçmek
renovate *v* yenilemek
renovation *n* yenileme
renowned *adj* yenilenmiş
rent *v* kiralamak
rent *n* kira
reorganize *v* ıslah etmek
repair *v* onarmak
reparation *n* tamirat
repay *v* ödemek
repayment *n* iade
repeal *v* feshetmek
repeal *n* feshetme
repeat *v* tekrarlamak
repel *v* geri atmak
repent *v* pişman olmak
repentance *n* pişmanlık
repetition *n* tekrar
replace *v* yerine koymak
replacement *n* ikame
replay *n* tekrar
replenish *v* ikmal etmek
replete *adj* dolgun
replica *n* kopya
replicate *v* yinelemek
reply *v* cevaplamak
reply *n* cevap
report *v* anlatmak
report *n* rapor
reporter *n* muhbir
repose *v* yatmak
repose *n* istirahat
represent *v* temsil etmek
repress *v* bastırmak
repression *n* baskı
reprieve *n* cezanın tecili
reprint *v* suret çıkarmak
reprint *n* yeni baskı
reprisal *n* misilleme
reproach *v* iftira etmek
reproach *n* ayıp

reproduce *v* tekrarlamak
reptile *n* sürüngen
republic *n* cumhuriyet
repudiate *v* reddetmek
repugnant *adj* iğrenç
repulse *v* defetmek
repulse *n* kovma
repulsive *adj* tiksindirici
reputation *n* ün
reputedly *adv* sözde
request *n* istek
require *v* gerekmek
requirement *n* gereklilik
rescue *v* kurtarmak
rescue *n* kurtarma
research *v* araştırmak
research *n* araştırma
resemblance *n* benzerlik
resemble *v* benzemek
resent *v* içerlemek
resentment *n* gücenme
reservation *n* rezervasyon
reserve *v* ayırmak
reservoir *n* sarnıç; depo
reside *v* ikamet etmek
residence *n* ikametgah
residue *n* bakiye; kalıntı
resign *v* terk etmek
resignation *n* istifa
resilient *adj* esnek
resist *v* dayanmak
resistance *n* dayanıklılık
resolute *adj* kararlı
resolution *n* çözünürlük
resolve *v* çözmek
resort *v* müracaat etmek
resounding *adj* çınlayan
resource *n* kaynak
respect *v* saygı duymak
respect *n* saygı
respectful *adj* saygılı
respective *adj* ayrı ayrı
respiration *n* solunum
respite *n* ertelemek
respond *v* cevap vermek
response *n* cevap
responsibility *n* sorumluluk
responsible *adj* sorumlu
responsive *adj* hevesli
rest *v* dinlenmek
rest *n* istirahat
rest room *n* tuvalet
restaurant *n* restaurant
restful *adj* dinlendirici
restitution *n* onarma
restless *adj* huzursuz

restoration *n* onarma
restrain *v* geri tutmak
restraint *n* yasaklama
restrict *v* kısmak
result *n* sonuç
resume *v* devam etmek
resurface *v* ortaya çıkmak
resurrection *n* diriliş
resuscitate *v* ölüyü diriltmek
retain *v* alıkoymak
retaliate *v* kısas etmek
retaliation *n* misilleme
retarded *adj* gecikmiş
retention *n* alıkoyma
retire *v* emekli olmak
retirement *n* emeklilik; inziva
retract *v* geri çekmek
retreat *v* geri adım atmak
retreat *n* sığınak; tenha yer
retrieve *v* erişmek
retroactive *adj* geçmişe dönük
return *v* geri dönmek
return *n* dönüş
reunion *n* kavuşma
reveal *v* açığa çıkarmak
revealing *adj* açıkta bırakan
revel *v* eğlenmek
revelation *n* ifşa
revenge *v* öç almak
revenge *n* öç
revenue *n* ciro
reverence *n* saygı göstermek
reversal *n* tersine çevirme
reverse *n* feshetmek
reversible *adj* dönüşür
revert *v* dönmek
review *n* teftiş; eleştiri
revise *v* düzeltmek
revision *n* düzeltme
revoke *v* geçersiz kılmak
revolt *v* isyan etmek
revolt *n* isyan
revolting *adj* tiksindirici
revolve *v* döndürmek
revolver *v* tabanca
revue *n* revü
revulsion *n* tiksinti
reward *v* ödüllendirmek
reward *n* ödül
rewarding *adj* tatmin edici
rheumatism *n* romatizma
rhinoceros *n* gergedan
rhyme *n* kafiye
rhythm *n* ritm
rib *n* kaburga
ribbon *n* kurdela

rice *n* pirinç
rich *adj* zengin
rid of *iv* kurtulmak
riddle *n* bilmece
ride *iv* sürmek
ridge *n* bayır
ridicule *v* dalga geçmek
ridicule *n* alay
ridiculous *adj* saçma
rifle *n* tüfek
rift *n* yarık
right *adv* sağda
right *adj* sağ; doğru
right *n* doğru
rigid *adj* soğuk
rigor *n* sertlik
rim *n* kenar; tekerlek
ring *iv* çaldırmak
ring *n* yüzük; halka
ringleader *n* elebaşı
rinse *v* durulamak
riot *v* başkaldırmak
riot *n* başkaldırı
rip *v* parçalamak
rip off *v* yürütmek
ripe *adj* olgun
ripen *v* olgunlaştırmak
ripple *n* çağıldamak
rise *iv* yükselmek
risk *v* riske atmak
risk *n* risk
risky *adj* riskli
rite *n* tören
rival *n* rakip
rivalry *n* rekabet
river *n* nehir
rivet *v* perçinlemek
riveting *adj* çok ilginç
road *n* yol
roam *v* dolaşmak
roar *v* kükremek
roar *n* gürleme
roast *v* kavurmak
roast *n* rosto
rob *v* soymak
robber *n* soyguncu
robbery *n* hırsızlık
robe *n* elbise
robust *adj* sağlam
rock *n* kaya
rocket *n* roket
rocky *adj* kayalık
rod *n* çubuk
rodent *n* kemirgen
roll *v* rolo yapmak
romance *n* romans

roof *n* çatı
room *n* oda; yer
roomy *adj* ferah
rooster *n* horoz
root *n* kök
rope *n* ip
rosary *n* tesbih
rose *n* gül
rosy *adj* pembe
rot *v* çürümek
rot *n* çürümüş
rotate *v* döndürmek
rotation *n* rotasyon
rotten *adj* çürümüş
rough *adj* kaba
round *adj* yuvarlak
roundup *n* toparlama
rouse *v* kaldırmak
route *n* rota
routine *n* rutin
row *v* kürek çekmek
row *n* kürek
rowdy *adj* gürültücü
royal *adj* krala ait
royalty *n* krallık
rub *v* ovalamak
rubber *n* kauçuk
rubbish *n* çöp
rubble *n* moloz
ruby *n* yakut
rudder *n* dümen
rude *adj* terbiyesiz
rudeness *n* terbiyesizlik
rudimentary *adj* temel
rug *n* halı
ruin *v* mahvetmek
ruin *n* harabe
rule *v* yönetmek
rule *n* yönetim
ruler *n* cetvel; hükümdar
rum *n* rom
rumble *v* gürüldemek
rumble *n* bagaj yeri;
rumor *n* söylenti
run *iv* koşmak
run away *v* kaçmak
run into *v* karşılaşmak
run out *v* eksilmek
run over *v* adam çiğnemek
run up *v* birikmek
runner *n* koşucu
runway *n* pist
rupture *n* kopma
rupture *v* koparmak
rural *adj* kırsal
ruse *n* hile

rush *v* acele etmek
Russia *n* Rusya
Russian *adj* Rus
rust *v* paslanmak
rust *n* pas
rustic *adj* kırsal
rust-proof *adj* pas tutmaz
rusty *adj* paslı
ruthless *adj* insafsız
rye *n* çavdar

S

sabotage *v* sabote etmek
sabotage *n* sabotaj
sack *v* kovmak
sack *n* çuval; işten atma
sacrament *n* ayin
sacred *adj* kutsal
sacrifice *n* kurban
sad *adj* üzgün
sadden *v* üzmek
saddle *n* semer
sadist *n* sadist
sadness *n* elem
safe *adj* güvenli
safety *n* güvenlik
sail *v* yelken açmak
sail *n* yelken
sailboat *n* yelkenli
sailor *n* gemici
saint *n* aziz
salad *n* salata
salary *n* maaş
sale *n* indirim
sale slip *n* satış fişi
salesman *n* satıcı
saliva *n* salya
salmon *n* som balığı
saloon *n* meyhane
salt *n* tuz
salty *adj* tuzlu
salvage *v* mal kurtarmak
salvation *n* kurtuluş
same *adj* aynı
sample *n* örnek
sanctify *v* kutsallaştırmak
sanction *v* tasdik etmek
sanction *n* tasdik
sanctity *n* kutsallık
sanctuary *n* tapınak
sand *n* kum
sandal *n* sandal

sandpaper *n* zımpara kağıdı
sandwich *n* sandviç
sane *adj* aklıbaşında
sanity *n* aklıbaşındalık
sap *n* dirilik
sap *v* tüketmek
saphire *n* safir
sarcasm *n* istihza
sarcastic *adj* iğneleyici
sardine *n* sardalya
satanic *adj* şeytanca
satellite *n* uydu
satire *n* hiciv
satisfaction *n* memnuniyet
satisfactory *adj* hoşnut edici
satisfy *v* tatmin etmek
saturate *v* doymak
Saturday *n* Cumartesi
sauce *n* salça; sos
saucepan *n* tava
saucer *n* çay tabağı
sausage *n* sosis
savage *adj* vahşi
savagery *n* vahşilik
save *v* kurtarmak
savings *n* birikim
savior *n* kurtarıcı
savor *v* zevk almak
saw *iv* doğramak
saw *n* testere
say *iv* söylemek
saying *n* deyiş
scald *v* haşlamak
scale *v* ölçeklemek
scale *n* pul; terazi
scalp *n* kafa derisi
scam *n* dolandırıcılık
scan *v* taramak
scandal *n* skandal
scapegoat *n* günah keçisi
scar *n* yara izi
scarce *adj* seyrek
scarcely *adv* nadiren
scarcity *n* kıtlık
scare *v* korkutmak
scare *n* korku
scarf *n* şal; atkı
scary *adj* korkunç
scatter *v* dağıtmak
scenario *n* senaryo
scene *n* sahne; manzara
scenery *n* manzara
scenic *adj* manzaralı
scent *n* koku
sceptic *adj* kuşkucu
schedule *v* planlamak

schedule *n* program
scheme *n* proje
schism *n* bölünme
scholar *n* bilgin
scholarship *n* irfan
school *n* okul
science *n* bilim
scientific *adj* bilimsel
scientist *n* bilim adamı
scissors *n* makas
scoff *v* hakaret
scold *v* azarlamak
scolding *n* azar
scooter *n* skuter
scope *n* kapsam
scorch *v* yakmak
score *n* puan
scorn *v* hor görmek
scornful *adj* küçümseyen
scorpion *n* akrep
scoundrel *n* hergele
scourge *n* kırbaçlamak
scout *n* izci
scramble *v* tırmanmak
scrambled *adj* talan edilmiş
scrap *n* hurda
scrape *v* kazımak
scratch *v* kaşımak
scratch *n* karalama
scream *v* çığlık atmak
scream *n* çığlık
screen *n* ekran; siper
screen *v* görüntülemek
screw *v* vidalamak
screw *n* vida
screwdriver *n* tornavida
scribble *v* karalamak
script *n* betik
scroll *n* tomar
scrub *v* ovalamak
scruples *n* tereddüt
scrupulous *adj* vicdanlı
scuffle *n* didişme
sculptor *n* heykeltıraş
sculpture *n* heykel
sea *n* deniz
seafood *n* deniz ürünleri
seagull *n* martı
seal *v* mühürlemek
seal *n* fok; mühür
seal off *v* tıkamak
seam *n* dikiş yeri
seamless *adj* kusursuz
seamstress *n* kadın terzi
search *v* aramak
search *n* arayış

S

seashore *n* sahil
seasick *adj* deniz tutmuş
seaside *adj* deniz kenarı
season *n* mevsim
seasonal *adj* mevsimlik
seasoning *n* çeşnilik
seat *n* oturacak yer
seated *adj* oturan
secede *v* çekilmek
secluded *adj* tenha
seclusion *n* çekilme
second *n* saniye
secondary *adj* ikinci
secrecy *n* gizlilik
secret *n* gizli
secretary *n* sekreter
secretly *adv* gizlice
sect *n* mezhep
section *n* bölüm
sector *n* kesim
secure *v* korumak
secure *adj* güvenli
security *n* güvenlik
sedate *v* yatıştırmak
sedation *n* yatıştırma
seduce *v* ayartmak
seduction *n* ayartma
see *iv* görmek
seed *n* tohum
seedless *adj* çekirdeksiz
seedy *adj* kılıksız
seek *iv* aramak
seem *v* görünmek
see-through *adj* saydam
segment *n* kesim
segregate *v* ayırmak
segregation *n* fark gözetme
seize *v* ele geçirmek
seizure *n* kriz
seldom *adv* nadiren
select *v* seçmek
selection *n* seçim
self-concious *adj* utangaç
self-esteem *n* özsaygı
self-evident *adj* besbelli
self-interest *n* kişisel çıkar
selfish *adj* bencil
selfishness *n* bencillik
self-respect *n* özsaygı
sell *iv* satmak
seller *n* satıcı
sellout *n* elden çıkarma
semblance *n* biçim
semester *n* sömestre
senate *n* senato
senator *n* senatör

send *iv* göndermek
sender *n* gönderen
senile *adj* bunak
senior *adj* kıdemli
seniority *n* kıdem
sensation *n* sansasyon
sense *v* algılamak
sense *n* duyu; zeka
senseless *adj* saçma
sensible *adj* mantıklı
sensitive *adj* hassas
sensual *adj* tensel
sentence *v* mahkum etmek
sentence *n* cümle; hüküm
sentiment *n* duygu
sentimental *adj* duygusal
sentry *n* nöbetçi
separate *v* ayırmak
separate *adj* ayrı
separation *n* ayırma
September *n* Eylül
sequel *n* devam
sequence *n* ardışıklık
serenade *n* serenat
serene *adj* dingin
serenity *n* dinginlik
sergeant *n* çavuş
series *n* dizi
serious *adj* ciddi; tehlikeli
seriousness *n* ciddiyet
sermon *n* vaaz
serpent *n* yılan
serum *n* serum
servant *n* hizmetçi
serve *v* hizmet etmek
service *n* servis
service *v* hizmet vermek
session *n* sezon
set *n* küme
set *iv* kurmak;
set about *v* girişmek
set off *v* yola çıkmak
set out *v* koyulmak
set up *v* kurmak
setback *n* aksama
setting *n* ayar
settle *v* yerleşmek
settle down *v* dibe oturmak
settle for *v* razı olmak
settlement *n* köy
settler *n* göçmen
setup *n* düzenek
seven *adj* yedi
seventeen *adj* onyedi
seventh *adj* yedinci
seventy *adj* yetmiş

sever *v* kesmek
several *adj* birçok
severance *n* kesme
severe *adj* haşin
severity *n* zorluk
sew *v* dikmek
sewage *n* lağım suyu
sewer *n* kanalizasyon
sewing *n* dikim
sex *n* cinsel ilişki
sexuality *n* cinsellik
shabby *adj* pejmürde
shack *n* baraka
shackle *n* engel
shade *n* gölge; göz siperi
shadow *n* gölge
shady *adj* gölgeli
shake *iv* sarsmak
shaken *adj* sarsılmış
shaky *adj* titrek
shallow *adj* sığ
sham *n* yapmacık
shame *v* utanmak
shame *n* utanç
shameful *adj* utanç verici
shameless *adj* utanmaz
shape *v* şekillendirmek
shape *n* şekil
share *v* paylaşmak
share *n* paylaşım; hisse
shareholder *n* hissedar
shark *n* köpekbalığı
sharp *adj* keskin; kurnaz
sharpen *v* bilemek
sharpener *n* kalemtraş
shatter *v* mahvetmek
shattering *adj* yıkıcı
shave *v* traş olmak
she *pro* o kız
shear *iv* kaykılma
shed *iv* dökmek
sheep *n* koyun
sheets *n* yelken iskotası
shelf *n* sergen; raf
shell *n* kabuk
shellfish *n* su kabuklusu
shelter *v* sığınmak
shelter *n* sığınak
shelves *n* kaya tabakası
shepherd *n* çoban
sherry *n* şeri
shield *v* kalkan
shield *n* siper etmek
shift *n* kayma; hile
shift *v* ötelemek
shine *iv* parlatmak

S

shiny *adj* parlak
ship *n* gemi
shipment *n* gönderilen mal
shipwreck *n* gemi enkazı
shipyard *n* tersane
shirk *v* yan çizmek
shirt *n* gömlek
shiver *v* ürpermek
shiver *n* ürperti
shock *v* şoke olmak
shock *n* şok; darbe
shocking *adj* inanılmaz
shoddy *adj* kalitesiz
shoe *n* ayakkabı
shoelace *n* ayakkabı bağı
shoestore *n* ayakkabıcı
shoot *iv* kurşun atmak
shop *v* alışveriş yapmak
shop *n* dükkan
shoplifting *n* mal aşırma
shopping *n* alışveriş yapmak
shore *n* sahil
short *adj* kısa; parasız
shortage *n* eksiklik
shortcoming *n* noksan
shortcut *n* kestirme
shorten *v* kısaltmak
shorthand *n* steno
shortlived *adj* kısa ömürlü
shortly *adv* kısa sürede
shorts *n* şort
shortsighted *adj* miyop
shot *n* atış; iğne
shotgun *n* av tüfeği
shoulder *n* omuz
shout *v* bağırmak
shout *n* bağırış
shouting *n* feryat
shove *v* sokmak
shove *n* itiş
shovel *n* kürek
show *iv* göstermek
show off *v* gösteriş yapmak
show up *v* ortaya çıkmak
shower *n* duş
shrapnel *n* şarapnel
shred *v* kıymak
shred *n* ince şerit
shrewd *adj* kurnaz
shriek *v* çığlık atmak
shriek *n* feryat
shrimp *n* karides
shrine *n* tapınak
shrink *iv* küçültmek
shroud *n* kefen
shrouded *adj* örtülü

shrub *n* çalılık
shrug *v* omuz silkmek
shudder *n* ürperti
shudder *v* ürpermek
shuffle *v* karıştırmak
shun *v* uzak durmak
shut *iv* kapatmak
shut off *v* durdurmak
shuttle *v* mekik dokumak
shy *adj* utangaç
shyness *n* çekingenlik
sick *adj* hasta
sicken *v* tiksindirmek
sickening *adj* tiksindirici
sickle *n* orak
sickness *n* kusma
side *n* yan; taraf
sideburns *n* favori
sidestep *v* yan çizmek
sidewalk *n* kaldırım
sideways *adv* yandan
siege *n* kuşatma
siege *v* kuşatmak
sift *v* elemek
sigh *n* iç çekme
sigh *v* iç çekmek
sight *n* görüş
sign *v* işaret etmek
sign *n* işaret; levha
signal *n* sinyal
signature *n* imza
significance *n* önem
significant *adj* önemli
signify *v* anlamına gelmek
silence *n* sessizlik
silence *v* susmak
silent *adj* sessiz
silhouette *n* silüet
silk *n* ipek
silly *adj* aptal
silver *n* gümüş
silversmith *n* gümüşçü
silverware *n* gümüş eşya
similar *adj* benzer
similarity *n* benzerlik
simmer *v* kaynamak
simple *adj* kolay; sade
simplicity *n* sadelik
simplify *v* sadeleştirmek
simulate *v* benzeştirmek
simultaneous *adj* simültane
sin *v* günaha girmek
sin *n* günah
since *c* olduğundan
since *pre* den beri
sincere *adj* samimi

sincerity *n* samimiyet
sinful *adj* günahkar
sing *iv* şarkı söylemek
singer *n* şarkıcı
single *n* tek
single *adj* bekar; tek
singlehanded *adj* tek elli
singleminded *adj* hilesiz
singular *adj* tekil
sinister *adj* netameli
sink *iv* batmak
sink in *v* nüfuz etmek
sinner *n* günahkar
sip *v* yudumlamak
sip *n* yudum
sir *n* beyefendi
siren *n* siren
sirloin *n* sığır filetosu
sissy *adj* hanım evladı
sister *n* abla
sister-in-law *n* görümce
sit *iv* oturmak
site *n* site
sitting *n* oturma
situated *adj* bulunan
situation *n* durum
six *adj* altı
sixteen *adj* onaltı
sixth *adj* altıncı
sixty *adj* altmış
sizable *adj* oldukça büyük
size *n* ölçü
size up *v* ölçüp biçmek
skate *v* paten kaymak
skate *n* paten
skeleton *n* iskelet
skeptic *adj* şüpheci
sketch *v* taslak çizmek
sketch *n* taslak
sketchy *adj* kabataslak
ski *v* kayak yapmak
skill *n* beceri
skillful *adj* becerikli
skim *v* sıyırmak
skin *n* deri
skinny *adj* sıska
skip *v* sıçramak
skip *n* sıçrama
skirmish *n* çarpışma
skirt *n* etek
skull *n* kafatası
sky *n* gökyüzü
skylight *n* dam penceresi
skyscraper *n* gökdelen
slab *n* taraça
slack *adj* özensiz

slacken *v* yavaşlatmak
slacks *n* bol pantolon
slander *n* iftira
slanted *adj* eğik
slap *n* tokat
slap *v* tokatlamak
slash *n* eğik çizgi
slash *v* indirmek
slate *n* kayrak
slaughter *v* katletmek
slaughter *n* katliam
slave *n* köle
slavery *n* kölelik
slay *iv* öldürmek
sleazy *adj* çürük
sleep *iv* uyumak
sleep *n* uyku
sleeve *n* elbise kolu
sleeveless *adj* kolsuz
sleigh *n* kızak
slender *adj* narin
slice *v* dilimlemek
slice *n* dilim
slide *iv* kaymak
slightly *adv* birazcık
slim *adj* zayıf; ince uzun
slip *v* kaymak
slip *n* fiş; külot
slipper *n* terlik
slippery *adj* kaygan
slit *iv* yarmak
slob *adj* serseri
slogan *n* slogan
slope *n* yamaç
sloppy *adj* yarım yamalak
slot *n* dar uzun delik
slow *adj* yavaş
slow down *v* yavaşlamak
slow motion *n* ağır çekim
slowly *adv* yavaşça
sluggish *adj* durgun
slum *n* harabe
slump *v* çöküvermek
slump *n* düşüş
sly *adj* kurnaz
smack *n* tokat
smack *v* tokat atmak
small *adj* küçük
smart *adj* akıllı
smear *n* leke
smear *v* sürmek
smell *iv* koklamak
smelly *adj* pis kokulu
smile *v* gülümsemek
smile *n* gülümseme
smith *n* nalbant

S

smoke *v* sigara içmek
smoked *adj* füme
smoker *n* sigara içen
smooth *v* düzleştirmek
smooth *adj* pürüzsüz
smoothness *n* pürüzsüzlük
smother *v* boğmak
smuggler *n* kaçakçı
snail *n* salyangoz
snake *n* yılan
snapshot *n* enstantane
snare *n* tuzak
snatch *v* kapmak
sneak *v* sinsice ilerlemek
sneeze *v* aksırmak
sneeze *n* aksırık
sniff *v* koklamak
sniper *n* keskin nişancı
snitch *v* çalmak
snore *v* horlamak
snore *n* horultu
snow *v* kar yağmak
snow *n* kar
snowfall *n* kar yağışı
snowflake *n* kar tanesi
snub *v* hiçe saymak
snub *n* kötü muamele
soak *v* suya bastırmak
soak in *v* emmek
soak up *v* ıslanmak
soar *v* hızla yükselmek
sob *n* hıçkırık
sober *adj* ayık
so-called *adj* sözde
sociable *adj* sosyal
socialism *n* sosyalizm
socialist *adj* sosyalist
socialize *v* sosyalleşmek
society *n* topluluk
sock *n* çorap
sod *n* çim
soda *n* gazoz
sofa *n* kanepe
soft *adj* yumuşak
soften *v* yumuşatmak
softness *n* yumuşaklık
soggy *adj* sırsıklam
soil *v* kirletmek
soil *n* toprak
soiled *adj* lekelenmiş
solace *n* teselli
solar *adj* güneşe ait
solder *v* lehimlemek
soldier *n* asker
sold-out *adj* satılıp biten
sole *n* taban

sole *adj* tek
solely *adv* yalnızca
solemn *adj* ağırbaşlı
solicit *v* rica etmek
solid *adj* sert; somut
solidarity *n* dayanışma
solitary *adj* yalnız
solitude *n* yalnızlık
soluble *adj* çözünür
solution *n* çözüm
solve *v* çözmek
solvent *adj* çözücü
somber *adj* kasvetli
some *adj* biraz
somebody *pro* birisi; birileri
someday *adv* bir gün
somehow *adv* bir şekilde
someone *pro* birine; birini
something *pro* bir şey
sometimes *adv* bazen
son *n* oğul
song *n* şarkı
son-in-law *n* damat
soon *adv* yakında
soothe *v* sakinleştirmek
sorcerer *n* sihirbaz
sorcery *n* büyücülük
sore *n* ağrıyan
sore *adj* hassas
sorrow *n* keder
sorrowful *adj* kederli
sorry *adj* üzgün
sort *n* çeşit
sort out *v* seçip ayırmak
soul *n* ruh
sound *n* ses; ima
sound *v* dillendirmek
sound out *v* ağzını aramak
soup *n* çorba
sour *adj* ekşi
source *n* kaynak
south *n* güney
southbound *adv* güneye giden
southeast *n* güneydoğu
southern *adj* güneye ait
southerner *n* güneyli
southwest *n* güneybatı
souvenir *n* andaç
sovereign *adj* özerk
sovereignty *n* özerklik
soviet *adj* sovyet
sow *iv* tohum ekmek
spa *n* kaplıca
space *n* uzay; boşluk
space out *v* dalıp gitmek
spacious *adj* ferah

spade *n* kürek
Spain *n* İspanya
span *v* yayılmak
span *n* süre; genişlik
Spaniard *n* İspanyol
Spanish *adj* İspanyol
spank *v* şaplak atmak
spanking *n* şaplak atma
spare *adj* yedek
spare part *n* yedek parça
spark *n* kıvılcım
spark off *v* neden olmak
spark plug *n* buji
sparkle *v* pırıldamak
sparrow *n* serçe
sparse *adj* seyrek
spasm *n* spazm
speak *iv* konuşmak
speaker *n* konuşmacı;
spear *n* mızrak
spearhead *v* öncülük etmek
special *adj* özel
specialize *v* özelleşmek
specialty *n* uzmanlık alanı
species *n* madeni para
specific *adj* belirli
specimen *n* numune
speck *n* benek
spectacle *n* görünüş
spectator *n* seyirci
speculation *n* spekülasyon
speech *n* konuşma
speechless *adj* dili tutulmuş
speed *iv* hız yapmak
speed *n* hız
speedily *adv* hızlıca
speedy *adj* hızlı
spell *iv* hecelemek
spell *n* büyü; nöbet vakti
spelling *n* belirtmek
spend *iv* harcamak
spending *n* harcama
sperm *n* sperm
sphere *n* küre
spice *n* baharat
spicy *adj* baharatlı
spider *n* örümcek
spiderweb *n* örümcek ağı
spill *iv* dökmek
spill *n* döküntü
spin *iv* döndürmek
spine *n* omurga
spineless *adj* cesaretsiz
spinster *n* kız kurusu
spirit *n* ruh
spiritual *adj* ruhani

spit *iv* tükürmek
spite *n* garez
spiteful *adj* garazlı
splash *v* sıçratmak
splendid *adj* şahane
splendor *n* ihtişam
splint *n* kırık çıkık
splinter *n* kıymık
split *n* yarık
split *iv* bölmek
split up *v* bölüştürmek
spoil *v* yıkmak
spoils *n* randıman
sponge *n* sünger
sponsor *n* sponsor
spontaneous *adj* spontane
spooky *adj* ürkütücü
spool *n* makara
spoon *n* kaşık
spoonful *n* kaşık dolusu
sporadic *adj* tek tük
sport *n* spor
sportman *n* sporcu
sporty *adj* sportmen
spot *v* tanımak
spot *n* leke; mevki
spotless *adj* lekesiz
spotlight *n* projektör ışığı
spouse *n* eş
sprain *v* burkmak
sprawl *v* yayılıp yatmak
spray *v* püskürtmek
spread *iv* yaymak
spring *iv* ileri atılmak
spring *n* yay; ilkbahar
springboard *n* tramplen
sprinkle *v* püskürtmek
sprout *v* filizlenmek
spruce up *v* düzenlemek
spur *v* dürtüklemek
spur *n* mahmuz
spy *v* casusluk etmek
spy *n* casus
squalid *adj* bakımsız
squander *v* boşa harcamak
square *adj* kare
square *n* gönye
squash *v* eşmek
squeak *v* gıcırdamak
squeaky *adj* gıcırtılı
squeeze *v* sıkıştırmak
squeeze in *v* sokuşturmak
squeeze up *v* sıkışmak
squirrel *n* sincap
stab *v* bıçaklamak
stab *n* saplama

stability *n* istikrar
stable *adj* durağan
stable *n* ahır
stack *v* istif etmek
stack *n* büyük yığın
staff *n* kurmay; çalışan
stage *n* sahne; posta arabası
stage *v* sahnelemek
stagger *v* tereddüt etmek
staggering *adj* çok şaşırtıcı
stagnant *adj* durgun
stagnate *v* durgunlaşmak
stagnation *n* durgunlaşma
stain *v* leke sürmek
stain *n* leke
stair *n* basamak
staircase *n* merdiven
stairs *n* merdiven
stake *n* kazık; bahis
stale *adj* bayat
stalemate *n* çıkmaz
stalk *v* iz sürmek
stalk *n* azametle yürüme
stall *n* ahır; stand
stall *v* ertelemek
stammer *v* kekelemek
stamp *v* damgalamak
stamp *n* damga
stampede *n* ayaklanma
stand *iv* ayakta durmak
stand *n* duruş
stand for *v* desteklemek
stand out *v* göze çarpmak
stand up *v* ayağa kalkmak
standard *n* standart;
standing *n* sabit olmak
standpoint *n* açı
standstill *adj* durgun
staple *v* zımbalamak
staple *n* zımba
stapler *n* zımba
star *n* yıldız
starch *n* nişasta
starchy *adj* nişastalı
stare *v* gözlerini dikmek
stark *adj* sert
start *v* başlamak
start *n* başlangıç
startle *v* korkutmak
startled *adj* korkmuş
starvation *n* açlıktan ölme
starve *v* acıkmak
state *n* durum; devlet
state *v* beyan etmek
statement *n* beyanname
station *n* istasyon

stationary *adj* durağan
stationery *n* kırtasiye
statistic *n* istatistik
statue *n* heykel
status *n* hal; medeni hal
statute *n* kanun
staunch *adj* sadık
stay *v* kalmak
stay *n* kalış
steady *adj* sabit; muntazam
steak *n* biftek
steal *iv* çalmak
stealthy *adj* gizli
steam *n* buhar
steel *n* çelik
steep *adj* sarp
stem *n* ağaç gövdesi
stem *v* başvermek
stench *n* taaffün
step *n* adım; basamak
step down *v* inmek
step out *v* dışarı çıkmak
step up *v* kuvvetlendirmek
step-by-step *adv* adım adım
stepdaughter *n* üvey kız
stepfather *n* üvey baba
stepladder *n* ayaklı merdiven
stepmother *n* üvey anne
stepsister *n* üvey kızkardeş
sterile *adj* steril
sterilize *v* sterilize etmek
stern *n* sandal kıçı
stern *adj* yavuz
stew *n* güveç
stewardess *n* hostes
stick *n* sopa
stick *iv* yapıştırmak
stick out *v* çıkarmak
stick to *v* ayrılmamak
sticker *n* etiket
sticky *adj* yapışkan
stiff *adj* katı
stiffen *v* sertleşmek
stiffness *n* katılık
stifle *v* boğmak
stifling *adj* boğucu
still *adj* durgun
stimulant *n* uyarıcı
stimulate *v* uyarmak
stimulus *n* uyarıcı unsur
sting *iv* sokmak
sting *n* iğne; dürtü
stinging *adj* batan
stingy *adj* cimri
stink *iv* kokmak
stink *n* pis koku

stinking *adj* pis kokan
stipulate *v* söz vermek
stir *v* karıştırmak;
stir up *v* kışkırtmak
stitch *v* dikmek
stitch *n* dikiş
stock *v* depolamak
stock *n* hisse senedi
stocking *n* çorap; stoklama
stockpile *n* stok yığını
stockroom *n* mal deposu
stoic *adj* stoacı
stomach *n* mide
stone *n* taş
stone *v* taşlamak
stool *n* iskemle
stop *v* durmak
stop *n* durak
stop by *v* uğramak
stop over *v* kısa ziyaret
storage *n* depo
store *v* depolamak
store *n* ambar
stork *n* leylek
storm *n* fırtına
stormy *adj* fırtınalı
story *n* öykü; kat
stove *n* soba
straight *adj* dümdüz
straighten out *v* düzeltmek
strain *v* germek
strain *n* germe
strained *adj* zoraki
strainer *n* süzgeç
strait *n* geçit
strange *adj* garip
stranger *n* yabancı
strangle *v* boğmak
strap *n* kayış
strategy *n* strateji
straw *n* çöp
strawberry *n* çilek
stray *adj* aylak
stray *v* yoldan çıkmak
stream *n* dere; cereyan
street *n* sokak
streetcar *n* tramvay
streetlight *n* sokak lambası
strength *n* kuvvet
strenuous *adj* yorucu
stress *n* gerilim; stres
stressful *adj* stres verici
stretch *n* hapis süresi
stretch *v* esnetmek
stretcher *n* sedye
strict *adj* sert

strife *n* çekişme
strike *n* vuruş; grev
strike *iv* vurmak
strike back *v* karşılık vermek
strike out *v* çıkartmak
strike up *v* başlamak
striking *adj* göze çarpan
string *n* şerit; seri
stringent *adj* zorlu
strip *n* şerit
strip *v* soymak
stripe *n* çubuk
striped *adj* çizgili
strive *iv* gayret etmek
stroke *n* darbe; hat
stroll *v* gezinmek
strong *adj* güçlü
structure *n* yapı
struggle *v* mücadele etmek
struggle *n* mücadele
stub *n* izmarit
stubborn *adj* inatçı
student *n* öğrenci
study *v* ders çalışmak
stuff *n* madde; eşya
stuff *v* tıkıştırmak
stuffing *n* dolgu
stuffy *adj* havasız
stumble *v* tökeslemek
stun *v* şaşırtmak
stunning *adj* nefis
stupendous *adj* muazzam
stupid *adj* aptal
stupidity *n* aptallık
sturdy *adj* sağlam
stutter *v* kekelemek
style *n* biçem
subdued *adj* bastırılmış
subject *v* maruz kalmak
subject *n* özne; konu
sublime *adj* yüce
submerge *v* batırmak
submissive *adj* uysal
submit *v* arz etmek
subpoena *n* celpname
subscribe *v* imzalamak
subscription *n* abonelik
subsequent *adj* sonraki
subsidiary *adj* yardımcı
subsidy *n* sübvansiyon
subsist *v* geçinmek
substance *n* madde
substandard *adj* acemi
substantial *adj* dayanıklı
substitute *v* yerine koymak
substitute *n* yedek

subtitle *n* altbaşlık
subtle *adj* kurnaz
subtraction *n* çıkarma
suburb *n* şehir dışı
subway *n* tünel
success *n* başarı
successful *adj* başarılı
successor *n* varis
succulent *adj* sulu
such *adj* bunun gibi
suck *v* emmek
sucker *adj* enayi
sudden *adj* ani
suddenly *adv* aniden
sue *v* dava açmak
suffer *v* acı çekmek
suffering *n* ıstırap
sufficient *adj* yeterli
suffocate *v* boğulmak
sugar *n* şeker
suggest *v* önermek
suggestion *n* öneri
suggestive *adj* anlamlı
suicide *n* intihar
suit *n* hukuk davası
suitable *adj* uygun
suitcase *n* valiz
sullen *adj* somurtkan
sulphur *n* kükürt
sum *n* toplam
sum up *v* toplamak
summarize *v* özetlemek
summary *n* özet
summer *n* yaz
summit *n* zirve
summon *v* çağırmak
sumptuous *adj* görkemli
sun *n* güneş
sunblock *n* güneş kremi
sunburn *n* güneş yanığı
Sunday *n* Pazar
sundown *n* gurup
sunglasses *n* güneş gözlüğü
sunken *adj* çökük
sunny *adj* güneşli
sunrise *n* gündoğumu
sunset *n* günbatımı
superb *adj* süper
superfluous *adj* fuzuli
superior *adj* üstün
superiority *n* üstünlük
supermarket *n* süpermarket
superpower *n* süper devletler
supersede *v* yerini almak
superstition *n* batıl inanç
supervise *v* teftiş etmek

supervision *n* teftiş
supper *n* akşam yemeği
supple *adj* esnek
supplier *n* tedarikçi
supplies *n* erzak
supply *v* tedarik etmek
support *v* desteklemek
supporter *n* destekçi
suppose *v* farzetmek
supposing *c* faraza
supposition *n* zan
suppress *v* sindirmek
supremacy *n* üstünlük
supreme *adj* ulu
sure *adj* güvenilir
surely *adv* elbette
surf *v* sörf yapmak
surface *n* yüzey
surge *n* büyük dalga
surgeon *n* cerrah
surgical *adv* cerrahi
surname *n* soyisim
surpass *v* baskın çıkmak
surplus *n* fazlalık
surprise *v* sürpriz yapmak
surprise *n* sürpriz
surrender *v* teslim olmak
surrender *n* teslimiyet
surround *v* çevrelemek
surroundings *n* çevre
surveillance *n* gözetme
survey *n* anket
survival *n* kurtuluş
survive *v* hayatta kalmak
survivor *n* sağ kalanlar
susceptible *adj* alıngan
suspect *v* kuşkulanmak
suspect *n* kuşku
suspend *v* askıya almak
suspenders *n* askı
suspense *n* askıda kalış
suspension *n* asılma
suspicion *n* kuşku
suspicious *adj* şüpheli
sustain *v* tedarik etmek
sustenance *n* gıda
swallow *v* yutmak
swamp *n* batak
swamped *adj* batmış
swan *n* kuğu
swap *n* değiş tokuş
swarm *n* küme
sway *v* sallamak
swear *iv* küfretmek
sweat *n* ter
sweat *v* terlemek

sweater *n* kazak
Sweden *n* İsveç
Sweedish *adj* İsveçli
sweep *iv* süpürmek
sweet *adj* tatlı
sweeten *v* tatlılaştırmak
sweetheart *n* sevgili
sweetness *n* tatlılık
sweets *n* şeker
swell *iv* şişmek
swelling *n* büyümek
swift *adj* atik
swim *iv* yüzmek
swimmer *n* yüzücü
swimming *n* yüzme
swindle *v* dolandırmak
swindle *n* dolandırıcılık
swindler *n* dolandırıcı
swing *iv* sallanmak
swing *n* salıncak; devre
Swiss *adj* İsviçreli
switch *v* değiştirmek
switch *n* anahtar
switch off *v* kapatmak
switch on *v* açmak
Switzerland *n* İsviçre
swollen *adj* şiş
sword *n* kılıç
swordfish *n* kılıçbalığı
syllable *n* hece
symbol *n* sembol
symbolic *adj* sembolik
symmetry *n* simetri
sympathy *n* sempati
symphony *n* senfoni
symptom *n* semptom
synagogue *n* sinagog
synod *n* sinod
synonym *n* eşanlamlı
synthesis *n* sentez
syphilis *n* frengi
syringe *n* şırınga
syrup *n* şurup
system *n* sistem
systematic *adj* sistemli

T

table *n* masa
tablecloth *n* sofra örtüsü
tablespoon *n* büyük kaşık
tablet *n* tablet
tack *n* pünez

tact *n* ince bir anlayış
tactful *adj* nazik
tactical *adj* taktiksel
tactics *n* taktik
tag *n* etiket
tail *n* kuyruk; tuğ
tail *v* peşine takılmak
tailor *n* terzi
tainted *adj* lekeli
take *iv* almak
take apart *v* ayırmak
take away *v* alıp götürmek
take back *v* geri almak
take in *v* daraltmak
take off *v* havalanmak
take out *v* çıkarmak
take over *v* devralmak
tale *n* masal
talent *n* yetenek
talk *v* konuşmak
talkative *adj* konuşkan
tall *adj* uzun boylu
tame *v* ehlileştirmek
tangent *n* teğet
tangerine *n* mandalina
tangible *adj* gerçek
tank *n* tank
tanned *adj* serili
tantamount to *adj* eşanlamlı
tantrum *n* öfke nöbeti
tap *n* tapa
tap into *v* pençe vurmak
tape *n* kaset
tape recorder *n* teyp kaydedici
tapestry *n* resimli örtü
tar *n* katran
tarantula *n* tarantula
target *n* hedef; nişan
tariff *n* tarife
tarnish *v* karartmak
tart *n* turta
tartar *n* tartar
task *n* görev
taste *v* denemek
taste *n* tat
tasteful *adj* zevk sahibi
tasteless *adj* tatsız
tasty *adj* leziz
tavern *n* taverna
tax *n* vergi
tea *n* çay
teach *iv* öğretmek
teacher *n* öğretmen
team *n* takım
teapot *n* çay fincanı
tear *iv* yırtmak; kopmak

T

tear *n* gözyaşı
tearful *adj* ağlayan
tease *v* alay etmek
teaspoon *n* çay kaşığı
technical *adj* teknik
technicality *n* teknik detay
technician *n* teknisyen
technique *n* teknik
technology *n* teknoloji
tedious *adj* sıkıcı
tedium *n* can sıkıntısı
teenager *n* genç
teeth *n* dişler
telegram *n* telegram
telepathy *n* telepati
telephone *n* telefon
telescope *n* teleskop
television *n* televizyon
tell *iv* anlatmak
teller *n* veznedar
telling *adj* tesirli
temper *n* tabiat; öfke
temperature *n* ısı derecesi
tempest *n* bora
temple *n* tapınak
temporary *adj* geçici
temptation *n* günaha teşvik
tempting *adj* cezbedici
ten *adj* on
tenacity *n* azim
tenant *n* kiracı
tendency *n* eğilim
tender *adj* gevrek; narin
tenderness *n* şefkat; taravet
tennis *n* tenis
tenor *n* tenör
tense *adj* gergin
tension *n* gerilim
tent *n* çadır
tentacle *n* dokunaç
tentative *adj* farazi
tenth *n* onuncu
tenuous *adj* müphem
tepid *adj* ılık
term *n* terim; müddet
terminate *v* sonlandırmak
terminology *n* terminoloji
termite *n* termit
terms *n* şartlar
terrace *n* teras
terrain *n* arazi
terrestrial *adj* karasal
terrible *adj* korkunç
terrific *adj* harika
terrifying *adj* korkunç
territory *n* arazi

terror *n* terör
terrorism *n* terörizm
terrorist *n* terörist
terrorize *v* yıldırmak
terse *adj* özlü
test *v* test etmek
test *n* test
testament *n* ahit
testify *v* tanıklık etmek
testimony *n* şahadet
text *n* metin
textbook *n* ders kitabı
texture *n* doku
thank *v* teşekkür etmek
thankful *adj* minnet dolu
thanks *n* teşekkürler
that *adj* o; onu
thaw *v* buzları çözülmek
thaw *n* erime
theater *n* tiyatro
theft *n* hırsızlık
theme *n* tema
themselves *pro* kendileri
then *adv* o zaman
theologian *n* ilahiyatçı
theology *n* ilahiyat
theory *n* teori
therapy *n* terapi
there *adv* orada; oradan
therefore *adv* o yüzden
thermometer *n* termometre
thermostat *n* termostat
these *adj* bunlar; bunları
thesis *n* tez
they *pro* onlar
thick *adj* kalın; koyu
thicken *v* kalınlaştırmak
thickness *n* kalınlık
thief *n* hırsız
thigh *n* uyluk
thin *adj* ince; seyrek
thing *n* şey
think *iv* düşünmek
thinly *adv* ince şekilde
third *adj* üçüncü
thirst *v* susamak
thirsty *adj* susamış
thirteen *adj* onüç
thirty *adj* otuz
this *adj* bu
thorn *n* diken
thorny *adj* dikenli
thorough *adj* esaslı
those *adj* onlar
though *c* rağmen
thought *n* düşünce

thoughtful *adj* düşünceli
thousand *adj* bin
thread *v* ipliğe dizmek
thread *n* iplik
threat *n* tehdit
threaten *v* tehdit etmek
three *adj* üç
thresh *v* konuşmak
threshold *n* eşik; basamak
thrifty *adj* tutumlu
thrill *n* heyecan;
thrive *v* uğraşıp başarmak
throat *n* boğaz
throb *n* vuruş; ağrı
throb *v* zonklamak
thrombosis *n* tromboz
throne *n* taht
throng *n* kalabalık
through *pre* boyunca
throw *iv* fırlatmak
throw away *v* çöpe atmak
throw up *v* kusmak
thug *n* cani
thumb *n* başparmak
thumbtack *n* raptiye
thunder *n* gökgürültüsü
thunderbolt *n* yıldırım
Thursday *n* Perşembe
thus *adv* böylece
thwart *v* engellemek
thyroid *n* tiroit
tickle *v* gıdıklamak
tickle *n* gıdıklanma
ticklish *adj* gıdıklanan
tide *n* med cezir
tidy *adj* muntazam
tie *v* bağlamak
tie *n* düğüm; kravat
tiger *n* kaplan
tight *adj* sıkı
tighten *v* sıkılaştırmak
tile *n* fayans; kiremit
till *adv* e kadar
till *v* çift sürmek
tilt *v* eğmek
timber *n* kereste
time *n* vakit
time *v* zamanlamak
timeless *adj* ebedi
timely *adj* zamanında
times *n* süre
timetable *n* çizelge
timid *adj* ürkek
timidity *n* ürkeklik
tin *n* teneke
tiny *adj* ufacık

tip *n* uç; bahşiş
tired *adj* yorgun
tiredness *n* yorgunluk
tiresome *adj* yorucu
tissue *n* mendil; doku
title *n* başlık; unvan
to *pre* ona
toad *n* kara kurbağa
toast *v* ekmek kızartmak
toast *n* kutlama
toaster *n* tost makinesi
tobacco *n* tütün
today *adv* bugün
toddler *n* küçük çocuk
toe *n* ayak parmağı
toenail *n* ayak tırnağı
together *adv* birlikte
toil *v* zahmet çekmek
toilet *n* tuvalet
token *n* simge
tolerance *n* tahammül
tolerate *v* göz yummak
toll *n* sabit ücret
toll *v* çan çalmak
tomato *n* domates
tomb *n* mezar
tombstone *n* mezar taşı
tomorrow *adv* yarın
ton *n* ton
tone *n* ses
tongs *n* maşa
tongue *n* dil
tonic *n* tonik
tonight *adv* bu gece
tonsil *n* bademcik
too *adv* o da
tool *n* gereç
tooth *n* diş
toothache *n* diş ağrısı
toothpick *n* kürdan
top *n* üst giyecek
topic *n* konu
topple *v* devrilmek
torch *n* meşale; el feneri
torment *v* işkence etmek
torment *n* işkence
torrent *n* sel
torrid *adj* çok sıcak
torso *n* heykel gövdesi
tortoise *n* tosbağa
torture *v* işkence etmek
torture *n* işkence
toss *v* sallamak
total *adj* tamamen
totalitarian *adj* totaliter
totality *n* toplam

touch *n* dokunuş; tesir
touch *v* dokunmak
touch on *v* değinmek
touch up *v* rötuş yapmak
touching *adj* dokunaklı
tough *adj* zor
toughen *v* sertleştirmek
tour *n* tur; nöbet
tourism *n* turizm
tourist *n* turist
tournament *n* turnuva
tow *v* çekmek
towards *pre* a doğru
towel *n* havlu
tower *n* kule
towering *adj* kule gibi
town *n* kasaba
town hall *n* belediye binası
toxic *adj* toksinli
toxin *n* toksin
toy *n* oyuncak
trace *v* iz sürmek
track *n* iz; ray
track *v* takip etmek
traction *n* çekiş
tractor *n* traktör
trade *n* ticaret
trade *v* ticaret yapmak
trademark *n* ticari marka
trader *n* tüccar
tradition *n* gelenek
traffic *n* trafik
tragedy *n* trajedi
tragic *adj* trajik
trail *v* izlemek
trail *n* iz
trailer *n* film parçası
train *n* tren
train *v* talim ettirmek
trainee *n* stajyer
trainer *n* terbiyeci
training *n* talim
trait *n* özellik
traitor *n* vatan haini
trajectory *n* mermi yolu
tram *n* tramvay
trample *v* ezmek
trance *n* hipnoz
tranquility *n* sükunet
transaction *n* işlem
transcend *v* sınırını aşmak
transfer *v* taşımak
transfer *n* taşıma
transform *v* dönüşmek
transformation *n* dönüşüm
transfusion *n* kan nakil

transient *adj* geçici
transit *n* transit
transition *n* geçiş
translate *v* tercüme etmek
translator *n* tercüman
transmit *v* iletmek
transparent *adj* saydam
transplant *v* transplantasyon
transport *v* taşımak
trap *n* hendek; tuzak
trash *n* çerçöp
trash can *n* çöp sepeti
traumatic *adj* travmatik
travel *v* seyahat etmek
traveler *n* yolcu
tray *n* tepsi
treacherous *adj* hain
treachery *n* ihanet
tread *iv* basmak
treason *n* vatana ihanet
treasure *n* hazine
treasurer *n* haznedar
treat *v* davranmak
treat *n* ikram
treatment *n* tedavi; muamele
treaty *n* antlaşma
tree *n* ağaç
tremble *v* titremek
tremendous *adj* muazzam
tremor *n* ürperme
trench *n* hendek
trend *n* eğilim
trendy *adj* modaya uygun
trespass *v* ihlal etmek
trial *n* duruşma
triangle *n* üçgen
tribe *n* kabile
tribulation *n* felaket
tribunal *n* mahkeme
tribute *n* hediye
trick *v* hile yapmak
trick *n* hile; şaka
trickle *v* akıtmak
tricky *adj* ustalık isteyen
trigger *v* tetiklemek
trigger *n* tetik
trim *v* kesip düzeltmek
trimmings *n* mağlubiyet
trip *n* gezi; çelme
trip *v* gezmeye çıkmak
triple *adj* üçlü
triumph *n* zafer
triumphant *adj* galip
trivial *adj* önemsiz
trolley *n* el arabası
troop *n* tabur

trophy *n* ganimet; andaç
tropic *n* dönence; tropik
tropical *adj* tropik
trouble *n* zahmet; bela
trouble *v* canını sıkmak
trousers *n* pantolon
trout *n* alabalık
truce *n* ateşkes
truck *n* kamyon
trucker *n* kamyoncu
trumped-up *adj* yalan
trumpet *n* borazan
trunk *n* bagaj; gövde
trust *v* itimat etmek
trust *n* itimat
truth *n* gerçek
truthful *adj* samimi
try *v* denemek
tub *n* banyo küveti
tuberculosis *n* tüberküloz
Tuesday *n* Salı
tuition *n* öğretim
tulip *n* lale
tumble *v* yuvarlanmak
tummy *n* karın
tumor *n* tümör
tumult *n* gürültü
tumultuous *adj* düzensiz
tuna *n* tonbalığı
tune *n* ayar
tune *v* ayarlamak
tunic *n* tünik
tunnel *n* tünel
turbine *n* türbin
turbulence *n* çalkantı
turf *n* çim; kesek
Turk *adj* Türk
Turkey *n* Türkiye
turmoil *n* karışıklık
turn *n* dönüş
turn *v* dönmek
turn back *v* geri dönmek
turn down *v* reddetmek
turn in *v* teslim etmek
turn off *v* kapatmak
turn on *v* açmak
turn out *v* kovmak
turn over *v* değiştirmek
turn up *v* gelmek
turret *n* zırhlı gemi
turtle *n* kaplumbağa
tusk *n* fildişi
tutor *n* özel öğretmen
tweezers *n* cımbız
twelfth *adj* onikinci
twelve *adj* oniki

twentieth *adj* yirminci
twenty *adj* yirmi
twice *adv* iki kere
twilight *n* alacakaranlık
twin *n* ikiz
twinkle *v* ışıldamak
twist *v* bükmek
twist *n* sicim; değişiklik
twisted *adj* çarpık
twister *n* hortum
two *adj* iki
tycoon *n* büyük işadamı
type *n* çeşit; sınıf
type *v* daktiloda yazmak
typical *adj* tipik
tyranny *n* zulüm
tyrant *n* zalim

U

ugliness *n* çirkinlik
ugly *adj* çirkin
ulcer *n* ülser
ultimate *adj* nihai
ultimatum *n* ültimatom
ultrasound *n* ültrason
umbrella *n* şemsiye
umpire *n* hakem.
unable *adj* olanaksız
unanimity *n* oybirliği
unarmed *adj* silahsız
unattached *adj* bekar
unavoidable *adj* kaçınılmaz
unaware *adj* habersiz
unbeatable *adj* yenilmez
unbelievable *adj* inanılmaz
unbiased *adj* önyargısız
unbroken *adj* kırılmamış
uncertain *adj* şüpheli
uncle *n* amca; dayı
uncommon *adj* nadir
unconscious *adj* habersiz
undecided *adj* kararsız
under *pre* altında
undercover *adj* gizli
underdog *n* güçsüz takım
undergo *v* geçirmek
underground *adj* yeraltı
underlie *v* altında yatmak
underline *v* altını çizmek
underlying *adj* altında yatan
undermine *v* altını kazmak
underneath *pre* altında

underpass *n* altgeçit
understand *v* anlamak
understanding *n* anlayış
undertake *v* yüklenmek
underwear *n* iç çamaşırı
underwrite *v* sigorta etmek
undeserved *adj* hak edilmemiş
undesirable *adj* istenilmeyen
undisputed *adj* tartışılmaz
undo *v* geri almak
undoubtedly *adv* şüphesiz
undress *v* soyunmak
undue *adj* aşırı
uneasiness *n* huzursuzluk
uneasy *adj* huzursuz
uneducated *adj* cahil
unemployed *adj* işsiz
unemployment *n* işsizlik
unending *adj* sonsuz
unequal *adj* eşit olmayan
unequivocal *adj* belirsiz
uneven *adj* düz olmayan
uneventful *adj* olaysız
unexpected *adj* beklenmedik
unfailing *adj* yanılmaz
unfair *adj* adaletsiz
unfairly *adv* adaletsizce
unfairness *n* adaletsizlik
unfaithful *adj* sadakatsız
unfamiliar *adj* alışılmadık
unfasten *v* çözmek
unfavorable *adj* olumsuz
unfit *adj* uygun olmayan
unfold *v* açmak
unforeseen *adj* beklenmedik
unforgettable *adj* unutulmaz
unfounded *adj* temelsiz
unfriendly *adj* içtensiz
unfurnished *adj* mobilyasız
ungrateful *adj* nankör
unhappiness *n* mutsuzluk
unhappy *adj* mutsuz
unharmed *adj* sağ salim
unhealthy *adj* sağlıksız
unhurt *adj* incinmemiş
unification *n* birleşme
uniform *n* tekbiçimli
uniformity *n* tekbiçimlilik
unify *v* birleştirmek
unilateral *adj* tek yanlı
union *n* bileşim
unique *adj* tek
unit *n* birim
unite *v* birleşmek
unity *n* birlik
universal *adj* evrensel

universe *n* evren
university *n* üniversite
unjust *adj* adaletsiz
unjustified *adj* haksız
unknown *adj* bilinmeyen
unlawful *adj* kanunsuz
unleaded *adj* kurşunsuz
unleash *v* salıvermek
unless *c* meğer ki
unlike *adj* den farklı
unlimited *adj* sınırsız
unlock *v* kilidi açmak
unlucky *adj* şanssız
unmarried *adj* bekar
unmistakable *adj* aşikar
unnecessary *adj* gereksiz
unpleasant *adj* çirkin
unplug *v* prizden çekmek
unpopular *adj* sıradan
unprotected *adj* korunmasız
unreal *adj* gerçekdışı
unrealistic *adj* hayali
unreasonable *adj* mantıksız
unrelated *adj* ilgisiz
unreliable *adj* güvenilmez
unrest *n* tedirginlik
unsafe *adj* emniyetsiz
unselfish *adj* cömert
unspeakable *adj* tarifsiz
unstable *adj* dengesiz
unsteady *adj* istikrarsız
unsuccessful *adj* başarısız
unsuspecting *adj* masum
unthinkable *adj* olanaksız
untie *v* çözmek
until *pre* e kadar
untimely *adj* zamansız
untrue *adj* uydurma
unusual *adj* nadir
unwillingly *adv* isteksizce
unwise *adj* akılsızca
upcoming *adj* gelecek
update *v* güncellemek
upgrade *v* yükseltmek
upheaval *n* karışıklık
uphill *adv* yokuş
uphold *v* yukarı kaldırmak
upholstery *n* döşemelik
upkeep *n* bakım
upon *pre* üzerine
upper *adj* üst
upright *adj* dikey
uprising *n* ayaklanma
uproar *n* arbede
upset *v* keyfini bozmak
upside-down *adv* baş aşağı

upstairs *adv* yukarda
uptight *adj* sinirli
up-to-date *adj* güncel
upturn *n* yükseliş
upwards *adv* yukarıya doğru
urban *adj* kentsel
urge *n* dürtü
urge *v* zorlamak
urgency *n* aciliyet
urgent *adj* acil
urinate *v* işemek
urine *n* çiş
urn *n* semaver
us *pro* biz
usage *n* kullanım
use *v* kullanmak
use *n* kullanım
used to *adj* alışık
useful *adj* kullanışlı
usefulness *n* kullanışlılık
useless *adj* yararsız
user *n* kullanıcı
usher *n* yer gösterici
usual *adj* alışılmış
usurp *v* gaspetmek
utensil *n* alet
uterus *n* dölyatağı
utilize *v* faydalanmak
utmost *adj* en uzak
utter *v* dile getirmek

vacancy *n* boşluk
vacant *adj* boş
vacate *v* boşaltmak
vacation *n* tatil
vaccinate *v* aşı yapmak
vaccine *n* aşı
vacillate *v* bocalamak
vagrant *n* başıboş
vague *adj* belirsiz
vain *adj* boş; kibirli
vainly *adv* nafile
valiant *adj* yiğit
valid *adj* geçerli
validate *v* geçerli kılmak
validity *n* geçerlilik
valley *n* vadi
valuable *adj* değerli
value *n* değer
valve *n* vana
vampire *n* vampir

van *n* van
vandal *n* vandal
vandalism *n* vandalizm
vanguard *n* elebaşı
vanity *n* kibir
vanquish *v* mağlup etmek
vaporize *v* buharlaştırmak
variable *adj* değişken
varied *adj* çeşitli; değişik
variety *n* çeşit
various *adj* türlü
varnish *v* verniklemek
varnish *n* vernik
vary *v* değişmek
vase *n* vazo
vast *adj* engin
veal *n* dana
veer *v* sapmak
vegetable *v* sebze
vegetarian *v* vejetaryen
vegetation *n* bitki örtüsü
vehicle *n* araç
veil *n* peçe
vein *n* damar
velocity *n* sürat
velvet *n* kadife
venerate *v* saygı duymak
vengeance *n* intikam
venison *n* karaca
venom *n* hayvan zehiri
vent *n* menfez
ventilate *v* havalandırmak
ventilation *n* havalandırma
venture *n* tehlikeli girişim
verb *n* fiil
verbally *adv* sözle
verbatim *adv* aynen
verdict *n* hüküm
verge *n* sınır
verification *n* doğrulama
verify *v* doğrulamak
versatile *adj* çok yönlü
verse *n* mısra
versed *adj* beyit
version *n* sürüm
versus *pre* e karşı
vertebra *n* omur
very *adv* çok; tıpkısı
vessel *n* tekne; damar
vest *n* yelek
vestige *n* kalıntı
veteran *n* gazi
veterinarian *n* veteriner
veto *v* veto etmek
viaduct *n* viyadük
vibrant *adj* titreşimli

V

vibrate *v* titreşmek
vibration *n* titreşim
vice *n* muavin
vicinity *n* civar
vicious *adj* hırçın; berbat
victim *n* kurban
victimize *v* mağdur etmek
victor *n* galip
victorious *adj* muzaffer
victory *n* zafer
view *n* bakış
view *v* görüntüleme
viewpoint *n* bakış açısı
vigil *n* nöbet tutma
village *n* köy
villager *n* köylü
villain *n* hain
vindicate *v* haklı çıkarmak
vindictive *adj* kinci
vine *n* asma
vinegar *n* sirke
vineyard *n* bağ
violate *v* ihlal etmek
violence *n* şiddet
violent *adj* zorlu
violet *n* menekşe
violin *n* keman
violinist *n* kemancı
viper *n* engerek
virgin *n* bakire
virginity *n* bakirelik
virile *adj* erkekçe
virility *n* kuvvetlilik
virtually *adv* neredeyse
virtue *n* erdem
virtuous *adj* erdemli
virulent *adj* öldürücü
virus *n* virüs
visibility *n* görünürlük
visible *adj* görülebilir
vision *n* görüş
visit *n* ziyaret
visit *v* ziyaret etmek
visitor *n* ziyaretçi
visual *adj* görsel
vital *adj* hayati
vitality *n* canlılık
vitamin *n* vitamin
vivacious *adj* hayat dolu
vivid *adj* parlak
vocation *n* kabiliyet
vogue *n* rağbet
voice *n* ses
void *adj* geçersiz
volatile *adj* uçucu
volcano *n* yanardağ

volleyball *n* voleybol
voltage *n* voltaj
volume *n* hacim
volunteer *n* gönüllü
vomit *v* kusmak
vomit *n* kusmuk
vote *v* oy vermek
vote *n* oy
voting *n* oylama
vouch for *v* doğrulamak
voucher *n* makbuz
vow *v* yemin etmek
vowel *n* sesli harf
voyager *n* gezgin
vulgar *adj* müstehcen
vulgarity *n* müstehcenlik
vulnerable *adj* savunmasız
vulture *n* akbaba

W

wafer *n* yonga plakası
wag *v* sallamak
wage *n* ücret; maaş
wagon *n* vagon
wail *v* feryat etmek
wail *n* feryat
waist *n* bel
wait *v* beklemek
waiter *n* garson
waiting *n* bekleme
waitress *n* bayan garson
waive *v* feragat etmek
wake up *iv* uyanmak
walk *v* yürümek
walk *n* yürüyüş
walkout *n* grev
wall *n* duvar
wallet *n* cüzdan
walnut *n* ceviz
walrus *n* deniz aygırı
waltz *n* vals
wander *v* dolaşmak
wanderer *n* avare
wane *v* azalmak
want *v* istemek
war *n* savaş
ward *n* semt
warden *n* muhafız
wardrobe *n* gardırop
warehouse *n* ambar
warfare *n* savaşım
warm *adj* ılık

warm up *v* ısınmak
warmth *n* ısı
warn *v* uyarmak
warning *n* uyarı
warp *v* eğrilmek
warped *adj* eğri
warrant *v* izin vermek
warrant *n* gerekçe
warranty *n* garanti
warrior *n* savaşçı
warship *n* savaş gemisi
wart *n* siğil
wary *adj* temkinli
wash *v* yıkamak
washable *adj* yıkanabilir
wasp *n* eşekarısı
waste *v* kaybetmek
waste *n* harap
wasteful *adj* müsrif
watch *n* saat
watch *v* izlemek
watch out *v* sakınmak
watchful *adj* uyanık
watchmaker *n* saat üreticisi
water *n* su
water *v* sulamak
water down *v* sulandırmak
waterfall *n* şelale
waterheater *n* termosifon
watermelon *n* karpuz
waterproof *adj* su geçirmez
watertight *adj* su geçirmez
watery *adj* sulu
watt *n* vat
wave *n* dalga; hare
waver *v* sallanmak
wavy *adj* dalgalı
wax *n* mum; ağda
way *n* yol; durum
way in *n* giriş
way out *n* çıkış
we *pro* biz
weak *adj* zayıf
weaken *v* zayıflatmak
weakness *n* zayıflık
wealth *n* zenginlik
wealthy *adj* zengin
weapon *n* silah
wear *n* giyim eşyası
wear *iv* giyinmek
wear out *v* yormak
weary *adj* yorgun
weather *n* hava
weave *iv* dokumak
web *n* ağ; top
web site *n* web sitesi

wed *iv* evlenmek
wedding *n* düğün
wedge *n* takoz
Wednesday *n* Çarşamba
weed *n* ot
weed *v* ot yolmak
week *n* hafta
weekday *adj* hafta içi
weekend *n* hafta sonu
weekly *adv* haftalık
weep *iv* ağlamak
weigh *v* tartmak
weight *n* ağırlık
weird *adj* garip
welcome *n* sevindirici
weld *v* birleştirmek
welder *n* kaynakçı
welfare *n* refah
well *n* iyi
well-known *adj* iyi bilinen
west *n* batı
westbound *adv* batıya giden
western *adj* batılı
westerner *adj* batılı
wet *adj* ıslak
whale *n* balina
wharf *n* iskele
what *adj* ne
whatever *adj* hepsi
wheat *n* buğday
wheel *n* tekerlek
wheelbarrow *n* çekçek
wheeze *v* hırıldamak
when *adv* ne zaman
where *adv* nerede
whereabouts *n* nerelerde
whereas *c* iken
wherever *c* her nerede
whether *c* olup olmadığını
which *adj* hangi
while *c* iken; sırasında
whim *n* kapris
whine *v* anırmak
whip *v* fırlatmak
whip *n* kırbaç
whirl *v* fırıldanmak
whirlpool *n* girdap
whiskers *n* favori
whisper *v* fısıldamak
whisper *n* fısıltı
whistle *v* ıslık çalmak
whistle *n* ıslık
white *adj* beyaz
whiten *v* beyazlatmak
whittle *v* yontmak
who *pro* kim

whoever *pro* kim olursa
whole *adj* bütün
wholehearted *adj* samimi
wholesale *n* toptan satış
wholesome *adj* erdemli
whom *pro* kimi; kime
why *adv* neden
wicked *adj* fena
wickedness *n* fenalık
wide *adj* geniş
widely *adv* genişçe
widen *v* genişletmek
widespread *adj* yaygın
widow *n* dul
widower *n* dul erkek
width *n* genişlik
wield *v* kullanmak
wife *n* eş; karı
wig *n* peruk
wiggle *v* oynamak
wild *adj* vahşi
wild boar *n* yabandomuzu
wilderness *n* vahşi doğa
wildlife *n* vahşi hayat
will *n* maksat; irade
willfully *adv* taammüden
willing *adj* istekli
willingly *adv* istekle
willingness *n* isteklilik
willow *n* söğüt
wily *adj* düzenbaz
wimp *adj* pısırık
win *iv* kazanmak
win back *v* geri kazanmak
wind *n* rüzgar
wind *iv* rüzgar esmek
wind up *v* kurmak
winding *adj* dolambaçlı
windmill *n* yeldeğirmeni
window *n* pencere
windpipe *n* nefes borusu
windshield *n* rüzgar siperi
windy *adj* rüzgarlı
wine *n* şarap
winery *n* şaraphane
wing *n* kanat
wink *n* pırıldamak
wink *v* göz kırpmak
winner *n* kazanan
winter *n* Kış
wipe *v* silmek
wipe out *v* temizlemek
wire *n* tel; telgraf
wireless *adj* kablosuz
wisdom *n* bilgelik
wise *adj* bilge

wish *v* dilemek
wish *n* dilek
wit *n* nükte
witch *n* cadı
witchcraft *n* büyücülük
with *pre* ile birlikte
withdraw *v* fesh etmek
withdrawal *n* iptal
withdrawn *adj* iptal edilmiş
wither *v* solmak
withhold *iv* kısıtlamak
within *pre* içerden
without *pre* siz suz eki
withstand *v* dayanmak
witness *n* şahit
witty *adj* esprili
wives *n* eşler; karılar
wizard *n* büyücü
wobble *v* sallanmak
woes *n* acılar
wolf *n* kurt
woman *n* kadın
womb *n* dölyatağı
women *n* kadınlar
wonder *v* merak etmek
wonder *n* merak
wonderful *adj* harika
wood *n* tahta
wooden *adj* tahtadan
wool *n* yün
woolen *adj* yünden
word *n* kelime; sözcük
wording *n* üslup
work *n* iş
work *v* işlemek
work out *v* halletmek
workable *adj* işletilebilir
workbook *n* alıştırma kitabı
worker *n* işçi
workshop *n* seminer
world *n* dünya
worldly *adj* dünyevi
worm *n* solucan
worn-out *adj* bitkin
worrisome *adj* üzücü
worry *v* üzülmek
worry *n* üzüntü
worse *adj* daha kötü
worsen *v* kötüleşmek
worship *n* tapmak
worst *adj* en kötü
worth *adj* kıymetli
worthless *adj* değersiz
worthwhile *adj* değerli
worthy *adj* layık
would-be *adj* sözde

wound *n* yara
wound *v* yaralanmak
woven *adj* örülü
wrap *v* sarmak
wrap up *v* sarmalamak
wrapping *n* özel ambalaj
wrath *n* öfke
wreath *n* çember
wreck *v* harap etmek
wreckage *n* enkaz
wrench *n* İngiliz anahtarı
wrestle *v* güreşmek
wrestler *n* güreşçi
wrestling *n* güreş
wretched *adj* perişan
wring *iv* burmak
wrinkle *v* kırıştırmak
wrinkle *n* kırışık
wrist *n* bilek
write *iv* yazmak
write down *v* not etmek
writer *n* yazar
writhe *v* kıvranmak
writing *n* yazı
written *adj* yazılı
wrong *adj* yanlış

X-mas *n* Noel
X-ray *n* röntgen ışını

yacht *n* yat
yam *n* yün ipliği
yard *n* yarda
yarn *n* yün ipliği
yawn *n* esneme
yawn *v* esnemek
year *n* yıl
yearly *adv* yıllık
yearn *v* can atmak
yeast *n* maya
yell *v* bağırmak
yellow *adj* sarı
yes *adv* evet
yesterday *adv* dün
yet *c* henüz
yield *v* teslim olmak
yield *n* hasılat

yoke *n* boyundurluk
yolk *n* yumurta sarısı
you *pro* sen
young *adj* genç
youngster *n* delikanlı
your *adj* senin; sizin
yours *pro* seninki
yourself *pro* kendin
youth *n* gençlik
youthful *adj* genç

Z

zap *v* vurmak
zeal *n* gayret
zealous *adj* gayretli
zebra *n* zebra
zero *n* sıfır
zest *n* zevk
zinc *n* çinko
zip code *n* posta kodu
zipper *n* fermuar
zone *n* bölge
zoology *n* zooloji

Turkish-English

Abbreviations

English - Turkish

a - article - nesne

adj - adjective - sıfat

adv - adverb - belirteç

c - conjunction - bağlaç

e - exclamation - ünlem

n - noun - ad

pre - preposition - edat

pro - pronoun - zamir

v - verb - eylem

A

a doğru *pre* towards
abajur *n* lampshade
abartılı *adj* overdone
abartmak *v* exaggerate
abla *n* sister
abluka *n* blockade
abluka etmek *v* blockade
abonelik *n* subscription
abuk sabuk *adj* incoherent
aç *adj* hungry
acayip *adj* bizarre
acele *adv* quickly
acele *n* haste
acele etmek *v* hurry up, rush
acele ettirmek *v* hurry
acele şekilde *adv* hastily
aceleci *adj* impetuous
aceleyle *adv* hurriedly
aceleyle girmek *v* burst into
acemi *adj* substandard
acemi *n* beginner
acemi asker *n* recruit
acı *adj* bitter
açı *n* standpoint, angle
acı çekmek *v* suffer
acı çektirmek *v* inflict
acı duymak *v* deplore
acı söz *n* lash
acı veren *adj* painful
acı vermek *v* afflict
açığa çıkarmak *v* reveal
açığa vurmak *v* disclose
açık *adj* open
açık fikirli *adj* open-minded
açık havada *adv* outdoors
açık saçık *adj* obscene
açık saçık laf *n* obscenity
açık seçik *adj* lucid
açık sözlü *adj* outspoken, forthright
açık yürekli *adj* outgoing
açıkça *adv* clearly
açıklama *n* remark
açıklamak *v* explain
açıklanamaz *adj* inexplicable
açıklayıcı not *n* annotation
acıklı *adj* harrowing
açıklık *n* openness
acıkmak *v* starve
açıkta *adv* off
açıkta bırakan *adj* revealing
acil *adj* urgent
acil *n* emergency
acılar *n* woes

acılık *n* bitterness
açılış *n* inauguration
açılış yapmak *v* inaugurate
aciliyet *n* urgency
açılmak *v* open up
açım *n* incision
acımasız *adj* cruel
acımasızlık *n* cruelty
acınası *adj* pathetic
aciz bırakmak *v* incapacitate
acizlik *n* inability
açlık *n* hunger
açlıktan ölme *n* starvation
açmak *v* switch on, open
ad çekimi *n* declension
ada *n* island
adacık *n* isle
adak *n* dedication
adalet *n* justice
adaletli *adj* judicious
adaletlilik *n* fairness
adaletsiz *adj* unfair, unjust
adaletsizce *adv* unfairly
adaletsizlik *n* unfairness
adam *n* guy, man
adam çiğnemek *v* run over
adam kaçırma *n* kidnapping
adam kaçırmak *v* kidnap
adam öldürme *n* manslaughter
adamak *v* devote, commit
adap *n* manners
adaptasyon *n* adaptation
adaptör *n* adapter
aday *n* applicant
adaylık *n* candidacy
adeta *adv* merely
adi *adj* despicable
adı çıkmış *adj* notorious
adil *adj* lawful
adil bir şekilde *adv* justly
adım *n* pace, step
adım adım *adv* step-by-step
adliye sarayı *n* courthouse
adres *n* address
Advent *n* Advent
af *n* absolution
afacan *adj* mischievous
afacan *n* brat
afet *n* catastrophe
affedilir *adj* forgivable
affetmek *v* forgive
afrodizyak *adj* aphrodisiac
afyon *n* opium
ağ *n* net, web
ağaç *n* tree
ağaç gövdesi *n* stem

ağaç kesmek *v* log
ağaç tokmak *v* maul
ağartmak *v* bleach
ağda *n* wax
ağdalı *adj* redundant
ağır *adj* heavy
ağır basan *adj* overbearing
ağır basmak *v* outweigh
ağır çekim *n* slow motion
ağır silah *n* artillery
ağır suç *n* felony
ağırbaşlı *adj* solemn
ağırlık *n* weight
ağıt *n* lament
ağıt yakmak *v* lament
ağız *n* mouth
ağızdan *adv* orally
ağızlık *n* nozzle
ağlamak *v* cry, weep
ağlayan *adj* tearful
ağrı *n* ache
ağrı kesici *n* painkiller
ağrıyan *n* sore
Ağustos *n* August
ağustosböceği *n* locust
ağzını aramak *v* sound out
ahbap *n* buddy, pal
ahenk *n* rapport
ahenksiz *adj* dissonant
ahır *n* barn, stable
ahit *n* testament
ahlak *n* ethics, moral
ahlak bozukluğu *n* depravity
ahlak dışı *adj* amoral
ahlaki *adj* ethical, moral
ahlakı bozan *adj* noxious
ahlaksız *adj* immoral
ahlaksızlık *n* immorality
ahmak *n* jerk
ahtapot *n* octopus
ahududu *n* raspberry
aidat *n* dues
aile *n* family
aile içi *adj* domestic
ait olmak *v* belong
ajan *n* agent
ajanda *n* agenda
ajans *n* agency
akademi *n* academy
akademik *adj* academic
akbaba *n* vulture
akciğer *n* lung
akıbet *n* outcome
akıcı bir şekilde *adv* fluently
akıl hastanesi *n* asylum
akıllanmaz *adj* incorrigible

akıllı *adj* clever, smart
akılsız *adj* mindless
akılsızca *adj* unwise
akın *n* exodus
akıntı *n* leak
akıp gitmek *v* elapse
akış *n* flow
akıtmak *v* drain, trickle
akla getirmek *v* connote
akla yatkın *adj* plausible
aklamak *v* exonerate
aklen *adv* mentally
aklıbaşında *adj* sane
aklıbaşındalık *n* sanity
aklına takılmak *v* obsess
aklını çelmek *v* beguile
akmak *v* flow
akordeon *n* accordion
akraba *n* relative
akrabalık *n* kinship
akran *n* offspring
akre *n* acre
akrep *n* scorpion
akrobat *n* acrobat
aksak *adj* lame
akşam *n* evening
akşam yemeği *n* dinner
aksama *n* setback
aksan *n* accent
aksesuar *n* ornament
aksi takdirde *adv* otherwise
aksilik *n* misfortune
aksini kanıtlamak *v* disprove
aksırık *n* sneeze
aksırmak *v* sneeze
aktör *n* actor
aktris *n* actress
akustik *adj* acoustic
akut *adj* acute
akvaryum *n* aquarium
alabalık *n* trout
alabora etmek *v* overturn
alabora olmak *v* capsize
alacakaranlık *n* dusk
alacaklı *n* creditor
alaka *n* liking
alaka *pre* concerning
alakasız *adj* irrelevant
alamet *n* omen
alan *n* area, field
alarm *n* alarm
alaşağı edilme *n* overthrow
alaşım *n* alloy
alay *n* mockery, ridicule
alay etmek *v* deride, mock
alaycı *adj* ironic

albay *n* colonel
alçak *adj* dishonorable
alçakgönüllü *adj* lowly, modest
alçaklık *n* dishonor
alçaltıcı *adj* degrading
alçaltmak *v* demean
aldatıcı *adj* misleading
aldatma *n* deception
aldatmak *v* betray, fool
aldırmamak *v* overlook
alelade *adj* mediocre
aleladelik *n* mediocrity
alenen *adv* publicly
alerji *n* allergy
alerjik *adj* allergic
alet *n* gadget, utensil
alev *n* flame
alevlendirmek *v* kindle
alfabe *n* alphabet
algılama *n* perception
algılamak *v* sense
alıkoyma *n* detention
alıkoymak *v* detain
alın *n* forehead
alıngan *adj* susceptible
alıntı *n* quotation
alıntı yapmak *v* quote
alıp götürmek *v* take away
alıp satmak *n* merchandise
alışık *adj* used to
alışılmadık *adj* unfamiliar
alışılmış *adj* usual
alışkanlık *n* habit
alışma *n* orientation
alıştırma kitabı *n* workbook
alıştırma yapmak *v* exercise
alıştırmak *v* acclimatize, accustom
alışveriş yapmak *v* shop
alkış *n* applause
alkışlamak *v* applaud
alkolik *adj* alcoholic
alkolizm *n* alcoholism
alkollü *adj* intoxicated
almak *v* get, take
Alman *adj* German
almanak *n* almanac
Almanya *n* Germany
alt *n* bottom
alt etmek *v* overwhelm
altbaşlık *n* subtitle
alternatif *n* alternative
altgeçit *n* underpass
altı *adj* six
altın *n* gold
altın çağ *n* heyday
altıncı *adj* sixth

altında *adv* below
altında *pre* under, beneath
altında yatan *adj* underlying
altında yatmak *v* underlie
altından *adj* golden
altını çizmek *v* underline
altını kazmak *v* undermine
altmış *adj* sixty
altüst etmek *v* mess up
alüminyum *n* aluminum
ama *c* but
amaç *n* purpose, goal
amaçlamak *v* aim
amaçsız *adj* aimless
amansız *adj* relentless
amatör *adj* amateur
ambar *n* store
amblem *n* emblem
ambulans *n* ambulance
amca *n* uncle
Amerikan *adj* American
amfibi *adj* amphibious
amfiteatr *n* amphitheater
amiral *n* admiral
amirane *adj* bossy
amonyak *n* ammonia
amorti etmek *v* amortize
ampul *n* bulb
ampütasyon *n* amputation
ampüte etmek *v* amputate
an *n* moment, instance
ana *adj* leading, main
ana çizgiler *n* outline
ana kara *n* mainland
ana noktalar *n* guidelines
anaç *adj* maternal
anahtar *n* key, switch
anahtarlamak *v* relay
anahtarlık *n* key ring
anakent *n* metropolis
analiz *n* analysis
analiz etmek *v* analyze
analoji *n* analogy
ananas *n* pineapple
anarşi *n* anarchy
anarşist *n* anarchist
anat *n* collarbone
anatomi *n* anatomy
anayasa *n* constitution
anayol *n* highway
anca *adv* narrowly
ancak *c* however
ançüez *n* anchovy
andaç *n* souvenir, trophy
anekdot *n* anecdote
anemi *n* anemia

anemik *adj* anemic
anestezi *n* anesthesia
Anglikan *adj* Anglican
ani *adj* sudden
ani *n* instant
ani çekiş *v* jerk
aniden *adv* suddenly
anılar *n* recollection
animasyon *n* animation
anımsamak *v* recall
anında *adv* instantly
anırmak *v* whine
anıt *n* monument
anjin *n* angina
anket *n* survey
anlam *n* meaning
anlamak *v* figure out
anlamına gelmek *v* signify
anlamlı *adj* meaningful
anlamsız *adj* meaningless
anlaşılır *n* articulation
anlaşılıyor ki *adv* plainly
anlaşılması güç *adj* murky
anlaşılmaz *adj* occult
anlaşılmazlık *n* obscurity
anlaşma *n* deal, accord
anlaşmak *v* agree, deal
anlaşmamak *v* disagree
anlaşmazlık *n* disagreement
anlatım *n* expression
anlatmak *v* report, tell
anlayış *n* understanding
anma *n* remembrance
anmak *v* commemorate
anne *n* mother
annelik *n* motherhood,
anonim *adj* anonymous
anonim *v* incorporate
anonim şirket *n* corporation
anormal *adj* abnormal
anormallik *n* abnormality
ansiklopedi *n* encyclopedia
anten *n* antenna
antibiyotik *n* antibiotic
antidot *n* antidote
antik *adj* ancient
antikite *n* antiquity
antilop *n* antelope
antipati *n* antipathy
antlaşma *n* treaty
antrenör *n* coach
antrenörlük etmek *n* coaching
apandis *n* appendix
apandisit *n* appendicitis
apartman *n* apartment
apartman dairesi *n* flat

aperatif *n* aperitif
aptal *adj* stupid, silly
aptal *n* goof
aptallık *n* stupidity
ara bulmak *v* mediate
ara bulucu *n* mediator
ara dönem *n* interlude
ara kablosu *n* lead
ara sıra *adv* occasionally
ara vermek *v* lay off
araba *n* car
araba gezintisi *n* drive
arabulucu *n* arbiter
araç *n* vehicle
araç sürmek *v* drive
aracı *n* middleman
aracılık *n* intervention
arada bulunan *n* intermediary
araf *n* purgatory
aralık *adj* ajar
aralık *n* interval, break
Aralık *n* December
aralıksız *adj* incessant
aramak *v* search, seek
Arap *adj* Arabic
arapsaçı gibi *adj* mixed-up
arasında *pre* among
arasını kesme *n* interruption
araştırma *n* inquiry, quest
araştırmak *v* inquire, probe
araya girme *n* intercession
araya girmek *v* intervene
arayış *n* search
arazi *n* territory, land
arazi doldurma *n* landfill
arbede *n* brawl, uproar
ardıl *adj* consecutive
ardında *adv* beyond
ardışıklık *n* sequence
arı *n* bee
arı kovanı *n* beehive
arife *n* eve
arındırma *n* purification
aristokrasi *n* aristocracy
aristokrat *n* aristocrat
aritmetik *n* arithmetic
arıza *n* obstruction
arızalı çalışma *n* malfunction
arızalı çalışmak *v* malfunction
arka *n* back
arka kap *n* backdoor
arkadaş *n* fellow, friend
arkadaş olmak *v* befriend
arkadaşça *adj* folksy
arkadaşlık *n* friendship
arkaik *adj* archaic

arkaplan *n* background
arkasında *adv* back
arkasında *pre* behind
arkaya doğru *adv* backwards
arkeoloji *n* archaeology
arktik *adj* arctic
armağan etmek *v* bestow
armut *n* pear
aromatik *adj* aromatic
arpa *n* barley
arsa *n* plot
arsenik *n* arsenic
arşiv *n* archive
art *adj* rear
art niyetli *adj* malevolent
artan *adj* increasing
artı *adj* plus
artıklar *n* leftovers
artıkyıl *n* leap year
artırıcı *n* conditioner
artış *n* increase, raise
artistik *adj* artistic
artizan *n* artisan
artmak *v* increase
artrit *n* arthritis
arttırmak *v* raise
arz etmek *v* submit
arzu *n* craving, desire
arzulamak *v* desire, lust
as *n* ace
aşağı inmek *v* come down
aşağıda *adv* down
aşağılama *n* mortification
aşağılık *adj* inferior
aşağısında *pre* below
aşağıya eğilmek *v* bend down
asalet *n* dignity
aşamalı *adj* progressive
asansör *n* elevator
aşçı *n* cook
asfalt *n* asphalt
aşı *n* vaccine
aşı yapmak *v* vaccinate
aşikar *adj* unmistakable
asil *adj* noble, prime
asılı şey *n* pendant
asılma *n* suspension
asılsız *adj* groundless
asilzade *n* nobleman
asimilasyon *n* assimilation
asimile etmek *v* assimilate
aşındırmak *v* corrode
aşırı *adj* excessive
aşırı *adv* exceedingly
aşırı *n* glut
aşırı yüksek *adj* exorbitant

asit *n* acid
asitlik *n* acidity
asker *n* soldier
askere alınmış *n* conscript
askere alma *n* draft
askere kaydolmak *v* enlist
askeri yürüyüş *n* march
askı *n* hanger
askıda kalış *n* suspense
askıya almak *v* suspend
asla *adv* never
aslan *n* lion
aslında *adv* actually
asma *n* grapevine
aşmak *v* exceed, outrun
aspirin *n* aspirin
ast *adj* junior
asteroit *n* asteroid
astım *n* asthma
astımlı *adj* asthmatic
astrolog *n* astrologer
astroloji *n* astrology
astronom *n* astronomer
astronomi *n* astronomy
astronomik *adj* astronomic
astronot *n* astronaut
at *n* horse
at arabası *n* carriage
at başlığı *n* bridle
ata *n* ancestor
atak *n* rash
atalar *n* antecedents
atama *n* appointment
atamak *v* ordain
atardamar *n* artery
atasözü *n* maxim
ateist *n* atheist
ateizm *n* atheism
ateş *n* fire
ateş etme *n* gunfire
ateşlemek *v* loose, fire
ateşli silah *n* firearm
atik *adj* swift
atılgan *adj* dashing
atılma *n* plunge
atış *n* shot
atkı *n* scarf
atlamak *v* bypass, elude
atlet *n* athlete
atletik *adj* athletic
atmaca *n* hawk
atmak *v* discard
atmosfer *n* atmosphere
atmosferik *adj* atmospheric
atom *n* atom
atomik *adj* atomic

av *n* chase, prey
av tüfeği *n* shotgun
avantaj *n* advantage
avare *n* wanderer
avcı *n* hunter
avize *n* chandelier
avlanmak *v* hunt
avlu *n* backyard
Avrupa *n* Europe
Avrupalı *adj* European
avuç *n* palm
avukat *n* lawyer, attorney
avukatlık yapan *adj* practising
ay *n* month, Moon
ayağa kalkmak *v* stand up
ayak *n* foot
ayak bileği *n* ankle
ayak işi *n* errand
ayak parmağı *n* toe
ayak takımı *n* mob
ayak tırnağı *n* toenail
ayak uydurmak *v* keep up
ayakkabı *n* shoe
ayakkabı bağı *n* shoelace
ayakkabıcı *n* shoestore
ayakkabılar *n* footwear
ayaklanma *n* mutiny, uprising; stampede
ayaklar *n* feet
ayaklı merdiven *n* stepladder
ayakta durmak *v* stand
ayar *n* setting, tune
ayarlamak *v* calibrate, tune
ayartıcı *adj* deprave
ayartma *n* seduction
ayartmak *v* entice, lure
ayaz *n* frost
aybaşı *n* menstruation
aydınlatmak *v* light, ignite
aydınlık *adj* luminous
aygıt *n* device
ayı *n* bear
ayık *adj* sober
ayin *n* litany, liturgy, sacrament
ayıp *n* reproach
ayıplamak *v* lash
ayırma *n* separation
ayırmak *v* allocate; separate, detach
ayırtetmek *v* distinguish
aylak *adj* idle, stray
aylık *adv* monthly
ayna *n* mirror
aynen *adv* verbatim
aynı *adj* same
ayraç *n* bracket
ayrı *adj* separate
ayrı *adv* apart

ayrı ayrı *adj* respective
ayrıcalık *n* oracle; perogative
ayrılabilir *adj* detachable
ayrılamamak *v* linger
ayrılış *n* departure
ayrılmak *v* go away
ayrılmamak *v* stick to
ayrılmaz *adj* inseparable
ayrım *n* discrimination
ayrıntı *n* nuance
ayrıntıya inmek *v* detail
ayrıştırmak *v* decompose
ayyaş *adj* lush
az *adj* few
azad etmek *v* let out
azalma *n* moderation
azalmak *v* decrease
azametle yürüme *n* stalk
azametli *adj* ostentatious
azar *n* rebuke, scolding
azar azar *adv* little by little
azarlama *n* rebuff
azarlamak *v* rebuke, scold
azat *n* liberation
azat etmek *v* liberate
azgın *adj* lustful
azim *n* tenacity
azimli *adj* militant
azınlık *n* minority
aziz *adj* beloved
aziz *n* saint
aziz saymak *v* canonize
azman *adj* monstrous

B

baba *n* dad, father
babacan *adj* fatherly
babalık *n* fatherhood
baca *n* chimney
bacak *n* leg, limb
badem *n* almond
bademcik *n* tonsil
bağ *n* connection; vineyard
bagaj *n* baggage
baget *n* baguette
bağımlı *adj* addicted
bağımlılık *n* addiction
bağımsız *adj* independent
bağımsızlık *n* independence
bağır *n* bosom
bağırış *n* outcry, shout
bağırmak *v* shout, yell

bağırsak *n* intestine
bağırsaklar *n* bowels
bağış *n* donation
bağış yapmak *v* donate
bağışçı *n* benefactor
bağışık *adj* immune
bağışıklık *n* immunity
bağışlama *n* forgiveness
bağışlamak *v* absolve
bağışlanamaz *adj* inexcusable
bağlam *n* context
bağlamak *v* bind, connect
bağlantı *n* link
bağlantıyı kesmek *v* disconnect
bağlılık *n* attachment
baharat *n* condiment
baharatlı *adj* spicy
bahçe *n* garden
bahçıvan *n* gardener
bahis *n* bet
bahriye *n* navy
bahriyeli *adj* marine
bahse girmek *v* bet, gage
bahsetmek *v* mention
bakanlık *n* ministry
bakıcı *n* nanny
bakıcılık yapmak *v* nurse
bakım *n* maintenance
bakımsız *adj* squalid
bakımsızlık *n* disrepair
bakır *n* copper
bakire *n* maiden, virgin
bakirelik *n* virginity
bakış *n* glance, view
bakış açısı *n* perspective
bakiye *n* residue
bakkaliye *n* groceries
bakmak *v* look
bakmaksızın *adv* regardless
bakteri *n* bacteria
bal *n* honey
balayı *n* honeymoon
balık *n* fish
balıkçı *n* fisherman
balina *n* whale
balkon *n* balcony
balon *n* balloon
balta *n* ax
balya *n* bale
bambu *n* bamboo
band *n* band
bandaj *n* bandage
bandajlamak *v* bandage
bank *n* bank, bench
banyo *n* bathroom
banyo küveti *n* bathtub, tub

banyo yapmak *v* bathe
bar *n* bar
baraj *n* barrage
baraka *n* hut, shack
barbar *n* barbarian
barbarca *adj* barbaric
barbarlık *n* barbarism
barbunya *n* kidney bean
bardak *n* mug
bardak ağzı *n* brim
barikat *n* barricade
barışmak *v* make up
bariyer *n* barrier
barmen *n* bartender
barometre *n* barometer
barut *n* gunpowder
baş *n* head
baş ağrısı *n* headache
baş aşağı *adv* upside-down
baş eğdirmek *v* master
baş gösterme *n* outbreak
baş işareti *v* nod
baş vermek *v* stem
basamak *n* digit, stair
basamaklamak *n* cascade
başaramamak *v* fail
başarı *n* success
başarılı *adj* successful
başarısız *adj* unsuccessful
başarısızlık *n* failure
başarısızlıkla *adv* poorly
başarmak *v* achieve
başı çekmek *v* lead
başı dönen *n* dizziness
başıboş *n* vagrant
basık *adj* overcast
basın *n* press
basınç *n* pressure
başından savmak *v* bow out
başını kesmek *v* behead
basiret *n* providence
basit *adj* ordinary
başka *adj* another, other
başka *adv* else
başka bir yere *adv* elsewhere
başka olmak *v* differ
başkaldırı *n* riot
başkaldırmak *v* riot
başkan *n* president
başkanlık *n* presidency
başkent *n* capital
basketbol *n* basketball
baskı *n* repression
baskı hatası *n* misprint
baskı yapmak *v* press
baskın *n* raid

baskın çıkmak *v* surpass
baskın yapmak *v* raid
baskıncı *n* raider
başlamak *v* begin, start, commence
başlangıç *n* beginning, onset
başlıca *adv* chiefly, mainly
başlıca *adv* mostly
başlık *n* title
basma *n* printing
basmak *v* publish
başparmak *n* thumb
başpiskopos *n* archbishop
başrahip *n* abbot
başta gelen *adj* foremost
baştaki *adv* initially
baştan savma *adj* evasive
bastırılmış *adj* subdued
bastırmak *v* repress, quell
baston *n* cane
başvurmak *v* recourse
başvuru *n* recourse
başyapıt *n* masterpiece
batak *n* swamp
bataklık *n* quicksand
batan *adj* stinging
batı *n* west
batıl inanç *n* superstition
batılı *adj* western
batırmak *v* immerse
batıya giden *adv* westbound
batma *n* immersion
batmak *v* go under, sink
batmış *adj* swamped
battaniye *n* blanket
bay *n* mister
bayağı *n* banality
bayan *n* miss
bayan barmen *n* barmaid
bayan garson *n* waitress
bayan hizmetçi *n* maid
bayat *adj* stale
bayılmak *v* pass out, faint
bayır *n* ridge
baykuş *n* owl
bayrak *n* flag
bayrak direği *n* mast
bayram etmek *v* exult
bazen *adv* sometimes
bebek *n* baby, infant
bebeklik *n* infancy
beceri *n* know-how, skill
becerikli *adj* deft, skillful
beceriksiz *adj* clumsy
beceriksizlik *n* clumsiness
beden *n* body
bedeni *adj* corporal

beğenmek *v* admire
beğenmeme *n* distaste
behmen *n* parsnip
bekar *adj* unmarried
bekar *n* bachelor
bekarlık *n* celibacy
bekleme *n* waiting
beklemede *adj* pending
beklemek *v* anticipate
beklenmedik *adj* unexpected
beklenti *n* expectation
bel *n* waist
bel vermek *n* bulge
belagat *n* eloquence
Belçika *n* Belgium
Belçikalı *adj* Belgian
belediye *n* city hall
belediye başkanı *n* mayor
belediye binası *n* town hall
belgelemek *v* authenticate
belgesel *n* documentary
belgi *n* profile
belirsiz *adj* ambiguous
belirteç *n* marker
belirti *n* indication
belirtisi *n* portent
belirtmek *n* spelling
belirtmek *v* denote
belit *n* axiom
belki *adv* may-be
belki de *adv* perhaps
belli *adj* apparent, obvious
belli ki *adv* apparently
ben *pro* I
bencil *adj* selfish
bencillik *n* selfishness
benek *n* speck
benim *adj* my
benimki *pro* mine
benimseme *n* adoption
bent kapağı *n* floodgate
benzemek *v* resemble
benzer *adj* akin, alike
benzer *pre* like
benzer şekilde *adv* likewise
benzerlik *n* similarity
benzeştirmek *v* simulate
benzin *n* gasoline
beraat *n* acquittal
berbat *adj* awful
berbat etmek *v* botch
berber *n* barber
bere *n* beret
bereketsiz *adj* meager
berelemek *v* bruise
beri *adv* onwards

beş *adj* five
beş parasız *adj* broke
besbelli *adj* self-evident
beşgen *n* pentagon
beşik *n* cradle
beşinci *adj* fifth
beslemek *v* feed, nourish
beslenme *n* nourishment
besleyici *adj* nutritious
besteci *n* composer
bestelemek *v* compose
betik *n* script
betimlemek *v* depict, portray
beton *n* concrete
beyan etmek *v* proclaim
beyanname *n* statement
beyaz *adj* white
beyazlatıcı *n* bleach
beyazlatmak *v* whiten
beyefendi *n* sir
beyin *n* brain
beyin yıkamak *v* brainwash
beyinsel *adj* cerebral
beyit *adj* versed
beysbol *n* baseball
bez *n* cloth, rag
bezelye *n* pea
bezemeli *adj* ornamental
biber *n* pepper
bıçak *n* knife
bıçaklamak *v* stab
biçem *n* style, format
biçimini bozmak *v* distort
biçimsizlik *n* deformity
biçmek *v* mow, reap
biftek *n* steak
bıkkın *adj* bored
bıkkınlık *n* boredom
bilardo *n* billiards
bildiri *n* declaration, bulletin
bildirmek *v* declare
bile *adj* even
bilek *n* wrist
bilemek *v* sharpen
bilerek *adv* knowingly
bileşen *n* component
bileşik *n* compound
bileşim *n* union
bilezik *n* bracelet
bilge *adj* wise
bilgelik *n* wisdom
bilgi *n* information
bilgin *n* scholar
bilgisayar *n* computer
bilim *n* science
bilim adamı *n* scientist

bilimsel *adj* scientific
bilinçlilik *n* consciousness
bilinemezci *n* agnostic
bilinmeyen *adj* unknown
bilmece *n* puzzle, riddle
bilmek *v* know
bilye *n* marble
bin *adj* thousand
bina cephesi *n* frontage
binbaşı *n* major
binek *n* mount
bingo *n* jackpot
binmek *v* embark, board
bir *a* a, an, one
bir an için *adv* momentarily
bir de *adv* also
bir gecede *adv* overnight
bir gün *adv* someday
bir kere *c* once
bir kerede *adv* once
bir kullanımlık *adj* disposable
bir şekilde *adv* somehow
bir şekilde *pro* anyhow
bir şey *pro* something
bira *n* beer
birahane *n* brewery
bırakmak *v* let
biraz *adj* some
birazcık *adv* slightly
birçok *adj* lots, many
birden akmak *v* flush
birdenbire *adv* abruptly
biri *pre* oneself
birikim *n* backlog, savings
birikmek *v* run up
biriktirmek *v* hoard
birim *n* unit
birinci *adj* premier, first
birine *pro* someone
birinin namına *adv* behalf (on)
birisi *pro* somebody
birleşme *n* merger
birleşmek *v* merge, unite
birleştirmek *v* combine
birlik *n* unity
birlikte *adv* together
birlikte varolmak *v* coexist
bisiklet *n* bicycle
bisikletçi *n* cyclist
bisküvi *n* biscuit
bit *n* louse
bitirmek *v* finish
bitiş *n* expiration
bitişik *adj* adjacent
bitiştirmek *v* adjoin
bitki *n* plant

bitki örtüsü *n* vegetation
bitkin *adj* prostrate
bitler *n* lice
bitli *adj* lousy
bitmemiş *adj* incomplete
bıyık *n* mustache
biyografi *n* biography
biyoloji *n* biology
biyolojik *adj* biological
biz *pro* us, we
bizim *adj* our
bizimki *pro* ours
bizler *pro* ourselves
bizon *n* bison
blöf yapmak *v* bluff
bloke etmek *v* block
bluz *n* blouse
böbrek *n* kidney
böbürlenmek *v* boast
bocalamak *v* vacillate
böcek *n* insect, bug
bodrum *n* basement
boğa *n* bull
boğa güreşçisi *n* bull fighter
boğa güreşi *n* bull fight
boğaz *n* larynx, throat
boğmak *v* choke, strangle
boğucu *adj* stifling
boğuk *adj* hoarse
boğulma *n* asphyxiation
boğulmak *v* drown
böğür *n* flank
böğürtlen *n* blackberry
bohça *n* bundle
bohçalamak *v* bundle
bok *n* crap
boks *n* boxing
boksör *n* boxer
boktan *adj* crappy
bol *adj* abundant
bol olmak *v* abound
bol pantolon *n* slacks
bolca *n* plenty
bölge *n* region, zone
bölgesel *adj* regional
bolluk *n* abundance
bölme *n* compartment
bölmek *v* divide, split
bölüm *n* chapter, section
bölümlemek *n* partition
bölünebilir *adj* divisible
bölünme *n* schism
bölünme çizgisi *n* parting
bölünmez *adj* indivisible
bölüştürmek *v* split up
bomba *n* bomb

bomba mermisi *n* bombshell
bombalama *n* bombing
bombalamak *v* bomb
bonus *n* bonus
bora *n* gust, tempest
borazan *n* trumpet
borç *n* debit, debt
borçlu *n* debtor
borçlu olmak *adj* obliged
borçlu olmak *v* owe
bornoz *n* bathrobe
boru hattı *n* pipeline
boru tesisatı *n* plumbing
boş *adj* empty, hollow
boşa çıkarmak *v* let down
boşa harcamak *v* squander
boşaltma *n* discharge
boşaltmak *v* empty, vacate, evacuate
boşanan *n* divorcee
boşanma *n* divorce
boşanmak *v* divorce
boşluk *n* vacancy
bostan *n* orchard
botanik *n* botany
boy *n* height
boya *n* dye, paint
boya fırçası *n* paintbrush
boyamak *v* dye, paint
boykot etmek *v* boycott
boylam *n* longitude
böylece *adv* thus
boynuz *n* horn
boyun *n* neck
boyun atkısı *n* muffler
boyun eğdirmek *v* overpower
boyun eğmek *v* back down
boyunca *pre* through
boyundurluk *n* yoke
boyut *n* magnitude
bozma *n* disruption
bozmak *v* perturb, disrupt, defile
bozulmak *v* break down
bozulmamış *adj* intact
bozyap *n* jigsaw
brifing *n* briefing
Britanya *n* Britain
Britanyalı *adj* British
bronşit *n* bronchitis
bronz *n* bronze
broşür *n* brochure
bu *adj* this
bu arada *adv* meantime
bu gece *adv* tonight
bu sırada *adv* meanwhile
bu vesileyle *adv* hereby
bucaksız *adj* immense

budak *n* knob
budala *adj* fool
budamak *v* prune
bufalo *n* buffalo
büfe *n* kiosk
buğday *n* wheat
buğu *n* condensation
bugün *adv* today
bugünlerde *adv* nowadays
buhar *n* steam
buharlaştırmak *v* evaporate
buji *n* spark plug
bukle *adj* curly
büklüm *n* curl
bükmek *v* flex, twist
bulanık *adj* blurred
bulaşıcı *adj* contagious
bulaşık makinası *n* dishwasher
bulaştırmak *v* infect
bülbül *n* nightingale
bulmak *v* find
bülten *n* newsletter
buluğ *n* puberty
bulunan *adj* situated
buluş *n* invention
buluşma *n* date
buluşmak *v* meet
bulut *n* cloud
bulutlu *adj* cloudy
bulutsuz *adj* cloudless
bulvar *n* boulevard
bunak *adj* senile
bunlar *adj* these
bunun gibi *adj* such
bunun yanında *pre* bésides
burada *adv* here
burjuva *adj* bourgeois
burkmak *v* sprain
burmak *v* wring
burnunu sokmak *v* meddle
büro *n* bureau
bürokrasi *n* bureaucracy
bürokrat *n* bureaucrat
burun *n* nose
burun deliği *n* nostril
buruşturmak *v* crease
büst *n* bust, effigy
bütçe *n* budget, fund
bütün *adj* whole
bütünlük *n* integrity
buyruk *n* order
büyü yapmak *v* bewitch
büyücü *n* wizard
büyücülük *n* witchcraft
büyük *adj* big, great
büyük ayıp *n* outrage

büyük buluş *n* breakthrough
büyük dalga *n* surge
büyük harf *n* capital letter
büyük işadamı *n* tycoon
büyük kale *n* fortress
büyük kaşık *n* tablespoon
büyük parça *n* block
büyük yapı *n* edifice
büyük yığın *n* stack
büyükanne *n* grandmother
büyükbaba *n* grandfather
büyükelçi *n* ambassador
büyülemek *v* charm
büyüleyici *adj* enchanting
büyüme *adj* lateral
büyüme *n* buildup, growth
büyüme *v* grow up
büyümek *n* swelling
buyurma *n* ordination
buyurmak *v* decree
büyütme *n* enlargement
büyütmek *v* enlarge, magnify; nurture
buz *n* ice
buz gibi *adj* ice-cold
buz kalıbı *n* ice cube
buz pateni *v* ice skate
buzdağı *n* iceberg
buzları çözülmek *v* thaw
buzlarını çözmek *v* defrost
buzlu *adj* icy
buzluk *n* freezer
buzul *n* glacier

C

çaba *n* effort
çabuk *adj* prompt, quick
cadde *n* avenue
cadı *n* witch
çadır *n* tent
çadır bezi *n* canvas
çağ *n* era
çağdışı *adj* antiquated
çağıldamak *n* ripple
çağırmak *v* summon
çağrı *n* call
cahil *adj* ignorant
çakal *n* jackal
çakıl *n* gravel, pebble
çakmak *n* lighter
çalar saat *n* alarm clock
çaldırmak *v* ring
çalı *n* bush

çalılık *n* shrub
çalışan *n* employee
çalışmak *v* plug
çalıştırmak *v* coach
çalkantı *n* turbulence
çalmak *v* pilfer, steal
cam *n* glass
çam ağacı *n* pine
çamaşırhane *n* laundry
cami *n* mosque
çamur *n* mud
çamur atmak *v* malign
çamurlu *adj* muddy
çamurluk *n* fender
can alıcı *adj* crucial
can atmak *v* yearn
çan çalmak *v* toll
çan kulesi *n* belfry
can sıkıcı *adj* depressing
can sıkıntısı *n* tedium
can sıkmak *v* irritate
cana yakın *adj* affable, likable
çanak çömlek *n* crockery
canavar *n* beast
candan *adj* heartfelt
cani *n* thug
canını sıkmak *v* trouble
cankurtaran *n* lifeguard
canlandırmak *v* animate
canlı *adj* alive, lively
canlı hayvan *adj* live
canlı hayvan *n* livestock
canlılık *n* vitality
cansız *adj* lifeless
cansızlaşmak *v* languish
çanta *n* bag, case
çap *n* diameter
çapa *n* anchor
çapkın *adj* dissolute
çapraz ateş *n* crossfire
çapraz bulmaca *n* crossword
çaprazlama *v* criss-cross
çar *n* czar
çarmıh *n* crucifix
çarmıha germe *n* crucifixion
çarmıha germek *v* crucify
çarpı *n* cross
çarpıcı *adj* impressive
çarpık *adj* twisted
çarpılı *adj* cross
çarpış *n* clash, collision
çarpışma *n* skirmish
çarpıtma *n* distortion
çarpıtmak *v* falsify
çarpmak *v* clash, collide
Çarşamba *n* Wednesday

çarşı *n* downtown
casus *n* spy
casusluk *n* espionage
casusluk etmek *v* spy
çatal *n* fork
çatal bıçak *n* cutlery
çatı *n* roof
çatlak *n* crack
çatlamak *v* crack
çavdar *n* rye
çavuş *n* sergeant
çay *n* tea
çay fincanı *n* teapot
çay kaşığı *n* teaspoon
çay tabağı *n* saucer
çaydanlık *n* kettle
caydırma *n* deterrence
caydırmak *v* dissuade
çayır *n* meadow
çaylak *n* novice
caymak *v* recant
cazibe *n* allure, attraction
cazibeli *adj* charming
cazip *adj* appealing
cebir *n* algebra
cehalet *n* ignorance
cehennem *n* hell
çehre *n* countenance
çek defteri *n* checkbook
çekçek *n* wheelbarrow
ceket *n* jacket
çekiç *n* hammer
çekici *adj* attractive
çekilme *n* abdication
çekilmek *v* abdicate
çekilmez *adj* intolerable
çekingenlik *n* shyness
çekip almak *v* rash
çekirdeksiz *adj* seedless
çekiş *n* traction
çekişme *n* altercation
çekişmek *v* contend
çekmece *n* drawer
çekmek *v* haul, pull
çelenk *n* garland
çelik *n* steel
çelişki *n* contradiction
çelişkili *adj* conflicting
çelişmek *v* contradict
celpname *n* subpoena
çember *n* wreath
cenaze *n* funeral
cenaze arabası *n* hearse
cenaze töreni *n* burial
çene *n* chin, jaw
cenin *n* fetus

cennet *n* heaven
cennet gibi *adj* heavenly
cep *n* pocket
cep telefonu *n* cellphone
cephane *n* ammunition
cephanelik *n* arsenal
cephe *n* front
çerçeve *n* frame
çerçöp *n* trash
cereyan *n* stream
cerrah *n* surgeon
cerrahi *adv* surgical
cesaret *n* courage
cesaret etmek *v* dare
cesaret vermek *v* encourage
cesaretini kırmak *v* discourage
cesaretli *adj* courageous
cesaretsiz *adj* spineless
cesaretsizlik *n* discouragement
ceset *n* carcass, corpse
çeşit *adj* diverse
çeşit *n* variety, sort
çeşitlendirmek *v* diversify
çeşitli *adj* assorted
çeşitlilik *n* diversity
çeşme *n* fountain
çeşni *n* flavor
çeşnilik *n* seasoning
cesur *adj* brave
cesurca *adv* bravely
çete *n* gang
cetvel *n* ruler
cevap *n* answer, reply, response
cevap vermek *v* respond
cevaplamak *v* answer, reply
cevher *n* jewel
çevik *adj* agile
çevir sesi *n* dial tone
çevirmek *v* dial, flip
ceviz *n* walnut
çevre *n* surroundings
çevrelemek *v* surround
çevrim *n* conversion; network
çeyiz *n* dowry
çeyrek *n* quarter
ceza *n* punishment
cezalandırmak *v* chastise
cezanın tecili *n* reprieve
cezbedici *adj* enticing, tempting
cezbetmek *v* attract
cezir *v* ebb
çiçek *n* flower
çiçek açmak *v* bloom
çiçeklenmek *v* blossom
ciddi *adj* grave
ciddi şekilde *adv* gravely

ciddiyet *n* seriousness
ciddiyetle *adv* earnestly
çift *adj* double
çift *n* pair, couple
çift sürmek *v* plow, till
çiftçi *n* farmer
çiftlik *n* farm
çiğ *adj* raw
ciğer *n* liver
çığlık *n* scream, crying
çığlık atmak *v* exclaim
çiğnemek *v* chew
cihaz *n* appliance
çıkar *n* interest
çıkarcı *adj* pragmatist
çıkarma *n* subtraction
çıkartmak *v* extract, remove
çıkış *n* exit, way out
çıkmak *v* move out, quit
çıkmaz *n* stalemate
çıkmaz sokak *n* dead end
çıkmaza girmek *v* bog down
çikolata *n* chocolate
çıktı *n* output, print
çıktı almak *v* print
çil *n* freckle
cila *n* polish
cilalamak *v* polish
çıldırmak *v* rave
çile *n* ordeal
çileden çıkarmak *v* exasperate
çilek *n* strawberry
çılgın *adj* crazy, frenzy
çılgına dönmüş *adv* berserk
çılgınlık *n* craziness
çilingir *n* locksmith
cılız *adj* lean
çilli *adj* freckled
çim *n* sod, turf
cımbız *n* tweezers
çimdik *n* nip, pinch
çimdik atmak *v* nip
çimdiklemek *v* pinch, lawn
çimen *n* grass
çimento *n* cement
çimlenmek *v* germinate
cimri *adj* stingy
cinayet *n* murder
çingene *n* gypsy
çinko *n* zinc
çınlayan *adj* resounding
cinnet *n* lunacy
cins *n* species
cins *n* breed
cinsel *adj* carnal
cinsel ilişki *n* sex

cinsellik *n* sexuality
cinsiyet *n* gender
çıplak *adj* naked, nude
çıplak ayak *adj* barefoot
çıplaklık *n* nudity
cips *n* fries
çırak *n* apprentice
çirkin *adj* unpleasant
çirkinleştirmek *v* deface
çirkinlik *n* ugliness
ciro *n* endorsement, revenue
çırpınmak *v* flutter
çiş *n* urine
çiselemek *v* drizzle
çisenti *n* drizzle
cisim *n* matter
çit *n* fence
çıtır *adj* crunchy, crispy
cıva *n* mercury
civar *n* outskirts, vicinity
civarında *pre* about
civciv *n* chick
çivi *n* nail
çiy *n* dew
çizelge *n* timetable
çizgi *n* line
çizgi film *n* cartoon
çizgili *adj* striped
çizim *n* drawing
çizme *n* boot
çizmek *v* draw
çoban *n* shepherd
çocuk *n* child, juvenile
çocuk bakıcısı *n* babysitter
çocukça *adj* childish
çocuklar *n* children
çocukluk *n* childhood
çocuksuz *adj* childless
çoğalma *n* multiplication
çoğalmak *v* multiply
coğrafya *n* geography
çoğul *n* plural
çoğunluk *n* majority
çok *adv* much
çok *adj* plentiful
çok değerli *adj* invaluable
çok hevesli *adj* red-hot
çok ileri gitmek *v* overstep
çok ilginç *adj* riveting
çok korkmak *v* dread
çok mutlu *adj* ecstatic
çok öfkeli *adj* livid
çok pişman *adj* remorseful
çok şaşırtıcı *adj* staggering
çok sevinçli *adj* jubilant
çok sevinmek *v* rejoice

çok sıcak *adj* torrid
çok yavaş *adj* lingering
çok yönlü *adj* versatile
çok zayıf *adj* emaciated
çökertmek *v* overthrow
çokeşli *adj* polygamist
çokeşlilik *n* polygamy
çoklu *adj* multiple
çökmek *v* cave in
çökük *adj* sunken
çöküş *n* collapse
çöküvermek *v* slump
çöl *n* desert
çömelmek *v* crouch
cömert *adj* unselfish
cömertlik *n* generosity
çömez *n* disciple
çöp *n* junk, rubbish
çöp sepeti *n* trash can
çöpe atmak *v* throw away
coplamak *v* bludgeon
çöplük *n* garbage
çorak *adj* infertile
çorap *n* sock
çorba *n* soup
coşku *n* euphoria
coşkun *adj* effusive
çözmek *v* untie, solve
çözücü *adj* solvent
çözülmez *adj* insoluble
çözüm *n* solution
çözünür *adj* soluble
çözünürlük *n* resolution
cübbe *n* cassock
çubuk *n* rod, stripe
cüce *n* dwarf, midget
çukur *n* ditch, pit
Cuma *n* Friday
Cumartesi *n* Saturday
cumhuriyet *n* republic
cümle *n* sentence
çünkü *c* because
cüret *n* dare
çürük *n* cavity, decay
çürük *adj* sleazy
çürümek *v* decay, rot
çürümüş *n* rot
çürümüş *adj* rotten
çürütmek *v* debunk, rebut
çürütülemez *adj* irrefutable
çuval *n* sack
cüzam *n* leprosy
cüzdan *n* wallet, purse
cüzzamlı *n* leper

D

dadanmak *v* frequent
dağ *n* mountain
dağılım *n* dispersal
dağınık *adj* messy
dağınıklık *n* mess
dağıtım *n* distribution
dağıtımcı *n* dealer
dağıtma *n* dispensation
dağıtmak *v* scatter, dissipate
dağlık *adj* mountainous
daha *adj* more
daha alçak *adj* lower
daha az *adj* fewer, less
daha da *c* even more
daha iyi *adj* better
daha kötü *adj* worse
daha sonra *adj* later
daha sonra *adv* afterwards
daha uzak *adv* farther
dahası *adv* furthermore, moreover
dahil *adv* inclusive
dahil etmemek *v* omit
dahili *adj* implicit, inward
dakik *adj* punctual
dakika *n* minute
daktiloda yazmak *v* type
dal *n* bough, branch
dal salmak *v* branch out
dalalet *n* heresy
daldırma *v* offset
dalga geçmek *v* ridicule, wave
dalgalı *adj* wavy
dalgıç *n* diver
dalıp gitmek *v* space out
dalış *n* diving
dalkavuk *n* henchman
dalkavukluk *n* adulation
dallanma *n* ramification
dalmak *v* dive
dam penceresi *n* skylight
damak *n* palate, gum
damar *n* vein
damariçi *adj* intravenous
damat *n* bridegroom
damga *n* stamp
damgalamak *v* stamp
damıtmak *v* distill
damla *n* drip
damlamak *v* drop, drip
dana *n* calf, veal
Danimarka *n* Denmark
danışma *n* consultation
danışmak *v* consult

danışman *n* adviser
dans *n* dance, dancing
dans balo salonu *n* ballroom
dans etmek *v* dance
dantel *n* lace
dar *adj* narrow
dar geçit *n* bottleneck
dar uzun delik *n* slot
darağacı *n* gallows
daraltmak *v* take in
darbe *n* coup, knock, bump, shock
dart *n* dart
dava *n* lawsuit
dava açmak *n* litigation
dava açmak *v* prosecute, sue
davacı *n* plaintiff
davet *n* invitation
davet etmek *v* invite
davetsiz *n* intruder
davranış *n* behavior
davranmak *v* act, behave, treat
davul *n* drum
dayanıklı *adj* durable, hardy
dayanıklılık *n* resistance
dayanıksız *adj* perishable
dayanılır *adj* bearable
dayanılmaz *adj* excruciating
dayanışma *n* solidarity
dayanmak *v* endure, resist
de *pre* at
debriyaj *n* clutch
dede *n* granddad
dedikodu *n* gossip
dedikodu *v* gulp
defetmek *v* dispel, oust
değer *n* merit, value
değer biçmek *v* appraise
değerlendirme *n* assessment
değerlendirmek *v* evaluate
değerli *adj* worthwhile
değersiz *adj* worthless
değil *adv* not
değinmek *v* touch on
değirmen *n* mill
değiş tokuş *n* swap
değişik *adj* varied
değişim *n* alteration
değişken *adj* incalculable
değişmek *v* mutate, vary
değişmez *adj* irrevocable, literal
değiştirmek *v* alter, change, switch
değiştirmek *v* turn over
değnek *n* baton
deha *n* genius
dehşet *adj* dreaded
dehşet *n* consternation

dehşet verici *adj* appalling
dehşete düşmek *v* appall
dejenerasyon *n* degeneration
dejenere *adj* degenerate
dekan *n* dean
dekor *n* décor
dekoratif *adj* decorative
dekore etmek *v* decorate
delegasyon *n* delegation
delege *n* delegate
deli *adj* deranged, insane
deli *n* madman
delice *adv* madly
delik *n* hole, perforation
delikanlı *n* lad, youngster
delil *n* evidence
delilik *n* folly, insanity
delirtmek *v* madden
dellenmiş *adj* frantic
delme *n* piercing
delmek *v* prick
demek istemek *v* drive at, mean
demir *n* iron
demir atmak *v* moor
demirci *n* blacksmith
demiryolu *n* railroad, rail
demlemek *v* brew
demode *adj* outmoded
demokrasi *n* democracy
demokratik *adj* democratic
den *pre* from
den beri *pre* since
den farklı *adj* unlike
denemek *v* taste, try
denetim *n* check
denetlemek *v* audit, inspect
deney *n* experiment
deneyim *n* experience
deneyimsiz *adj* inexperienced
denge *n* balance
dengelemek *v* balance, poise
dengesiz *adj* unstable
dengesizlik *n* imbalance
deniz *n* sea
deniz aşırı *adv* overseas
deniz aygırı *n* walrus
deniz feneri *n* lighthouse
deniz kenarı *adj* seaside
deniz kızı *n* mermaid
deniz mavisi *adj* navy blue
deniz tutmuş *adj* seasick
deniz ürünleri *n* seafood
deniztarağı *n* clam
denklem *n* equation
deodorant *n* deodorant
departman *n* department

depo *n* storage, depot
depolamak *v* stock; store
deprem *n* earthquake
depresyon *n* depression
dere *n* creek
derece *n* degree, grade
deri *n* leather, skin
derin *adj* deep
derin çukur *n* pothole
derin yara *n* gash
derinlemesine *adv* in depth
derinleştirmek *v* deepen
derinlik *n* depth
derlemek *v* compile
ders *n* lecture, lesson
ders çalışmak *v* study
ders kitabı *n* textbook
dert *n* affliction, care
desen *n* pattern
despot *adj* despotic
despot *n* despot
deste *n* deck
destek *n* backing, crutch
destekçi *n* supporter
desteklemek *v* back, support
detay *n* detail
detaycı *adj* pedantic
detektif *n* detective
detektör *n* detector
deterjan *n* detergent
dev *n* giant
deva *n* remedy
deva olmak *v* remedy
devalüasyon *n* devaluation
devalüe etmek *v* devalue
devam *n* sequel
devam etmek *v* continue, carry on
devam ettirmek *v* maintain
devamı *n* continuation
devasa *adj* monumental
devasız *adj* incurable
deve *n* camel
devekuşu *n* ostrich
devir *n* epoch, cycle
devlet *n* state
devralmak *v* take over
devre *n* circuit
devretmek *v* hand down
devreye sokmak *v* call out
devrilmek *v* topple
deyim *n* idiom, phrase
deyiş *n* saying
dezavantaj *n* disadvantage
dezenfektan *n* disinfectant
dezenfekte etmek *v* fumigate
dibe oturmak *v* settle down

dibe vurmak *v* plummet
didişme *n* scuffle
diftong *n* diphthong
dijestif *adj* digestive
dik başlı *adj* obstinate
dik kafalı *adj* opinionated
dikdörtgen *adj* rectangular
dikdörtgen *n* rectangle
diken *n* thorn
dikenli *adj* thorny
dikey *adj* upright
dikim *n* sewing
dikiş *n* stitch
dikiş yeri *n* seam
dikizlemek *v* peep
dikkat dağınıklığı *n* distraction
dikkat etmek *v* look out
dikkat etmek *v* mind
dikkate almak *v* consider
dikkate değer *adj* remarkable
dikkatini dağıtmak *v* distract
dikkatle bakmak *v* behold
dikkatli *adj* careful
dikkatsiz *adj* careless
dikkatsizlik *n* negligence
dikmek *v* sew, stitch
diktatör *n* dictator
diktatörce *adj* dictatorial
diktatörlük *n* dictatorship
dil *n* language
dil dökmek *v* coax
dile getirmek *v* utter
dilek *n* wish
dilekçe *n* petition
dilemek *v* implore, wish
dilenci *n* beggar
dili tutulmuş *adj* speechless
dilim *n* slice
dilimlemek *v* slice
dillendirmek *v* sound
dilsiz *adj* mute
din *n* religion
din kardeşi *n* brethren
dinamik *adj* dynamic
dinamit *n* dynamite
dindar *adj* devout, pious
dindarlık *n* piety
dingil *n* axle
dingil başlığı *n* nave
dingil çivisi *n* linchpin
dingin *adj* serene
dinginlik *n* serenity
dinlemek *v* listen
dinlendirici *adj* restful
dinlenmek *v* rest
dinleyici *n* listener

dinozor *n* dinosaur
diploma *n* diploma
diplomasi *n* diplomacy
diplomat *n* diplomat
diplomatik *adj* diplomatic
dipnot *n* footnote
dipsiz *adj* abysmal
dırdır *adj* nagging
dırdır etmek *v* nag
dırdırcı *adj* grouchy
direk *n* pillar
direniş *n* opposition
direnme *n* persistence
dirilik *n* sap
diriliş *n* resurrection
dirsek *n* elbow
diş *n* tooth
dış *adj* external, outer
diş ağrısı *n* toothache
diş doktoru *n* dentist
dış hatlar *n* contour
diş ipliği *n* floss
dışa doğru *adj* outward
dışadönük *adj* extroverted
dışarı çıkmak *v* go out
dışarıda *adv* out, outside
dişi aslan *n* lioness
dışında *adv* aside from
disiplin *n* discipline
disk *n* disk
diskalifiye etmek *v* disqualify
dışlamak *v* exclude
dışlanmış *n* outsider
dişler *n* teeth
dişsel *adj* dental
diyabet *n* diabetes
diyabetik *adj* diabetic
diyagram *n* diagram
diyakoz *n* deacon
diyalog *n* dialogue
diyet *n* diet
diz *n* knee
diz çökmek *v* genuflect
diz kapağı *n* kneecap
dizgin *n* lining, rein
dizginlemek *v* rein
dizi *n* series
dizin *n* directory
dizlenmek *v* kneel
doğa *n* nature
doğaçlama *adv* impromptu
doğal *adj* natural
doğal olarak *adv* naturally
doğal sonuç *n* corollary
doğmak *v* be born
dogmatik *adj* dogmatic

doğmuş *adj* born
doğramak *v* chop, mince
doğru *adj* correct, right
doğrudan *adj* direct
doğrulama *n* correction
doğrulamak *v* affirm, correct, vouch for
doğrultmak *v* redress
doğruluk *n* accuracy
doğu *n* east, orient
doğulu *n* easterner
doğum *n* birth, delivery
doğum günü *n* birthday
doğurmak *v* procreate
doğusal *adj* eastern
doğuya doğru *adv* eastward
doğuya giden *adj* eastbound
doğuya özgü *adj* oriental
dökmek *v* spill, shed, pour
doksan *adj* ninety
doktor *n* doctor
doku *n* texture, tissue
dokuma tezgahı *n* loom
dokumak *v* weave
doküman *n* document
dökümhane *n* foundry
dokunaç *n* tentacle
dokunaklı *adj* touching
dokunmak *v* touch
döküntü *n* debris, spill
dokunuş *n* touch
dokuz *adj* nine
dokuzuncu *adj* ninth
dolamak *v* curl
dolambaçlı *adj* oblique; winding
dolambaçlı yol *n* detour
dolandırıcı *n* swindler
dolandırıcılık *n* scam, swindle
dolandırmak *v* cheat, defraud
dolap *n* cupboard
dolar *n* dollar
dolaşmak *v* wander, roam, hover
dolayısıyla *adv* hence
dolaylı *adj* indirect
doldurmak *v* pad, fill
doldurulmuş *adj* loaded
dolgu *n* filling, stuffing
dolgun *adj* replete
dolmalık biber *n* bell pepper
dolmuş uçak *n* charter
dolu *adj* full
doluşmak *v* crowd
dölyatağı *n* uterus, womb
domates *n* tomato
domuz *n* hog, pig
domuz eti *n* pork, ham
domuz yağı *n* lard

D

don *n* pants
donakalmış *adj* petrified
donanım *n* hardware
donanma *adj* fleeting
donatım *n* equipment
donatmak *n* furnishings
donatmak *v* equip, garnish
dondurma *n* ice cream
dondurmak *v* freeze
döndürmek *v* revolve, spin
dönem *n* mileage
dönemeç *n* crook
dönence *n* tropic
dönmek *v* go back, revert
donmuş *adj* frozen
donuk *n* faint
dönüş *n* comeback
dönüşlü *adj* reflexive
dönüşmek *v* transform
dönüştürmek *v* convert
dönüşüm *n* transformation
dönüşür *adj* reversible
dördüncü *adj* fourth
dört *adj* four
dörtnala gitmek *v* gallop
dörtyol *n* crossroads
doruk *n* peak
döşemek *v* furnish
döşemelik *n* upholstery
dost *n* mistress
dostane *adj* amicable
dosya *n* dossier
dosyalamak *v* file
döviz *n* currency
dövmek *v* batter, beat
dövüşçü *n* combatant
doymak *v* saturate
doymaz *adj* insatiable
dozaj *n* dosage
dozaşımı *n* overdose
dragon *n* dragon
dramatik *adj* dramatic
dramatize etmek *v* dramatize
dua *n* prayer
dua etmek *v* pray
dudak *n* lip
düdük *n* pipe
düello *n* duel
düğme *n* button
düğme iliği *n* buttonhole
düğüm *n* knot
düğün *n* wedding
düğüne ait *adj* bridal
dük *n* duke
dükkan *adj* laden
dükkan *n* shop

dul *n* widow
dul erkek *n* widower
duman *n* fumes
dumanlı *adj* hazy
dümdüz *adj* straight
dümen *n* helm, rudder
dün *adv* yesterday
dün gece *adv* last night
dünya *n* world, earth
dünyevi *adj* worldly
durağan *adj* stable
durak *n* stop
dürbün *n* binoculars
durdurma *n* holdup
durdurmak *v* abort, halt
durgun *adj* standstill
durgunlaşma *n* stagnation
durgunlaşmak *v* stagnate
durgunluk *n* lull
durmadan *adv* nonstop
durmak *v* stop
dürtmek *v* goad, prod
dürtü *n* impulse, urge
dürtüklemek *v* spur
durulamak *v* purify, rinse
durum *n* circumstance
durumsallık *n* contingency
duruş *n* stand
duruşma *n* hearing, trial
dürüst *adj* frank, honest
dürüstçe *adv* frankly
dürüstlük *n* frankness
duş *n* shower
düşes *n* duchess
düşkün *adj* affectionate
düşkünlük *n* affection
düşman *n* foe, enemy
düşman etmek *v* antagonize
düşmanca *adj* hostile
düşmanlık *n* hostility
düşmek *v* fall, go down
düşük yapmak *v* miscarry
düşünce *n* thought, notion
düşünceli *adj* thoughtful
düşüncesiz *adj* brusque
düşünmek *v* think
düşüş *n* drop, decrease
duvar *n* wall
duvarcı *n* bricklayer
duygu *n* emotion, feeling
duygusal *adj* emotional
duygusuz *adj* frigid
duyu *n* sense
duyulur *adj* audible
duyurmak *v* announce, give out
duyuru *n* announcement

düz *adj* flat, plain
düz olmayan *adj* uneven
düzeltme *n* amendment
düzeltmek *v* amend, revise
düzen *n* array, formation
düzenbaz *adj* wily
düzenek *n* setup
düzenleme *n* adjustment
düzenlemek *v* adjust, regulate
düzenlenebilir *adj* adjustable
düzenli *adj* methodical
düzenli şekilde *adv* regularly
düzensiz *adj* disorganized
düzey *n* level
düzgün *adj* proper
düzine *n* dozen
düzlem *n* platform
düzleştirmek *v* flatten, smooth
düzyazı *n* prose

E

e göre *pre* according to
e kadar *adv* till, until
e karşı *pre* versus
e yapışmak *v* adhere
ebe *n* midwife
ebedi *adj* timeless
ebediyen *adv* forever
ebediyet *n* eternity
ebeveyn *n* parents
eczacı *n* pharmacist
eczane *n* pharmacy
edebiyat *n* literature
edep *n* decency
edepli *adj* decent
edepsiz *adj* nasty
edinmek *v* adopt, procure
efendi *adj* gallant, genteel
efendi *n* gentleman
efsane *n* legend, myth
eften püften *adj* nitpicking
egemen olmak *v* dominate
egemenlik *n* mastery
eğer *c* if
eğik *adj* slanted
eğik çizgi *n* slash

eğilim *n* tendency
eğilimli *adj* predisposed
eğilmek *v* incline
eğilmez *adj* inflexible
eğitimsel *adj* educational
eğitmek *v* educate
eğlence *n* amusement
eğlenceli *adj* amusing
eğlenceli *n* fun
eğlendirmek *v* entertain
eğlenmek *v* revel, play
eğmek *v* tilt, bend
egoist *n* egoist
eğri *adj* warped
eğrilmek *v* warp
egzersiz *n* exercise
egzotik *adj* exotic
ehil *adj* competent
ehlileştirmek *v* tame
ehliyet *n* proficiency
ek *adj* additional
Ekim *n* October
ekin *n* crop
ekip *n* crew
ekip biçme *n* cultivation
eklem *n* joint
ekleme *n* addition
eklemek *v* add
ekmek *n* bread
ekmek *v* plant
ekmek kızartmak *v* toast
ekoloji *n* ecology
ekonomi *n* economy
ekonomik *adj* economical
ekran *n* screen
Ekselanslar *n* Highness
eksen *n* axis
eksi *adj* minus, sour
eksik *adj* absent, lack
eksiklik *n* deficiency
eksilmek *v* lack, run out
ekstra *adv* extra
ekvator *n* equator
el *n* hand
el altından *adj* clandestine
el arabası *n* cart, trolley
el bombası *n* grenade
el çantası *n* handbag
el çırpmak *v* clap
el feneri *n* flashlight
el kitabı *n* handbook
el koymak *v* confiscate
el sıkışma *n* handshake
el sürmek *n* handle
el yapımı *adj* handmade
el yazısı *n* manuscript

elastik *adj* elastic
elbette *adv* surely
elbise *n* robe
elbise kolu *n* sleeve
elçilik *n* embassy
elde etmek *v* acquire, gain
elden çıkarma *n* disposal
elden çıkarmak *v* dispose
eldiven *n* glove
ele geçirmek *v* capture
ele geçmez *adj* elusive
elebaşı *n* ringleader, vanguard
elek *n* hunting
elektrik *adj* electric
elektrik *n* electricity
elektrik direği *n* lamppost
elektrik kesintisi *n* blackout
elektrikçi *n* electrician
elektronik *adj* electronic
elem *n* sadness
eleman *n* element
elemek *v* sift
eleştiri *n* critique
eleştirmek *v* criticize
elle yapılan *adj* manual
elli *adj* fifty
elma *n* apple
elma şarabı *n* cider
elmacık kemiği *n* cheekbone
elmas *n* diamond
elveda *n* farewell
elverişli *adj* convenient
elverişlilik *n* convenience
elverişsiz *adj* cumbersome
emanet *n* deposit
emanet etmek *v* entrust
embriyon *n* embryo
emeklemek *v* creep
emekli aylığı *n* pension
emekli olmak *v* retire
emeklilik *n* retirement
emici *adj* absorbent
emir *n* commandment
emlak *n* realty
emmek *v* absorb, soak in
emniyetsiz *adj* unsafe
emretmek *v* direct, prescribe
emsal *n* precedent
en çok *adj* most
en iyi *adj* best
en kötü *adj* worst
en sonuncu *adj* latest
en ufak *adj* least
en uzak *adj* utmost
enayi *adj* sucker
endişe *n* anxiety, concern

endişe verici *adj* alarming
endişelenmek *v* distress
endişeli *adj* anxious
endişeli *n* insecurity
endüstri *n* industry
endüstriyel *adj* industrious
enerji *n* energy
enerji dolu *adj* energetic
enfeksiyon *n* infection
enfes *adj* fantastic
enflasyon *n* inflation
engellemek *v* hinder, thwart
engerek *n* viper
engin *adj* broad, vast
enginar *n* artichoke
enjeksiyon *n* injection
enkaz *n* wreckage
enlem *n* latitude
enstantane *n* snapshot
entrika *n* intrigue
erdem *n* virtue
erdemli *adj* virtuous
ergen *n* adolescent
ergenlik *n* adolescence
erik *n* plum
erime *n* dissolution, thaw
erimek *v* melt
erişilebilir *adj* accessible
erişim *n* access
erişmek *v* retrieve
eritmek *v* dissolve
erkek *n* male
erkek arkadaş *n* boyfriend
erkek torun *n* grandson
erkekçe *adj* virile
erkekler *n* men
erkeklik *n* boyhood
erkeksi *adj* manly
erken *adj* premature
erken *adv* early
eroin *n* heroin
erteleme *n* postponement
ertelemek *n* respite
ertelemek *v* defer, delay
ertelemek *v* stall
erzak *n* supplies
eş *n* spouse, wife
eşanlamlı *n* synonym
esas *adj* intrinsic
esas yemek *n* entree
esaslı *adj* thorough
eşdeğer *adj* equivalent
eşek *n* donkey
eşekarısı *n* wasp
eşik *n* brink, threshold
esin kaynağı *n* inspiration

E

E

esinlemek *v* inspire
esinti *n* blow
eşit *adj* equal
eşit olmayan *adj* unequal
eşitlemek *v* equate
eşitlik *n* equality
eşitsizlik *n* inequality, odds
eski *adj* obsolete
eski moda *adj* old-fashioned
eskiden *adv* formerly
eskrim *n* fencing
eşlemek *v* match
eşler *n* wives
eşlik etmek *v* accompany
eşmek *v* squash
esnek *adj* flexible, supple
esneme *n* yawn
esnemek *v* yawn
esnetmek *v* stretch
esprili *adj* witty
esrarengiz *adj* mystic
estetik *adj* aesthetic
eşya *n* stuff
eşyalar *n* belongings
et *n* flesh, meat
et yağı *n* grease
etap *n* lap
etek *n* skirt
etik *n* morality
etiket *n* label, sticker
etken *n* factor
etkenlik *n* efficiency
etki *n* jolt, impact
etkilemek *v* affect, impress
etkili *adj* effective
etkinleştirmek *v* enable
etkisiz *adj* ineffective
etrafında *pre* around
etrafını sarmak *v* beset
etrafta takılmak *v* hang around
etsuyu *n* broth
ev *n* home, house
ev dışında *adv* outdoor
ev halkı *n* household
ev hanımı *n* housewife
ev işi *n* housework
ev ödevi *n* homework
ev sahibesi *n* landlady
ev sahibi *n* host
ev yapımı *adj* homemade
evcil hayvan *n* pet
evcilleştirmek *v* domesticate
evet *adv* yes
evhamlı *adj* apprehensive
evini özlemiş *adj* homesick
evlenme *n* matrimony

evlenmek *v* marry, wed
evli *adj* married
evlilik *n* marriage
evlilikle ilgili *adj* marital
evrak çantası *n* briefcase
evre *n* phase
evren *n* universe
evrensel *adj* universal
evrim *n* evolution
evrim geçirmek *v* evolve
evsiz *adj* homeless
evvel *adj* prior
eylem *n* action
Eylül *n* September
eyvallah *e* bye
ezberlemek *v* memorize
ezik *n* bruise
eziyet *n* pain
ezme *n* pulp
ezmek *v* crush, mash

F

faal *adj* active
faaliyet *n* activity; play
fabrika *n* factory
facia *n* holocaust
fail *n* maker
fakir *n* poor
fakülte *n* faculty
fanatik *adj* fanatic
fanilik *n* mortality
fantezi *n* fantasy
fanus *n* lantern
faraza *c* supposing
farazi *adj* tentative
fare *n* mouse
fareler *n* mice
fark *n* difference
fark gözetme *n* segregation
farketmek *v* notice
farkına varmak *v* realize
farkında *adj* aware
farkındalık *n* awareness
farklı *adj* different
farklı *n* disparity
fars *n* farce
farz etmek *v* reckon

farzetmek *v* suppose, deem
fasıl *n* episode
fasulye *n* bean
fatih *n* conqueror
fatura *n* invoice, bill
favori *adj* favorite
favori *n* sideburns
fayans *n* tile
fayda *n* benefit
fayda *v* avail
fayda sağlamak *v* court
faydalanan kişi *n* beneficiary
faydalanmak *v* utilize
faydası olmak *v* benefit
faydasızlık *n* futility
fazla kilolu *adj* overweight
fazlalık *n* excess, surplus
fazlasıyla uzun *adj* lengthy
feci *adj* disastrous
federal *adj* federal
felaket *n* calamity
felç *n* paralysis
felç olmak *v* paralyze
felsefe *n* philosophy
fena *adj* wicked
fena halde *adv* grossly
fenalık *n* mischief, wickedness
fener *n* beacon
feragat etmek *v* relinquish
ferah *adj* roomy, spacious
ferahlama *n* relief
ferahlamak *v* relieve
feribot *n* ferry
ferman *n* mandate
fermuar *n* zipper
feryat *n* cry, shouting
feryat etmek *v* wail
fesat *n* malice
fesh etmek *v* withdraw
feshetme *n* repeal
feshetmek *n* reverse
feshetmek *v* abolish, annul
fesih *n* annulment
fethetmek *v* conquer
fetih *n* conquest
feveran *n* outburst
fevkalade *n* greatness
fiber *n* fiber
fıçı *n* barrel, keg
fiil *n* verb
fikir *n* idea, opinion
fıkra *n* joke
fil *n* elephant
fildişi *n* ivory, tusk
filizlenmek *v* sprout
film *n* movie

film parçası *n* trailer
filo *n* fleet
filozof *n* philosopher
filtre *n* filter
filtrelemek *v* filter
finans *v* finance
finansal *adj* financial
fincan *n* cup
Fince *adj* Finnish
fındık *n* hazelnut
fındık *n* nut
fındık kabuğu *n* nut-shell
Finlandiya *n* Finland
firar *n* flight
firar etmek *v* flee
fırça *n* brush
fırçalamak *v* brush
fırıldanmak *v* whirl
fırın *n* bakery, oven
fırıncı *n* baker
fırında pişirmek *v* bake
firkateyn *n* frigate
fırlatmak *v* hurl, throw, cast
firma *n* firm
fırsat *n* occasion
fırtına *n* storm
fırtınalı *adj* stormy
fiş *n* slip
fısıldamak *v* whisper
fısıltı *n* whisper
fışkırtmak *v* eject
fıtık *n* hernia
fitnecilik *n* incitement
fiyasko *n* flop
fiyat *n* price
fiyat aralığı *n* gap
fiyat düşürmek *v* mark down
fiyat teklifi *n* bid
fiyort *n* fjord
fizik *n* physics
fiziksel olarak *adv* physically
flaş *n* flash
flört etmek *v* flirt
flüt *n* flute
fobi *n* phobia
fok *n* seal
formalite *n* paperwork
formül *n* formula, notation
fosfor *n* phosphorus
fosil *n* fossil
fotoğraf *n* photography
fotoğraf çekmek *v* photograph
fotoğraf makinesi *n* camera
fotoğrafçı *n* photographer
fotokopi *n* photocopy
fotokopi makinesi *n* copier

Fransa *n* France
Fransız *adj* French
frapan *adj* flamboyant
fren *n* brake
frengi *n* syphilis
frenlemek *v* brake
fuar *n* fair
füme *adj* smoked
futbol *n* football
fuzuli *adj* superfluous

G

gaf *n* blunder
gaga *n* beak
galaksi *n* galaxy
galeri *n* gallery
galip *adj* triumphant
galip *n* victor
galon *n* gallon
galvanizlemek *v* galvanize
gangster *n* gangster
ganimet *n* booty, loot
ganimetlemek *v* loot
garaj *n* garage
garanti *n* guarantee
garanti etmek *v* ensure
garantör *n* guarantor
garaz *n* bile
garazlı *adj* spiteful
gardırop *n* wardrobe
gardiyan *n* jailer
garez *n* grudge, rancor
gargara yapmak *v* gargle
garip *adj* odd, queer
gariplik *n* oddity
garnitür *n* garnish
garnizon *n* garrison
garson *n* waiter
gaspetmek *v* usurp
gayret *n* endeavor, zeal
gayret etmek *v* strive
gayretli *adj* diligent
gayri meşru *adj* illegitimate
gayri şahsi *adj* impersonal
gaz *n* gas
gazap *n* fury
gazete *n* newspaper
gazete bayii *n* newsstand
gazeteci *n* journalist
gazi *n* veteran
gazino *n* casino
gazlı bez *n* gauze

gazoz *n* soda
gebe kalma *n* conception
gebe kalmak *v* conceive
gebelik *n* gestation
geç *adv* late
geç kahvaltı *n* brunch
geç kalmış *adj* belated
gece *n* night
geceleyin *adj* nocturnal
gecelik *n* nightgown
geçerli *adj* valid, binding
geçerli kılmak *v* validate
geçerlilik *n* validity
geçersiz *n* invalid
geçersiz *adj* void
geçersiz kılmak *v* overrule
geceyarısı *n* midnight
geçici *adj* provisional
geçici heves *n* fad
gecikme *n* delay
gecikmiş *adj* overdue,
geçim *n* livelihood
geçinmek *v* subsist
geçirgen *adj* porous
geçirmek *v* undergo
geçiş *n* pass, transition
geçit *n* gorge, ravine
geçme *n* lapse
geçmek *v* get by, pass
geçmiş *adj* past, recent
geçmişe dönük *adj* retroactive
geğirmek *v* belch, burp
geğirti *n* belch, burp
gelecek *n* future
gelecek *adj* upcoming
gelen *adj* coming
gelenek *n* custom, tradition
geleneksel *adj* customary
gelin *n* bride
gelincik *n* poppy
gelir *n* income
gelişme *n* improvement
gelişmek *v* prosper
geliştirmek *v* improve, enhance
gelmek *v* come, turn up
gemi *n* boat, ship
gemi enkazı *n* shipwreck
gemi yolculuğu *v* cruise
gemici *n* sailor
gen *n* gene
genç *n* teenager
genç *adj* youthful
gençleştirmek *v* rejuvenate
gençlik *n* youth
genel *n* general
genel *adj* public; common

genel af *n* amnesty
genel bakış *n* overview
genelde *adv* ordinarily
genelev *n* brothel
genellemek *v* generalize
genetik *adj* genetic
geniş *adj* large, wide
geniş görüşlü *adj* broadminded
genişçe *adv* widely
genişletmek *v* widen
genişlik *n* breadth, width
genleşme *n* expansion
genleşmek *v* expand
geometri *n* geometry
gerçek *n* fact, truth
gerçek *adj* tangible, real
gerçekçi *adj* down-to-earth
gerçekçilik *n* realism
gerçekdışı *adj* unreal
gerçekten *adv* really, indeed
gereç *n* tool
gerek *n* need
gerekçe *n* warrant
gereken *adj* due
gerekli *adj* necessary
gerekli kılmak *v* necessitate
gereklilik *n* necessity
gerekmek *v* must, need
gereksiz *adj* needless
gergedan *n* rhinoceros
gergin *adj* jumpy, tense
geri *n* rear
geri adım atmak *v* retreat
geri almak *v* take back, undo
geri atmak *v* repel
geri çekilme *n* recession
geri çekilmek *v* move back
geri çekmek *v* retract
geri çevirme *n* refusal
geri dönmek *v* return, turn back
geri gelmek *v* come back
geri getirmek *v* bring back
geri kalan *adj* remaining
geri kazanmak *v* win back
geri ödeme *n* refund
geri ödemek *v* pay back, refund
geri tepme *n* backlash
geri tepmek *v* backfire
geri tutmak *v* restrain
geri yaslanmak *v* lean back
geribildirim *n* feedback
geride bırakmak *v* leave
geride kalmak *v* fall behind
gerilim *n* tension
gerilla *n* guerrilla
geriye sayım *n* countdown

gerizekalı *n* idiot
gerizekalı *adj* moron
germe *n* strain
germek *v* strain
getirmek *v* bring
geveze *adj* garrulous
gevezelik etmek *v* babble
gevrek *n* cereal
gevşek *n* limp
gevşetmek *v* loosen
geyik *n* deer
gezegen *n* planet
gezgin *adj* medicinal
gezgin *n* voyager
gezi *n* trip
gezinmek *v* stroll
gezinti *n* excursion
gezmeye çıkmak *n* trip
gibi *adv* as
gıcırdamak *v* creak, squeak
gıcırtı *n* creak
gıcırtılı *adj* squeaky
gıda *n* sustenance
gidermek *v* eliminate
gidici *adj* bound
gıdıklamak *v* tickle
gıdıklanan *adj* ticklish
gıdıklanma *n* tickle
girdap *n* whirlpool
girdi *n* input
girinti *n* dent
giriş *n* preamble
girişim *n* enterprise
girişimci *n* entrepreneur
girişken *adj* gregarious
girişmek *v* set about
girmek *v* enter, go in
gişe *n* box office
gitar *n* guitar
gitmek *v* go
gitmek üzere *adj* bound for
gittikçe küçülmek *v* dwindle
giydirmek *v* clothe
giyim eşyası *n* wear
giyinmek *v* dress, wear
giyotin *n* guillotine
giysi *n* clothes, garment
gizem *n* mystery
gizemli *adj* mysterious
gizleme *n* coverup
gizleme yeri *n* hideaway
gizlemek *v* conceal
gizlenmek *v* hide
gizli *adj* covert, hidden
gizli *n* secret
gizlice *adv* secretly

gizlilik *n* privacy
gladyatör *n* gladiator
glikoz *n* glucose
göbek *n* belly, hub
göbek deliği *n* belly button
göç *n* immigration
göç etmek *v* immigrate
göçmek *v* emigrate, migrate
göçmen *n* immigrant, settler, migrant
göğüs *n* breast, chest
gök tutulması *n* eclipse
gökdelen *n* skyscraper
gökgürültüsü *n* thunder
gökkuşağı *n* rainbow
göklere çıkarmak *v* enthuse
gökyüzü *n* sky
göl *n* lake
gol *n* goal
gölcük *n* lagoon
gölet *n* pond
gölge *n* shadow
gölgeli *adj* shady
gömlek *n* shirt
gömmek *v* bury
gönder *n* flagpole
gönderen *n* sender
gönderilen mal *n* shipment
göndermek *v* relegate, send
gönlünü almak *v* conciliate
gönüllü *n* volunteer
gönüllülük *n* readiness
gönülsüz *adj* reluctant
gönülsüzlükle *adv* reluctantly
gönye *n* square
göreli *adj* relative
göreneksel *adj* orthodox
görev *n* mission, task
görev yapmak *v* officiate
görevden almak *v* depose
görevli *n* attendant
görgü kuralları *n* etiquette
görgü tanığı *n* eyewitness
görgüsüz *adj* coarse, crass
goril *n* gorilla
görkemli *adj* magnificent
görmek *v* see
görsel *adj* visual
görülebilir *adj* visible
görümce *n* sister-in-law
görüngü *n* phenomenon
görünmek *v* seem, appear
görünmez *adj* invisible
görüntü *n* image, display
görüntüleme *v* view
görüntülemek *v* display, screen
görünüm *n* appearance

görünürlük *n* visibility
görünüş *n* aspect, looks
görüş *n* sight, vision
görüş sahası *n* reach
görüş yeteneği *n* eyesight
gösteriş *n* parade
gösteriş yapmak *v* show off
göstermek *v* indicate, show
göstermelik *adj* conspicuous
göt *n* butt
götürü *n* lump sum
gövde *n* trunk
göz *n* eye
göz alan *adj* eye-catching
göz atmak *v* glance, browse
göz dağı *n* menace
göz doktoru *n* optician
göz kamaştıran *adj* dazzling
göz kamaştırmak *v* blind, dazzle
göz kapağı *n* eyelid
göz kırpmak *v* blink, wink
göz siperi *n* shade
göz yummak *v* condone
gözardı etmek *v* ignore
gözden düşmek *v* disgrace
gözden geçirmek *v* look over
göze çarpan *adj* outstanding
göze çarpmak *v* stand out
gözenek *n* pore
gözetleme deliği *n* loophole
gözetme *n* surveillance
gözetmek *v* look after
gözlem *n* observation
gözlemek *v* await
gözlemevi *n* observatory
gözlemlemek *v* observe
gözleri bağlı *n* blindfold
gözlerini dikmek *v* stare
gözlük *n* eyeglasses
gözü kapalı *n* blindness
gözü pek *adj* daunting
gözüne ilişme *n* glimpse
gözüne ilişmek *v* glimpse
gözünü dikmek *v* gaze
gözyaşı *n* tear
grafik *adj* graphic, chart
gram *n* gram
gramer *n* grammar
granit *n* granite
gresleme *n* lubrication
grev *n* walkout, strike
greyfurt *n* grapefruit
gri *adj* gray
grimsi *adj* grayish
grip *n* flu
Grönland *n* Greenland

grup *n* fellowship, group
gübre *n* dung, manure
gübrelemek *v* fertilize
güç *adj* arduous
güç *n* power, force

güç kullanmak *v* exert
güçbela *adv* barely
gücendirmek *v* embitter
gücenme *n* offense
güçlendirmek *v* boost
güçlü *adj* mighty, strong
güçlük *n* hangup
güçsüz *adj* powerless
güçsüz takım *n* underdog
gül *n* rose
güldürücü *adj* humorous
güle güle *n* bypass
gülmek *v* laugh
gülümseme *n* smile
gülümsemek *v* smile
gülünç *adj* laughable, ludicrous
gümbürdemek *v* boom
gümbürtü *n* boom, rumble
gümrük *n* customs
gümüş *n* silver
gümüş eşya *n* silverware
gümüşçü *n* silversmith
gün *n* day
gün ortası *n* midday
günah *n* sin
günah keçisi *n* scapegoat
günaha girmek *v* sin
günaha teşvik *n* temptation
günahkar *adj* sinful
günahkar *n* sinner
günbatımı *n* sunset
günce *n* diary
güncel *adj* up-to-date
güncellemek *v* update
gündoğumu *n* sunrise
güneş *n* sun
güneş gözlüğü *n* sunglasses
güneş kremi *n* sunblock
güneş yanığı *n* sunburn
güneşe ait *adj* solar
güneşlenmek *v* bask
güneşli *adj* sunny
güney *n* south
güneybatı *n* southwest
güneydoğu *n* southeast
güneye ait *adj* southern
güneye giden *adv* southbound
güneyli *n* southerner
günlük *adv* daily
güreş *n* wrestling
güreşçi *n* wrestler

güreşmek *v* wrestle
gürleme *n* roar
gürüldemek *v* rumble
gürültü *n* noise, tumult
gürültücü *adj* noisy, rowdy
gurulu biçimde *adv* proudly
gurup *n* sundown
gurur *n* pride
gururlu *adj* proud
gut *n* gout
güve *n* moth
güveç *n* casserole, stew
güvence *n* assurance
güvenilir *adj* reliable, sure
güvenilirlik *n* credibility
güvenilmez *adj* unreliable
güvenli *adj* safe, secure
güvenlik *n* safety, security
güvenmemek *v* mistrust
güvercin *n* dove, pigeon
güvey *n* groom
güzel *adj* beautiful, nice
güzelce *adv* nicely
güzelleştirmek *v* beautify
güzellik *n* beauty

haber bülteni *n* newscast
haber vermek *v* inform
haberci *n* messenger
habercisi olmak *v* foreshadow
haberdar *n* acquaintance
haberdar olmak *v* acquaint
haberler *n* news
habersiz *adj* unaware
habislik *n* malignancy
hac *n* pilgrimage
hacı *n* pilgrim
hacim *n* volume
hacimli *adj* bulky
Haçlı *n* crusader
haçlı seferi *n* crusade
haczetmek *n* confiscation
hadise *n* incident
hafif *adj* mild, light
hafif sıklet *n* lightweight
hafif uyku *n* doze
hafiflemiş *adj* extenuating
hafifletici *adj* attenuating
hafifletme *n* remission
hafifletmek *v* deaden
hafıza *n* memory

H

hafıza kaybı *n* amnesia
hafta *n* week
hafta içi *adj* weekday
hafta sonu *n* weekend
haftalık *adv* weekly
haham *n* rabbi
hain *adj* treacherous
hain *n* villain
hak edilmemiş *adj* undeserved
hak etmek *v* deserve
hak kazanmak *v* qualify
hakaret *n* affront, insult
hakaret *v* scoff
hakaret edici *adj* offensive
hakaret etmek *v* affront, insult
hakem *n* referee, umpire
hakemlik *n* arbitration
hakikat *n* reality
hakiki *adj* genuine
hakim *n* judge
hakimiyet *n* domination
hakkında *pre* about, regarding
haklı çıkarmak *v* vindicate
haksız *adj* unjustified
haksızlık *n* injustice
hal *n* predicament
hala *n* aunt
halı *n* carpet, rug
haliç *n* estuary
halk *n* people
halletmek *v* work out
ham *adj* crude
hamak *n* hammock
hamamböceği *n* cockroach
hamburger *n* hamburger
hamile *adj* pregnant
hamilelik *n* pregnancy
hamilik *n* patronage
hamle *n* onslaught
hamlık *n* immaturity
hamur *n* dough
hamur işi *n* pastry
han *n* inn
hançer *n* dagger
hanedan *n* dynasty
hangi *adj* which
hanım *n* lady
hanım evladı *adj* sissy
hanım gibi *adj* ladylike
hanımefendi *n* madam
hapis *n* prison, jail
hapis süresi *n* stretch
hapse atmak *v* imprison, jail
hapsedilme *v* incarcerate
hapsedilmiş *adj* pent-up
hapsetmek *v* confine, lock up

harabe *n* ruin, slum
haraç *n* extortion
harap *adj* dilapidated
harap *n* waste
harap edici *adj* devastating
harap etmek *v* destroy, wreck
haraplık *n* desolation
hararetli *adj* fervent
harcama *n* spending
harcamak *v* spend
harçlık *n* allowance
hardal *n* mustard
hareket *n* motion, movement
hareket *n* move
hareket etmek *v* move
hareketli *adj* mobile
hareketsiz *adj* motionless
harici *adj* exterior, foreign
haricinde *pre* barring; except
harika *adj* fabulous, terrific
harika *n* marvel, prodigy
harita *n* map
harman *n* blend
harmanlamak *v* blend
harp *n* harp
hasar *n* havoc, injury
hasat *n* harvest
hasat etmek *v* harvest
haset *n* envy
haset etmek *v* envy
haşhaş *n* hashish
hasılat *n* proceeds, yield
haşin *adj* severe
hasır *n* mat
hasis *n* miser
haşlamak *v* scald
hassas *adj* sensitive, sore
hasta *adj* ill, sick
hastalık *n* ailment, disease
hastane *n* hospital
hat *n* stroke
hata *n* error, mistake
hata yapmak *v* goof, mistake
hatalı *adj* erroneous
hatalı kullanım *n* misuse
hatasız *adj* impeccable
hatıra *n* memento
hatırlamak *v* remember
hatırlatma *n* reminder
hatırlatmak *v* remind
hav hav *n* bark
hava *n* weather, air
hava akımı *n* circulation
hava boşluğu *n* airspace
hava geçirmez *adj* airtight
havaalanı *n* airfield

havacı *n* aviator
havacılık *n* aviation
havageçirmez *adj* hermetic
havai fişek *n* fireworks
havalandırma *n* ventilation
havalandırmak *v* air
havalanmak *v* lift off, take off
havale *n* remittance
havale etmek *v* hand over
havalimanı *n* airport
havan topu *n* mortar
havanın akması *v* circulate
havari *n* apostle
havasız *adj* stuffy
havayolu *n* airline
havlamak *v* bark
havlu *n* towel
havuç *n* carrot
havuz *n* pool
hayal *n* delusion
hayal etmek *v* imagine
hayal kırıklığı *n* disillusion
hayal kurmak *v* dream
hayalet *n* ghost
hayalgücü *n* imagination
hayali *adj* unrealistic
hayat dolu *adj* vivacious
hayati *adj* vital
hayatta kalmak *v* survive
haydut *n* bandit
hayırlı *adj* auspicious
hayırsever *adj* charitable
hayırseverlik *n* charity
haykırmak *v* cry out
hayran *n* admirer
hayret *n* amazement
hayret verici *adj* astounding
hayvan *adj* brute
hayvan *n* animal
hayvan çiftliği *n* ranch
hayvan zehiri *n* venom
hayvani *adj* bestial
hazımsızlık *n* indigestion
hazin *adj* pitiful
hazine *n* treasure
hazır *adj* ready
Haziran *n* June
hazırlamak *v* prepare
hazırlayıcı *adj* preliminary
hazırlık *n* preparation
haznedar *n* treasurer
hece *n* syllable
hecelemek *v* spell
hedef *n* destination
hediye *n* gift, tribute
hediye etmek *v* give away

hekim *n* physician
helikopter *n* helicopter
helvacı kabağı *n* pumpkin
hemen *adv* immediately
hemşire *n* nurse
hendek *n* trench
henüz *c* yet
hep beraber *adj* altogether
hepsi *adj* all, entire
hepsi *adv* lot
her *adj* each, every
her bir *adj* each other
her gün *adj* everyday
her ikisi de *adj* both
her nerede *c* wherever
her şey *pro* everything
her zaman *adv* always
hergele *n* scoundrel
herhangi bir *adj* any
herkes *pro* everybody
hesap *n* account
hesap defteri *n* ledger
hesap makinesi *n* calculator
hesap vermek *v* account for
hesaplama *n* calculation
hesaplamak *v* calculate
hesapsız *adj* innumerable
hesaptan düşmek *v* deduct
hevesli *adj* eager
heveslilik *n* eagerness
heybetli *adj* imposing
heyecan *n* excitement
heyecan verici *adj* exciting
heyecanlı *adj* hectic
heyelan *n* avalanche
heykel *n* statue
heykel gövdesi *n* torso
heykeltıraş *n* sculptor
hiç biri *adv* ever
hiç biri *pro* anyone
hiçbir şey *n* nothing
hiçbir yerde *adv* nowhere
hiçbiri *adj* neither
hiçbiri *adv* neither
hiçbiri *pro* none
hiçe saymak *v* snub
hiciv *n* satire
hıçkırık *n* hiccup, sob
hiddetlenmek *v* flare-up
hidrojen *n* hydrogen
hidrolik *adj* hydraulic
hijyen *n* hygiene
hikaye *n* novel
hile *n* deceit, ruse
hilebaz *n* juggler
hilekar *adj* deceitful

hilekar *n* cheater
hileli *adj* fraudulent
hilesiz *adj* singleminded
hindistancevizi *n* coconut
hipnotize etmek *v* hypnotize
hipnoz *n* hypnosis
hırçın *adj* harsh, vicious
hırçınlık *n* harshness
hırıldamak *v* wheeze
hırıltı *n* murmur
hırlamak *v* growl
hırs *n* ambition, greed
hırsız *n* burglar, thief
hırsızlık *n* burglary, theft
hırsızlık yapmak *v* break in
hırslı *adj* greedy
his *n* feelings
hisse *n* ration
hisse senedi *n* stock
hissedar *n* shareholder
hissedilebilir *adj* palpable
hissetmek *v* feel
hissiz *adj* callous
histeri *n* hysteria
hitabe *n* homily
hitap etmek *v* address
hiyerarşi *n* hierarchy
hız *n* speed, rate
hız vermek *v* hasten
hız yapmak *v* speed
hiza *n* alignment
hizaya getirmek *v* align
hızla yükselmek *v* soar
hızlandırıcı *n* accelerator
hızlandırmak *v* accelerate
hızlı *adj* fast, rapid
hızlı içmek *v* guzzle
hızlı koşmak *v* dash
hızlı yemek *v* gobble
hızlıca *adv* speedily
hizmet etmek *v* minister, serve
hizmet vermek *v* service
hizmetçi *n* servant
hobi *n* hobby
hol *n* hallway
holigan *n* hooligan
Hollanda *n* Holland
Hollandalı *adj* Dutch
homurdanma *v* grumble
hoparlör *n* loudspeaker
hor görmek *v* despise
hor kullanmak *v* mistreat
horlamak *v* snore
hormon *n* hormone
horoz *n* cock, rooster
horoz ötüşü *v* crow

hortum *n* twister
horultu *n* snore
hoş *adj* delightful
hoş *n* delight
hoşa giden *adj* favorable
hoşgörülü *adj* lenient
hoşlanma *n* predilection
hoşlanmak *v* care for, like
hoşlanmama *n* dislike
hoşlanmamak *v* dislike
hoşnut edici *adj* satisfactory
hoşnut etmek *v* gratify
hoşnutsuzluk *adj* discontent
hostes *n* stewardess
Hristiyan *adj* Christian
Hristiyanlık *n* Christianity
hudut *n* frontier, border
hukuk davası *n* suit
hüküm *n* ascendancy
hükümdar *n* monarch
hükümet *n* government
hülasa *n* compendium
humma *n* fever
hummalı *adj* feverish
hurda *n* scrap
hürmet *n* homage
hüsran *n* frustration
huşu *n* awe, hush
husumet *n* animosity
huysuz *adj* grumpy
huzur *n* peace
huzurlu *adj* peaceful
huzursuz *adj* restless, uneasy
huzursuzluk *n* uneasiness

I

iade *n* extradition
iade etmek *v* extradite
iç *adj* inner
iç bahçe *n* courtyard
iç çamaşırı *n* underwear
iç çekme *n* sigh
iç çekmek *v* sigh
icap ettirmek *v* entail
icat etmek *v* invent
içecek *n* beverage
içedönük *adj* introvert
içeri almak *v* let in
içeri girmek *v* come in, get in
içeriden *pre* within
içerik *adj* content
içerilerde *adv* inland

içerlemek *v* resent
içermek *v* contain, include
içgüdü *n* instinct
içilir *adj* drinkable
için *pre* for
içinde *adj* inside, interior
içinde *adv* aboard
içinde *pre* inside, in
içindekiler *n* index
içine çekmek *v* engulf, inhale
içine dökme *n* infusion
içine işlemek *v* perforate
içki *n* booze, liquor
içkici *n* drinker
içmek *v* drink
icra etmek *v* perpetrate
içtensiz *adj* unfriendly
içtima yapmak *v* muster
idare *n* conduct
idare etmek *v* conduct
iddia *n* allegation, claim
iddia etmek *v* allege
ideal *adj* ideal
ideoloji *n* ideology
idol *n* idol
idrak etmek *v* apprehend
ifade *n* recital
ifade etmek *v* articulate, frame
iffet *n* chastity
iflas *n* bankruptcy
iflas etmek *v* bankrupt
iflas etmiş *adj* bankrupt
ifşa *n* revelation
ifşa etmek *v* divulge
iftira *n* slander, libel
iftira etmek *v* reproach
iğne *n* needle, pin
iğneleyici *adj* sarcastic
iğrenç *adj* disgusting
iğrenmek *n* disgust, abhor
ihanet *n* betrayal
ihbar etmek *v* denounce
ihbarcı *n* informer
ihlal *n* infraction, breach
ihlal etmek *v* trespass, violate
ihmal *n* neglect, omission
ihmal etmek *v* neglect
ihmalkar *adj* negligent
ihraç *n* expulsion
ihracat *v* export
ihtar *n* notice
ihtimal *n* likelihood
ihtişam *n* splendor
ihtiva etmek *v* comprise
ihtiyatla *adv* gingerly
ihtiyatlı *adj* cautious

ihya etmek *v* recreate
ikame *n* replacement
ikamet etmek *v* reside, dwell
ikametgah *n* residence
iken *c* whereas
iki *adj* two
iki ayda bir *adj* bimonthly
iki dilli *adj* bilingual
iki kere *adv* twice
ikieşlilik *n* bigamy
ikilem *n* dilemma
ikili *adj* dual
ikinci *adj* secondary
ikisinden biri *adj* either
ikisinden biri *adv* either
ikiyüzlü *adj* hypocrite
ikiyüzlülük *n* hypocrisy
ikiz *n* twin
iklim *n* climate
iklimsel *adj* climatic
ikmal etmek *v* replenish
ikna *n* persuasion
ikna edici *adj* persuasive
ikna etmek *v* persuade
ikon *n* icon
ikram *n* treat
iktidarsız *adj* impotent
ilaç *n* drug, medicine
ilaç tedavisi *n* medication
ilaç vermek *v* drug
ilahi *adj* divine, holy
ilahi *n* chant, hymn
ilahilik *n* divinity
ilahiyat *n* theology
ilahiyatçı *n* theologian
ilan *n* proclamation
ilave *v* augment
ilçe *n* county
ile birlikte *pre* with
ileri atılmak *v* spring
ileri gelen *adj* prominent
ileri gitmek *v* proceed
ileride *adv* forward
ileride *pre* ahead
ileriyi görmek *v* foresee
ilerleme *n* progress
ilerlemek *v* advance
iletişim *n* communication
iletişim kurmak *v* communicate
iletken *n* conductor
iletmek *v* transmit
ilgeç *n* preposition
ilgi çekici *adj* intriguing
ilgilendiren şey *n* concern
ilgili *adj* interested
ilginç *adj* interesting

I

ilgisiz *adj* indifferent, aloof
ilgisizlik *n* apathy
ilhak *n* annex
ilik *n* marrow
ılık *adj* warm, tepid
ılımlı *adj* moderate
ilişik *adj* attached
ilişki *n* association
ilişkilendirmek *v* associate
ilişkili *adj* related
iliştirmek *v* attach
ilkbahar *n* spring
ilke *n* motto, principle
ilkel *adj* primitive
ilmihal *n* catechism
iltica etmek *v* defect
iltifat *n* compliment
iltihap *n* pus
iltihaplanmak *v* fester
ima *n* allusion, mention
ima etmek *v* imply
imal etmek *v* manufacture
iman *n* creed
imha *n* annihilation
imha etmek *v* annihilate
imkansız *adj* impossible
imkansızlık *n* impossibility
imparator *n* emperor
imparatoriçe *n* empress
imparatorluk *n* imperialism
imrenmek *v* covet
imtiyaz *n* privilege
imza *n* autograph
imzalamak *v* subscribe
inanan *n* believer
inanç *n* belief, faith
inançlı *adj* faithful
inanılır *adj* believable
inanılmaz *adj* incredible
inanmak *v* believe
inanmama *n* disbelief
inat *n* obstinacy
inatçı *adj* persistent
inç *n* inch
ince *adj* thin
ince bir anlayış *n* tact
ince şekilde *adv* thinly
ince şerit *n* shred
incelemek *v* go over, look into
inci *n* pearl
incil *n* bible, gospel
incilden *adj* biblical
incinmemiş *adj* unhurt
incir *n* fig
indirgemek *v* demote
indirim *n* discount

indirim yapmak *v* discount
indirimli *adj* deductible
indirmek *v* slash
inek *n* cow
infilak *n* blast
İngiliz *adj* English
İngiliz anahtarı *n* wrench
İngiltere *n* England
inilti *n* moan
iniş *n* descent
inisiyatif *n* initiative
inkar *n* denial
inkar etmek *v* deny
inlemek *v* groan, moan
inmek *v* descend, get off
inşa etmek *v* construct, build
inşaat *n* building, construction
inşaat işçisi *n* builder
insaf *n* mercy
insaflı *adj* merciful
insafsız *adj* merciless
insafsızca *adv* harshly
insan avı *n* manhunt
insan gücü *n* manpower
insan soyu *n* mankind
insancıl *adj* human
insanlık *n* humanities
insanoğlu *n* humankind
intihar *n* suicide
intikal etmek *v* lapse
intikam *n* vengeance
intikam almak *v* avenge
ip *n* rope
ipek *n* silk
ipliğe dizmek *v* thread
iplik *n* thread
ipotek *n* mortgage
iptal *n* cancellation
iptal edilmiş *adj* withdrawn
iptal etmek *v* call off, cancel, quash
ipucu *n* clue, inkling
ipucu vermek *v* hint
irfan *n* scholarship
iriyarı *adj* burly
ırkçı *adj* racist
ırkçılık *n* racism
İrlanda *n* Ireland
İrlandalı *adj* Irish
ironi *n* irony
ırsi *adj* hereditary
irtibat *n* liaison
iş *n* work, job, deed
iş adamı *n* businessman
iş arkadaşı *n* colleague
iş gücü *n* labor
isabet *n* precision, hit

işaret *n* mark, sign
işaret etmek *v* designate, sign
işaretle çağırmak *v* beckon
işaretlemek *v* mark
işbirliği *n* collaboration
işbirliği yapmak *v* cooperate
işbirlikçi *n* collaborator
işçi *n* laborer, worker
işe almak *v* recruit
işemek *v* urinate
işgal etmek *v* occupy
ishal *n* diarrhea
ısı *n* heat, warmth
ısı derecesi *n* temperature
ışık *n* glimmer, light
ışıklı bölüm *n* highlight
ışıldamak *v* twinkle
ışıltılı *adj* ablaze
isim *n* name, noun
ışın *n* beam, ray
ısınmak *v* warm up
ısırık *n* bite
ısırmak *v* bite
ısıtıcı *n* heater
ısıtmak *v* heat
işitmek *v* hear
iskele *n* wharf
iskelet *n* skeleton
iskemle *n* stool
işkence *n* torture
işkence etmek *v* torment
ıslah etmek *v* reorganize
ıslahat *v* reform
ıslak *adj* wet
İslami *adj* Islamic
ıslanmak *v* soak up
işlem *n* transaction
işlemek *v* perform, work
işlemeli *adj* inlaid
işletilebilir *adj* workable
işletmek *v* operate
işlev *n* function
ıslık *n* whistle
ıslık çalmak *v* whistle
ısmarlama *adj* custom-made
İspanya *n* Spain
İspanyol *adj* Spanish
İspanyol *n* Spaniard
ispat etmek *v* demonstrate
israf *n* extravagance
israf etmek *v* lavish
ısrar *n* insistence
ısrar etmek *v* insist
ısrarcı *adj* demanding
işsiz *adj* jobless
işsizlik *n* unemployment

işţah *n* appetite
ıstakoz *n* lobster
istasyon *n* station
istatistik *n* statistic
isteğe bağlı *adj* optional
istek *n* request
istekle *adv* willingly
istekli *adj* willing
isteklilik *n* willingness
isteksiz *adj* averse
isteksizce *adv* unwillingly
isteksizlik *n* aversion
istemek *v* want
istemeyerek *adv* grudgingly
işten çıkarma *n* dismissal
istenilmeyen *adj* undesirable
isteri *adj* hysterical
istiare *n* metaphor
istif etmek *v* stack
istifa *n* resignation
istihza *n* sarcasm
istikrar *n* stability
istikrarsız *adj* unsteady
istikrarsızlık *n* instability
istila *n* invasion, influx
istila et *adj* infested
istila etmek *v* invade
istilacı *n* invader
iştira *n* purchase
istirahat *n* repose, rest
ıstırap *n* agony, anguish
ıstırap çekmek *v* agonize
ıstırap verici *adj* agonizing
istiridye *n* oyster
istismar *n* exploit
istisna *n* exception
istisnai *adj* exceptional
İsveç *n* Sweden
İsveçli *adj* Swedish
işveren *n* employer
İsviçre *n* Switzerland
İsviçreli *adj* Swiss
isyan *n* rebellion
isyan etmek *v* rebel, revolt
isyancı *n* rebel
itaat *n* obedience
itaat *v* abide by
itaat etmek *v* conform
itaat etmemek *v* disobey
itaatkar *adj* obedient
itaatsiz *adj* disobedient
itaatsizlik *n* disobedience
italik *adj* italics
İtalya *n* Italy
İtalyan *adj* Italian
itfa *n* redemption

I

itfaiyeci *n* fireman
ithaf *v* deduce
ithal etmek *v* import
ithalat *n* importation
itham etmek *v* indict
itibar *v* esteem
itibarsızlık *n* degradation
itici *n* projectile
itilaf *n* conflict
itimat *n* reliance, trust
itimat etmek *v* rely on, trust
itimat etmemek *v* distrust
itimatsız *adj* distrustful
itiraf *n* confession
itiraf etmek *v* confess, profess
itiraz *n* objection
itiş *n* shove
itmek *v* push
ittifak *n* alliance
ittifak etmek *v* ally
iyi *adj* fine, good
iyi *adv* fine
iyi *n* well, fine
iyi bilinen *adj* well-known
iyi kalpli *adj* benign
iyi niyet *n* goodwill
iyi niyetli *adj* benevolent
iyileşen *adj* convalescent
iyileşme *n* recovery
iyileştirici *n* healer
iyileştirmek *v* heal
iyilik *n* favor, goodness
iyimser *adj* optimistic
iyimserlik *n* optimism
iyot *n* iodine
iz *n* trail, track
iz sürmek *v* stalk, trace
izci *n* scout
izdiham *adj* crushing
izdiham *n* multitude
ızgara *adj* charbroiled
ızgara *n* broiler, grill
ızgara yapmak *v* broil, grill
izin *n* permission
izin vermek *v* allow, permit
izlemek *v* monitor, watch
izlemek *v* trail
izleyici *n* onlooker
izmarit *n* stub
izolasyon *n* isolation
izole etmek *v* isolate

J

jaguar *n* jaguar
Japon *adj* Japanese
Japonya *n* Japan
jartiyer *n* garter
jean pantolon *n* jeans
jeneratör *n* generator
jeoloji *n* geology
jest *n* gesture
jestler yapmak *v* gesticulate
jilet *n* razor
jinekoloji *n* gynecology
jüri *n* jury

K

kaba *adj* impolite, rough
kabadayı *n* hoodlum
kabahat *n* misconduct, misdemeanor
kabahatli *n* culpability
kabakulak *n* mumps
kabarcık *n* blister, bubble
kabarık *adj* puffy
kabartmak *v* emboss
kabataslak *adj* sketchy
kabile *n* clan, tribe
kabiliyet *n* aptitude, competence
kabiliyetsiz *adj* incapable
kabin *n* booth, cabin
kabız *adj* constipated
kabızlık *n* constipation
kabızlık vermek *v* constipate
kablo *n* cable, cord
kablosuz *adj* wireless
kabuk *n* crust, peel, shell
kabuklu *adj* crusty
kabul *n* acceptance, recognition
kabul edilebilir *adj* acceptable
kabul edilemez *adj* inadmissible
kabul etmek *v* accept, admit
kabul etmemek *v* dissent
kaburga *n* rib
kaçak *n* contraband
kaçakçı *n* smuggler
kaçamak *n* evasion
kaçık *adj* demented, mental
kaçınılabilir *adj* avoidable
kaçınılmaz *adj* inevitable
kaçınmak *v* abstain, refrain
kaçırma *n* abduction, hijack
kaçırmak *v* abduct

kaçmak *v* get away, escape
kadar etmek *v* amount to
kadeh *n* chalice
kademeli *adj* gradual
kader *n* destiny, fate
kadife *n* velvet
kadın *n* woman, female
kadın iç çamaşırı *n* lingerie
kadın mirasçı *n* heiress
kadın terzi *n* seamstress
kadınlar *n* women
kadınsı *adj* feminine
kadran *n* dial
kafa derisi *n* scalp
kafa karıştıran *adj* confusing
kafa tutmak *v* defy
kafa ütülemek *v* pester
kafadar *n* crony
kafası karışmış *adj* disoriented
kafasını karıştırmak *v* confuse
kafatası *n* skull
kafein *n* caffeine
kafeinsiz *adj* decaff
kafes *n* cage
kafeterya *n* cafeteria
kafile *n* procession
kafir *adj* heretic, profane
kafir *n* heathen
kafiye *n* rhyme
kağıt *n* paper
kağıt raptiyesi *n* paperclip
kahkaha *n* laugh, laughter
kahkül *n* fringe
kahraman *n* hero
kahramanlık *n* heroism
kahretmek *v* damn
kahvaltı *n* breakfast
kahve *n* coffee
kahverengi *adj* brown
kahya *n* housekeeper
kakao *n* cocoa
kalabalık *adj* crowded
kalabalık *n* crowd, throng
kalbe ait *adj* cardiac
kalça *n* hip
kaldıraç *n* crowbar
kaldırım *n* pavement
kaldırma *n* removal
kaldırmak *v* lift, pick up
kale *n* castle, fort
kaleci *n* goalkeeper
kalem *n* pencil
kalemtıraş *n* sharpener
kalibrasyon *v* gauge
kalibre *n* caliber
kalıcı *adj* permanent

kalın *adj* thick
kalın kafalı *adj* dull
kalınlaştırmak *v* thicken
kalınlık *n* thickness
kalıntı *n* relic, vestige
kalıp *n* mold
kalıp dökmek *v* mold
kalış *n* stay
kalıt *n* inheritance
kalitesiz *adj* shoddy
kalkan *v* shield
kalkık *adj* erect
kalkınma *n* development
kalkış *n* lift-off
kalkmak *v* erect, get up
kalmak *v* remain, stay
kalori *n* calorie
kalorifer *n* heating
kalp *n* heart
kalp atışı *n* heartbeat
kalp krizi *n* cardiac arrest
kalple ilgili *adj* coronary
kalpsiz *adj* heartless
kambur *adj* hunched
kambur *n* hunchback
kamp *n* camp
kamp ateşi *n* campfire
kamp yapmak *v* camp
kampanya *n* campaign
kamuflaj *n* camouflage
kamufle etmek *v* camouflage
kamulaştırmak *v* expropriate
kamyon *n* truck
kamyoncu *n* trucker
kamyonet *n* pickup
kan *n* blood
kan davası *n* feud
kan nakil *n* transfusion
kana susamış *adj* bloodthirsty
kanal *n* canal, channel
kanalizasyon *n* drainage
kanama *n* hemorrhage
kanamak *v* bleed
kanarya *n* canary
kanat *n* wing
kanayan *n* bleeding
kanca *n* hook
kandırmak *v* deceive
kanepe *n* couch, sofa
kangren *n* gangrene
kanguru *n* kangaroo
kanıt *n* proof
kanıtlamak *v* prove
kanıtlanmış *adj* proven
kanıtlayan *adj* demonstrative
kanlı *adj* bloody, gory

kano *n* canoe
kanser *adj* cancerous
kanser *n* cancer
kantin *n* canteen
kanun *n* law, statute
kanun yapmak *v* legislate
kanuni *n* lawmaker
kanunsuz *adj* unlawful
kanyon *n* canyon, chasm
kaos *n* chaos
kap *n* pot
kapak *n* lid, cap
kapalı *adj* close, closed
kapalı çarşı *n* mall
kapanış *n* closure
kapasite *n* capacity
kapatmak *v* close, shut
kapı *n* door, port
kapı aralığı *n* doorway
kapı çalmak *v* knock
kapı girişi *n* doorstep
kapı zili *n* doorbell
kapıcı *n* janitor, porter
kapitalizm *n* capitalism
kapkara *adj* pitch-black
kaplan *n* tiger
kaplıca *n* spa
kaplumbağa *n* turtle
kapmak *v* snatch
kapris *n* whim
kapsam *n* coverage, extent
kapsamak *v* enclose, cover
kapsamak *v* embody
kapsamlı *adj* comprehensive
kapsül *n* capsule
kaptan *n* captain
kar *n* profit, snow
kar etmek *v* profit
kar getiren *adj* profitable
kar tanesi *n* snowflake
kar yağışı *n* snowfall
kar yağmak *v* snow
kara çalmak *v* defame
kara ile çevrili *adj* landlocked
kara kurbağa *n* toad
karaağaç *n* elm
karabasan *n* nightmare
karaca *n* venison
karakol *n* patrol
karakter *n* character
karakter *v* char
karakteristik *adj* characteristic
karakulak *n* lynx
karalama *n* scratch
karalamak *v* scribble
karalık *n* blackness

karamsar *adj* pessimistic
karamsarlık *n* pessimism
karanfil *n* carnation
karanlık *n* darkness
karar *n* decision, judgement
karar vermek *v* decide
kararlı *adj* adamant, decisive
kararlılık *n* determination
kararname *n* decree
kararsız *adj* undecided
kararsızlık *n* indecision
karartmak *v* tarnish
karasal *adj* terrestrial
karat *n* carat
karatahta *n* blackboard
karate *n* karate
karavan *n* caravan
karaya çıkarma *n* landing
karbüratör *n* carburetor
kardeş *n* brother
kardeşçe *adj* brotherly
kardeşlik *n* fraternity
kardiyoloji *n* cardiology
kare *adj* square
karga *n* crow
kargaşa *n* disorder
kargo *n* cargo
karides *n* shrimp
karikatür *n* caricature
karın *n* abdomen
karınca *n* ant
karışık *adj* intricate
karışıklık *n* upheaval
karışım *n* assortment
karışmak *v* interfere
karıştırmak *v* embroil, stir
kariyer *n* career
karizma *n* charisma
karizmatik *adj* charismatic
karmakarışık *adj* chaotic,
karmaşık *adj* complex
karmaşıklık *n* complexity
karnabahar *n* cauliflower
karpuz *n* watermelon
karşı *n* opposite
karşı *pre* against
karşı çıkmak *v* object
karşı koymak *v* oppose
karşıda *adv* opposite
karşılamak *v* afford
karşılanabilir *adj* affordable
karşılaşma *n* encounter
karşılaşmak *v* run into
karşılaştırma *n* comparison
karşılaştırmak *v* compare
karşılaştırmalı *adj* comparative

karşılık *n* provision
karşılık vermek *v* strike back
karşılıklı *adj* reciprocal
karşılıklı olarak *adv* mutually
karşıt *adj* contrary
karşıtlık *n* contrast
karşıya geçmek *v* cross
kart *n* postcard
kartal *n* eagle
kas *n* muscle
kasaba *n* borough, town
kasap *n* butcher
kase *n* bowl
kaset *n* tape
kaşif *n* explorer
kasık *n* spoon
kaşık dolusu *n* spoonful
kasılma *n* contraction
Kasım *n* November
kaşımak *v* scratch
kaşınmak *v* itch
kaşıntı *n* itchiness
kasırga *n* hurricane, cyclone
kasıt *n* premeditation
kasiyer *n* cashier
kaşlarını çatmak *v* frown
kast *n* caste
kasten *adv* purposely
kastetmek *v* intend
kasvetli *adj* bleak, gloomy
kat *n* story
katakomp *n* catacomb
katalog *n* catalog
katalog yapmak *v* catalog
katedral *n* cathedral
kategori *n* category
kati *adj* definitive, stiff
katı *adj* solid
katil *n* murderer
katılık *n* stiffness
katılım *n* attendance
katılma *n* participation
katılmak *v* participate
katılmak *v* attend, join
katip *n* clerk
katır *n* mule
katkı *n* contribution
katkı *v* contribute
katlamak *v* fold
katlanabilir *adj* pliable
katletmek *n* carnage
katletmek *v* slaughter
katliam *n* slaughter
katman *n* layer
Katolik *adj* catholic
Katolik *n* Catholicism

katran *n* tar
katsayı *n* coefficient
kauçuk *n* rubber
kavanoz *n* jar
kavga *n* fight, quarrel
kavga etmek *adj* contentious
kavga etmek *v* quarrel, fight
kavgacı *adj* quarrelsome
kavgacı *n* fighter
kavgacı *v* comprehend
kavramak *v* grab
kavrayışlı *adj* receptive
kavşak *n* junction
kavun *n* cantaloupe
kavurmak *v* roast, parch
kavuşma *n* reunion
kavuz *n* hull
kaya *n* boulder, rock
kaya tabakası *n* shelves
kayak yapmak *v* ski
kayalık *adj* rocky
kaybetmek *v* misplace, waste
kayda değer *adv* notably
kaydetmek *v* matriculate
kaydolmak *v* register
kaygan *adj* slippery
kayınbirader *n* brother-in-law
kayınpeder *n* father-in-law
kayıp *adj* missing
kayıp *n* loss
kayış *n* strap
kayısı *n* apricot
kayıt *n* registration
kaykılma *v* shear
kayma *n* shift
kaymak *v* slip, slide
kaynaç *n* geyser
kaynak *n* basis, source
kaynakça *n* bibliography
kaynakçı *n* welder
kaynamak *v* boil, simmer
kaynana *n* mother-in-law
kaynaşma *n* fusion
kayrak *n* slate
kaz *n* geese, goose
kaza *n* accident
kaza yapmak *v* crash
kazak *n* sweater
kazan *n* boiler
kazanan *n* winner
kazanç *n* increment, gain
kazançlı *adj* lucrative
kazanım *n* acquisition
kazanmak *v* earn, win
kazazede *n* casualty
kazı *n* engraving

kazı yapmak *v* excavate
kazık *n* stake
kazık atmak *v* double-cross
kazımak *v* engrave
kazmak *v* dig
keçi *n* goat
keder *n* grief, sorrow
kederlen *v* grieve
kederli *adj* dejected, dismal
kedi *n* cat, kitten
kefalet *n* bail
kefaret *n* expiation
kefaret *v* expiate
kefaret etmek *v* atone
kefen *n* shroud
kehanet *n* prophecy
kek *n* cake
kekelemek *v* stammer
keklik *n* partridge
kel *adj* bald
kelebek *n* butterfly
kelepçe *n* handcuffs
kelepçelemek *v* handcuff
kelime *n* word
keman *n* violin
kemancı *n* violinist
kemer *n* arch, belt
kemik *n* bone
kemik iliği *n* bone marrow
kemirgen *n* rodent
kemirmek *v* gnaw, nibble
kenar *n* rim
kenara *adv* aside
kendi *adj* own
kendileri *pro* themselves
kendim *pro* myself
kendinden emin *adj* confident
kendine özgü *adj* distinctive
kendini tutmak *v* hold back
kendisine *pro* herself
kentsel *adj* urban
kereste *n* timber, lumber
kereviz *n* celery
kerpeten *n* pincers, pliers
kertenkele *n* lizard
keşfetmek *v* find out
kesici *n* cutter
keşif *n* discovery
keşif gezisi *n* expedition
kesik *n* cut
kesim *n* sector, segment
kesin *adj* certain, definite
kesinlik *n* certainty
kesir *n* fraction
keşiş *adj* monastic
keşiş *n* hermit

kesişmek *v* intercept
keski *n* chisel
keskin *adj* acute, poignant
keskin *adv* bitterly
keskin nişancı *n* sniper
kesme *n* severance
kesme işareti *n* apostrophe
kesmek *v* cut off, sever
kestane *n* chestnut
kestanefişeği *n* firecracker
kestirme *n* shortcut
kestirmek *v* estimate
ket vurmak *v* inhibit
keten *n* linen
keyfi *adj* arbitrary
keyfini bozmak *v* upset
keyfini çıkarmak *v* enjoy
keyif *n* enjoyment
keyifli *adj* enjoyable
kibar *adj* gentle, kind
kibarca *adv* kindly
kibarlık *n* courtesy
kibir *adj* conceited
kibir *n* arrogance
kibirli *adj* arrogant
kibrini kırmak *v* bring down
kıç *n* bum
kıdem *n* seniority
kıdemli *adj* senior
kıkırdamak *v* giggle, chuckle
kil *n* clay
kılavuz *n* guide
kılavuzluk *n* guidance
kılavuzluk etmek *v* guide
kiler *n* pantry
kilerci *n* butler
kılıç *n* blade, sword
kılıçbalığı *n* swordfish
kilidi açmak *v* unlock
kılık *n* guise
kılıksız *adj* seedy
kilise *n* church
kilit *n* lock, padlock
kilitlemek *v* lock
kıllı *adj* hairy
kilogram *n* kilogram
kilometre *n* kilometer
kilovat *n* kilowatt
kim *pro* who
kim olursa *pro* whoever
kimi *pro* whom
kımıldamak *v* budge
kimlik *n* identity
kimse *pro* no one, nobody
kimsesiz *n* orphan
kimya *n* chemistry

kimyager *n* chemist
kimyasal *adj* chemical
kınama *n* blame
kınamak *v* censure
kinaye *n* allegory, innuendo
kinci *adj* vindictive
kinik *adj* cynic
kinizm *n* cynicism
kir *n* dirt, grime
kira *n* rent
kira sözleşmesi *n* lease
kiracı *n* lessee, tenant
kırağılı *adj* frosty
kiralamak *v* hire, rent
kiralayan *n* lessor
kiraz *n* cherry
kırbaç *n* whip
kırbaçlamak *n* scourge
kireç *n* lime
kireçtaşı *n* limestone
kırıcı *adj* hurtful
kırık *adj* broken
kırık *n* fracture
kırık çıkık *n* splint
kırılgan *adj* brittle, fragile
kırılır *adj* breakable
kırılmamış *adj* unbroken
kırım *n* massacre
kırıntı *n* crumb
kırıp açmak *v* break open
kırıp geçirmek *v* decimate
kırışık *n* furrow, wrinkle
kırıştırmak *v* wrinkle
kırk *adj* forty
kirletmek *v* pollute, soil
kirli *adj* dirty, foul
kirlilik *n* pollution
kırma *n* crease
kırmak *v* break
kırmalı *adj* pleated
kırmızı *adj* red
kırmızılaşmak *v* redden
kirpik *n* eyelash
kırpma *n* clipping
kırpmak *v* clip
kırsal *adj* pastoral, rural
kırsal bölge *n* countryside
kırtasiye *n* stationery
Kış *n* winter
kısa *adj* short
kısa çizgi *n* hyphen
kısa kesmek *v* curtail
kısa not *n* memo
kısa ömürlü *adj* shortlived
kısa sürede *adv* shortly
kısa uyku *n* nap

K

kısa ziyaret *v* stop over
kısaca *adv* briefly
kısalık *n* brevity
kısaltmak *v* abbreviate
kısas etmek *v* retaliate
kişi başına *pre* per
kısık *adj* husky
kişilik *n* personality
kişisel çıkar *n* self-interest
kişisel özellik *n* mannerism
kısıt *n* constraint
kısıtlamak *v* withhold
kıskaç *n* clamp
kıskanç *adj* envious, jealous
kıskançlık *n* jealousy
kışkırtıcı *n* agitator
kışkırtmak *v* incite, provoke
kışla *n* barracks, quarters
kısmak *v* restrict
kısmen *adv* partially
kısmet *n* fortune
kısmi *adj* partial
kısmi *adv* partly
kısrak *n* mare
kıssa *n* parable
kist *n* cyst
kıta *n* continent
kitabe *n* inscription
kitap *n* book
kitap evi *n* bookstore
kitapçı *n* bookseller
kitapçık *n* booklet
kitaplık *n* bookcase
kıtasal *adj* continental
kıtlık *n* famine, scarcity
kıvılcım *n* spark
kıvırmak *v* curve
kıvranmak *v* writhe
kıvrım *n* curve, pleat
kıyafet *n* clothing
kıyamet *n* apocalypse
kıyı *n* coastline
kıyı boyunca *adj* coastal
kıyıda *adv* ashore
kıyım *n* mistreatment
kıyma *n* mincemeat
kıymak *v* shred
kıymet tahmini *n* appraisal
kıymetli *adj* worth
kıymık *n* splinter
kız *n* gal, girl
kız arkadaş *n* girlfriend
kız çocuk *n* daughter
kız kurusu *n* spinster
kızak *n* sleigh
kızamık *n* measles

kızarmış *adj* fried
kızartmak *v* fry
kızdırıcı *adj* annoying
kızdırmak *v* annoy
kızgın *adj* fiery
kızgınlık *n* furor
klarnet *n* clarinet
klas *adj* classy
klasik *adj* classic
klasör *n* folder
klavye *n* keyboard
klinik *n* clinic
klon *n* cloning
klonlamak *v* clone
klozet *n* closet
koalisyon *n* coalition
koç *n* ram
koca *n* husband
kocaman *adj* enormous
kod *n* code
kodlamak *v* codify
köfte *n* meatball
kök *n* root
kokain *n* cocaine
köken *n* origin
koklamak *v* smell, sniff
kökleşmiş *adj* ingrained
kokmak *v* stink
kokmuş *adj* putrid
kokpit *n* cockpit
kokteyl *n* cocktail
koku *n* fragrance
kokulu *adj* fragrant
kokuşmuş *adj* fetid
kol *n* arm
kolay *adj* easy
kolayca *adv* easily
kolaylaştırmak *v* ease
köle *n* slave
kolej *n* college
koleksiyon *n* collection
koleksiyoncu *n* collector
kölelik *n* slavery
kolera *n* cholera
kolesterol *n* cholesterol
kolik *n* colic
kollateral *adj* collateral
kolluk *n* cuff
kolon *n* colon
kolonya *n* cologne
kolsuz *adj* sleeveless
koltuk *n* armchair
koltukaltı *n* armpit
kolye *n* necklace
koma *n* coma
komedi *n* comedy

komedyen *n* comedian
komik *adj* comical, funny
komisyon *n* commission
komite *n* committee
kompakt *adj* compact
komplikasyon *n* complication
kompliman *n* flattery
komplo *n* conspiracy
komplo kurmak *v* conspire
komplocu *n* conspirator
komposto *n* compost
kompozisyon *n* composition
kompresyon *n* compression
kompülsif *adj* compulsive
komrad *n* comrade
komşu *n* neighbor
komşuluk *n* neighborhood
komünist *adj* communist
komünizm *n* communism
kömür *n* coal
konak *n* mansion
konaklamak *v* lodge
konferans *n* conference
konfor *n* comfort
konforlu *adj* comfortable
konformist *adj* conformist
kongre *n* congress
koni *n* cone
konsept *n* concept
konser *n* concert
konserve *adj* canned
konsey *n* council
konsolos *n* consul
konsolosluk *n* consulate
kontes *n* countess
konteynır *n* container
kontrol *n* control
kontrol etmek *v* check, control
konu *n* topic
konudan ayrılmak *v* digress
konukseverlik *n* hospitality
konum *n* location
konuşkan *adj* talkative
konuşlandırma *n* deployment
konuşlanmak *v* deploy
konuşma *n* speech
konuşmacı *n* speaker
konuşmak *v* talk, speak
konvoy *n* convoy
konyak *n* brandy
kooperatif *adj* cooperative
koordinasyon *n* coordination
koordinatör *n* coordinator
koparmak *v* pluck, pick
köpek *n* dog
köpek evi *n* kennel

köpek yavrusu *n* puppy
köpekbalığı *n* shark
köpekdişi *n* fang
kopma *n* rupture
köprü *n* ligament, bridge
kopukluk *n* disunity
kopuvermek *v* come apart
kopya *n* copy, replica
kopyalamak *v* copy
kör *adj* blind
kör gibi *adv* blindly
kordon *n* braid, cordon
körelmek *v* atrophy
körelmiş *adj* blunt
körfez *n* bay, gulf
koridor *n* corridor, aisle
korkak *n* coward
korkakça *adv* cowardly
korkaklık *n* cowardice
korkmuş *adj* afraid
korku *n* fear, fright
korkunç *adj* dire, fearful
korkunç son *n* doom
korkutma *n* provocation
korkutmak *v* frighten, horrify
körlük *n* bluntness
korna çalmak *v* honk
kornet *n* cornet
koro *n* choir, chorus
korsan *n* hijacker, pirate
korsanlık *n* piracy
koruma *n* protection
korumak *v* protect, secure
korunmasız *adj* unprotected
koruyucu *n* guardian
köşe taşı *n* corner
köşegen *adj* diagonal
koşmak *v* hitch up, run
köstebek *n* mole
kostüm *n* costume
koşucu *n* runner
koşul *n* condition
koşullu *adj* conditional
koşuşturma *n* hustle
koşutzamanlı *adj* concurrent
kötü *adj* bad
kötü kalpli *adj* mean
kötü muamele *n* snub
kötü niyetli *adj* malignant
kötüleşme *n* deterioration
kötüleşmek *v* worsen
kötüleştirme *n* aggravation
kötüleştirmek *v* aggravate
kötüleyici *adj* abusive
kötülük *n* evil
kova *n* bucket, pail

kovalama *n* pursuit
kovalamak *v* pursue
kovboy *n* cowboy
kovma *n* repulse
kovmak *v* expel, dismiss
kovmak *v* turn out
köy *n* settlement
köylü *n* peasant
koymak *v* put
koyu *adj* bold
koyu renk *adj* dark
koyulmak *v* set out
koyuluk *n* boldness
koyun *n* sheep
köz *n* embers
kozmetik *n* cosmetic
kozmik *adj* cosmic
kozmonot *n* cosmonaut
kral *n* king
kral naibi *n* regent
krala ait *adj* regal, royal
kraliçe *n* queen
kraliyet *n* kingdom
krallık *n* royalty
kramp *n* cramp
kramp girmiş *adj* cramped
krank *n* crank
krater *n* crater
kravat *n* tie, necktie
krayon *n* crayon
kredi *n* credit
krem *n* cream
kremalı *adj* creamy
kremasyon *v* cremate
kreş *n* nursery
kriket *n* cricket
kristal *n* crystal
kriter *n* criterion
kritik *adj* critical
kriz *n* crisis, seizure
kronik *n* chronicle
kronoloji *n* chronology
kuaför *n* hairdresser
kubbe *n* dome
kübik *adj* cubic
kucak *n* embrace, hug
kucaklamak *v* cuddle, hug
kucaklaşmak *v* embrace
küçük *adj* little, small
küçük bölme *n* cubicle
küçük çocuk *n* toddler
küçük düşürmek *v* humiliate
küçük iş *n* chore
küçük kısım *n* bit
küçük köşk *n* chalet
küçüklük *n* pettiness

K

küçültmek *v* shrink
küçümsemek *v* belittle
küçümseyen *adj* scornful
kuduz *n* rabies
küf *n* mildew
küf mantar *n* fungus
küflü *adj* moldy
küfretmek *v* swear
küfür *v* cuss
kuğu *n* swan
kukla *n* puppet
kükremek *v* roar
kukuleta *n* hood
kükürt *n* sulphur
kül *n* cinder, ash
kulak *n* ear
kulak ağrısı *n* earache
kulak mumu *n* earwax
kulak zarı *n* eardrum
kulaklık *n* earphones
külçe *n* chunk
kule *n* tower
kule gibi *adj* towering
kulis yapmak *v* lobby
kullanıcı *n* user
kullanılırlık *n* availability
kullanılmazlık *n* disuse
kullanım *n* usage, use
kullanışlı *adj* handy, useful
kullanışlılık *n* usefulness
kullanmak *v* use, wield
küllük *n* ashtray
kült *n* cult
kültür *n* culture
kültürel *adj* cultural
kulübe *n* cottage
kulüp *n* club
kum *n* sand
kumandan *n* commander
kumar oynamak *v* gamble
kumaş *n* fabric, material
kumaşla örtmek *n* drape
kumbara *n* piggy bank
küme *n* cluster, set
kümelemek *v* heap
kümelenmek *v* cluster
kumral *adj* brunette
kundakçı *n* arsonist
kundakçılık *n* arson
kunduz *n* beaver
küp *n* cube
kupa *n* trophy
küpe *n* earring
kupon *n* coupon
kura *n* draw
kurabiye *n* cookie

K

kuraklık *n* drought
kural *n* norm
küratör *n* curator
kurbağa *n* frog
kurban *n* sacrifice
kürdan *n* toothpick
kurdele *n* ribbon
küre *n* globe, sphere
kürecik *n* globule
kürek *n* row, shovel
kürek çekmek *v* row
kürk *n* fur
kurmak *v* prefabricate
kurmay *n* staff
kurnaz *adj* cunning, shrewd
kurnazlık *n* guile
kürsü *n* lectern, pulpit
kurşun *n* bullet
kurşun atmak *v* shoot
kurşun kaplı *adj* leaded
kurşunsuz *adj* unleaded
kurt *n* wolf
kürtaj *n* abortion
kurtarıcı *n* savior
kurtarma *n* rescue
kurtarmak *v* recover, rescue
kurtarmak *v* save, rid of
kurtuluş *n* salvation
kuru *adj* arid, dried
kuru erik *n* prune
kuru temizlemek *v* dryclean
kuru üzüm *n* raisin
kurucu *n* founder
kurul başkanı *n* chairman
kuruluş *n* organization
kurutmak *v* dry
kurutucu *n* dryer
kurye *n* courier
kuş *n* bird
kuşam *n* apparel
kuşatma *n* siege
kuşatmak *v* besiege, encircle
kuşkonmaz *n* asparagus
kuşku *n* mistrust, suspect
kuşkucu *adj* skeptic
kuşkulanmak *v* suspect
kuşkulu *adj* dubious
küskün *adj* disgruntled
kusma *n* sickness
kusmak *v* throw up, vomit
kusmuk *n* vomit
küstah *adj* insolent
küstahlık *n* impertinence
kusur *n* blemish, defect
kusur bulmak *v* chide
kusurlu *adj* defective

kusursuz *adj* flawless, seamless
kutlama *n* celebration
kutlamak *v* celebrate
kütle *n* mass
kütlesel *n* molar
kutsal *adj* sacred
kutsallaştırmak *v* sanctify
kutsallık *n* holiness, sanctity
kutsama *n* benediction
kutsamak *v* bless
kutsanmış *adj* blessed
kutu *n* box
kutucuk *n* cartridge
kütük *n* log
kutup *n* pole
kütüphane *n* library
kutupsal *adj* polar
kuvvet *n* boost, strength
kuvvetli *adj* forceful
kuvvetlilik *n* virility
kuvvetsiz *adj* feeble
kuyruk *n* tail
kuyrukluyıldız *n* comet
kuyumcu *n* jeweler
kuzen *n* niece
kuzey *n* north
kuzeydoğu *n* northeast
kuzeye ait *adj* northern
kuzeyli *adj* northerner
kuzgun *n* raven
kuzu *n* lamb

L

labirent *n* labyrinth
laboratuar *n* lab
lağım suyu *n* sewage
lahana *n* cabbage
lakap *n* nickname
lale *n* tulip
lamba *n* lamp
lanet *n* damnation
lanetlemek *v* curse
lastik patlaması *n* blowout
lavabo *n* lavatory
lavaj *n* irrigation
layık *adj* deserving
layık olmak *v* merit
lazer *n* laser
leğen *n* basin
lehçe *n* dialect
lehimlemek *v* solder
leke *n* smear, stain

leke sürmek *v* stain
lekelemek *v* blemish, blot
lekelenmiş *adj* soiled
lekeli *adj* tainted
lekesiz *adj* spotless
leopar *n* leopard
leylek *n* stork
leziz *adj* tasty
lezzet vermek *v* relish
lezzetli *adj* delicious
libre *n* pound
lider *n* leader
liderlik *n* leadership
lig *n* league
likör *n* liqueur
liman *n* harbor
limit *n* limitation
limon *n* lemon
limonata *n* lemonade
linç etmek *v* lynch
lisans *n* licence
lisanslamak *v* license
liste *n* list
liste yapmak *v* list
listeleyici *n* browser
litre *n* liter, litre
lobi *n* lobby
lokalize etmek *v* localize
lokma *n* morsel
lonca *n* guild, lounge
lord *n* lord
lordluk *n* lordship
loş *adj* dim
lösemi *n* leukemia
losyon *n* lotion
lüks *adj* de luxe, posh
lüzum *n* calling

M

maaş *n* salary, wage
maaş bordrosu *n* payroll
maaş çeki *n* paycheck
maaş makbuzu *n* payslip
macera *n* adventure
madalya *n* medal
madalyon *n* medallion
madde *n* substance
maddecilik *n* materialism
maddi *adj* bodily
madem ki *c* inasmuch as
maden *n* ore
madeni para *n* coin, species

mağara *n* cave, cavern
magazin *n* magazine
mağdur etmek *v* victimize
mağlubiyet *n* trimmings
mağlup *adj* beaten
mağlup etmek *v* vanquish
mahal *n* lieu
mahalle *n* district, parish
mahcup *adj* ashamed
mahir *adj* proficient
mahkeme *n* tribunal
mahkum etmek *v* convict, sentence
mahkumiyet *adj* doomed
mahmuz *n* spur
mahrum *adj* devoid
mahrumiyet *n* deprivation
mahvetmek *v* ruin, shatter
majeste *n* majesty
makale *n* article
makara *n* pulley, spool
makas *n* scissors
makbul *adj* admissible
makbuz *n* voucher
maket *n* dummy
makine *n* engine, machine
maksimum *adj* maximum
makul *adj* advisable
makyaj *n* makeup
mal *n* asset, property
mal aşırma *n* shoplifting
mal deposu *n* stockroom
mal etmek *v* cost
mal kurtarmak *v* salvage
mal sahibi *n* owner
mallar *n* goods
malumat *n* dope
malvarlıkları *n* assets
malzeme *n* ingredient
mamut *n* mammoth
manastır *n* abbey, convent
mandal *n* latch
mandalina *n* tangerine
mandıra *n* dairy farm
manevra *n* maneuver
mangal *n* barbecue
mangal kömürü *n* charcoal
manifesto *v* manifest
manivela *n* lever
mantar *n* mushroom
mantık *n* logic
mantıklı *adj* coherent, sensible
mantıksal *n* loin
mantıksız *adj* illogical
manto *n* overcoat
manyak *adj* maniac
manyetik *adj* magnetic

manyetizma *n* magnetism
manzara *n* scenery
manzaralı *adj* scenic
marangoz *n* carpenter
marangozluk *n* carpentry
mareşal *n* marshal
marifet *n* feat
marine etmek *v* marinate
marjinal *adj* marginal
marka *n* brand
market *n* market
Marksçı *adj* Marxist
marmelat *n* marmalade
Mars *n* Mars
marş *n* anthem
Mart *n* March
martı *n* seagull
marul *n* lettuce
maruz *adj* exposed
maruz bırakmak *v* expose
maruz kalmak *v* subject, incur
masa *n* table, tongs
masaj *n* massage
masaj yapmak *v* massage
masal *n* fable, tale
maskara *n* laughing stock
maskaralık *n* charade
maske *n* mask
maskülen *adj* masculine
mason *n* mason
masör *n* masseur
masöz *n* masseuse
masraf *n* cost, expense
masum *adj* innocent
masumiyet *n* innocence
matem *n* bereavement
matematik *n* math
matkap *n* drill
matkaplamak *v* drill
mavi *adj* blue
mavi kopya *n* blueprint
mavna *n* barge
maya *n* ferment, yeast
mayalamak *v* ferment
maydanoz *n* parsley
mayın *n* mine
mayın döşemek *v* mine
mayın tarlası *n* minefield
mayıncı *n* miner
Mayıs *n* May
maymun *n* ape, monkey
mazeret *n* excuse
mazlum *adj* downtrodden
mazoşizm *n* masochism
mazur görmek *v* excuse
mecbur etmek *v* obligate

mecburi *adj* compulsory
mecburiyet *n* obligation
meclis *n* chamber
med cezir *n* tide
medeni *adj* civil
medeniyet *n* civilization
meditasyon *n* meditation
meğer ki *c* unless
mekanik *n* mechanic
mekanizma *n* mechanism
mekik dokumak *v* shuttle
Meksikalı *adj* Mexican
mektup *n* epistle
mektuplaşmak *v* correspond
melankoli *n* melancholy
melek *n* angel
meleksi *adj* angelic
meli malı eki *v* ought to
melodi *n* melody
melodik *adj* melodic
meltem *n* breeze
membran *n* membrane
meme ucu *n* nipple
memeli *n* mammal
memleket *n* hometown, realm
memnun *adj* glad
memnun etmek *v* please
memnun olmak *v* content
memnuniyet *n* satisfaction
memur *n* officer
mendil *n* napkin
menekşe *n* violet
menenjit *n* meningitis
menetmek *v* prohibit
menfaat *n* expediency
menfez *n* vent
menopoz *n* menopause
menteşe *n* hinge
menteşe takmak *v* hinge
menü *n* menu
merak *n* curiosity, wonder
merak etmek *v* care about
meraklı *adj* curious
mercek *n* lense
mercimek *n* lentil
merdiven *n* staircase
merhamet *n* clemency
merhem *n* balm, ointment
merhum *adj* deceased
merkez *n* center, navel
merkezi *adj* central
mermi yolu *n* trajectory
mesaj *n* message
meşale *n* torch
mesane *n* bladder
meşe ağacı *n* oak

meşgul *adj* busy
meşgul *adv* busily
meşgul *adj* engaged
meşgul etmek *v* engage
Mesih *n* Messiah
mesuliyet *n* liability
metal *n* metal
metalik *adj* metallic
metanetli *n* fortitude
meteor *n* meteor
metin *n* text
metot *n* method
metre *n* meter
mevcut *adj* forthcoming
mevki *n* spot
mevsim *n* season
mevsimlik *adj* seasonal
meydan okuma *n* challenge
meydan okumak *v* challenge
meydana çıkmak *v* emerge
meydana gelmek *v* consist
meyhane *n* saloon
meyil *n* leaning
meyus *adj* despondent
meyve *n* fruit
meyve suyu *n* juice
meyveli *adj* fruity
meyvesiz *adj* barren
mezar *n* grave
mezar kitabesi *n* epitaph
mezar taşı *n* gravestone
mezarlık *n* cemetery
mezatçı *n* auctioneer
mezbaha *n* butchery
meze *n* appetizer
mezhep *n* sect
mezra *n* hamlet
mezun olmak *v* graduate
mezuniyet *n* graduation
microwave *n* microwave
mide *n* gut, stomach
mide bulantısı *n* nausea
mide ekşimesi *n* heartburn
midesel *adj* gastric
miğfer *n* helmet
migren *n* migraine
mıknatıs *n* magnet
mikrofon *n* microphone
mikrop *n* germ, microbe
mikroskop *n* microscope
mikser *n* blender, mixer
miktar *n* amount
mil *n* mile
milenyum *n* millennium
miligram *n* milligram
milimetre *n* millimeter

millet *n* folks
millileştirmek *v* nationalize
milyar *n* billion
milyarder *n* billionaire
milyon *n* million
milyoner *n* millionaire
mimar *n* architect
mimari *n* architecture
mimik yapmak *v* mime
minder *v* bolster, cushion
mineral *n* mineral
mini etek *n* miniskirt
minimum *n* minimum
minnet dolu *adj* thankful
minnettar *adj* grateful
minnettarlık *n* gratitude
minyatür *n* miniature
miras *n* heritage, legacy
miras kalmak *v* inherit
mirasçı *n* heir
mırıldanmak *v* hum
misafir *n* guest
misafir etmek *v* put up
misil *n* missile
misilleme *n* reprisal
misilleme yapmak *v* hit back
mısır *n* corn
mısır koçanı *n* cob
mısra *n* verse
misyoner *n* missionary
miyop *adj* myopic
mizah *n* humor
mızrak *n* spear
mobilya *n* furniture
mobilyasız *adj* unfurnished
mod *n* mode
moda *n* fashion
modaya uygun *adj* trendy
model *n* model
modern *adj* modern, contemporary
modül *n* module
molekül *n* molecule
moloz *n* rubble
monarşi *n* monarchy
monolog *n* monologue
monopol *n* monopoly
monoton *adj* monotonous
monoton *n* monotony
mor *adj* purple
morali bozuk *adj* downcast
morfin *n* morphine
morg *n* mortuary
morina *n* cod
motel *n* motel
motive etmek *v* motivate
motor *n* motor

motosiklet *n* motorcycle
mozaik *n* mosaic
muaf *adj* exempt
muaf olma *n* impunity
muafiyet *n* exemption
muamele *n* dealings
muavin *n* vice
muayene *n* check up
muazzam *adj* colossal
mübaşir *n* bailiff
mücadele *n* struggle
mücadele etmek *v* combat
mücevher *n* gem
mucize *n* miracle
mucizevi *adj* miraculous
müddet *n* duration, period
müdür *n* manager
müessese *n* institution
müfettiş *n* inspector
muhabbet *n* conversation
muhabir *n* correspondent
muhafaza *n* custody
muhafaza etmek *v* conserve
muhafız *n* custodian
muhakeme *n* reasoning
muhalefet *n* defiance, defiant
muhalif *n* opponent
muhallebi *n* custard
muhasebe *n* bookkeeping
muhasebeci *n* accountant
muhatap *n* addressee
muhbir *n* reporter
mühendis *n* engineer
muhtaç *adj* dependent
muhtemelen *adv* likely
mühürlemek *v* seal
müjdeci *n* herald
müjdecisi olmak *v* herald
mukabil *n* counterpart
mükafat *n* recompense
mukavele *n* covenant
mukavva *n* cardboard
mükemmel *adj* excellent, brilliant
mükemmeliyet *n* perfection
muktedir *adj* able
mukus *n* mucus
mülakat *n* interview
mülayim *adj* bland
mülk *n* condo
mülkiyet *n* ownership
mülteci *n* refugee
mum *n* candle
mümkün *adj* feasible
mumyalamak *v* embalm
münakaşa *n* dispute
münasebetsiz *adj* improper

muntazam *adj* tidy, steady
münzevi *n* recluse
müphem *adj* tenuous
müracaat etmek *v* apply for
mürekkep *n* ink
mürekkepli kalem *n* pen
Musevi *adj* Jewish
Musevi alemi *n* Judaism
Musevilik *n* Jew
müşkülpesent *adj* choosy
musluk *n* faucet
Müslüman *adj* Muslim
müsrif *adj* wasteful
müstehcen *adj* lewd, vulgar
müstehcenlik *n* vulgarity
müşteri *n* buyer, client
mutabık *adj* corresponding
mütehakkim *adj* domineering
mütevazı şekilde *adv* humbly
mutfak *n* cuisine, kitchen
mutlu *adj* happy, merry
mutluluk *n* happiness
mutsuz *adj* unhappy
mutsuzluk *n* unhappiness
müttefik *adj* allied
müttefik *n* ally
müvekkiller *n* clientele
muz *n* banana
muzaffer *adj* victorious
müzakere etmek *v* confer
müzayede *n* auction
müze *n* museum
müzik *n* music
muziplik *n* prank
müzisyen *n* musician
müzmin *adj* chronic

N

nabız *n* pulse
nacak *n* hatchet
nadir *adj* rare, unusual
nadiren *adv* rarely, seldom
nafile *adj* futile
nafile *adv* vainly
nahoş *adj* disagreeable, displeasing
nakit para *n* cash
nakletmek *v* recite, recount, convey
nakliye *n* freight
nalbant *n* smith
namlu ağzı *n* muzzle
namuslu *adj* chaste
nane *n* mint

nankör *adj* ungrateful
nankörlük *n* ingratitude
nar *n* pomegranate
narin *adj* tender, frail
narkotik *n* narcotic
nasihat *n* advice
nazik *adj* courteous
ne *adj* what
ne de *c* nor
ne zaman *adv* when
neden *adv* why, how
neden *n* incentive
neden olmak *v* induce
nedeniyle *pre* because of
nedime *n* bridesmaid
nefes *n* breath
nefes alma *n* breathing
nefes almak *n* aspiration, breathe
nefes borusu *n* windpipe
nefes kesici *adj* breathtaking
nefesini tutmak *adj* catching
nefis *adj* stunning
nefret *n* hatred, loathing
nefret dolu *adj* hateful
nefret etmek *v* detest, hate
negatif *adj* negative
nehir *n* river
nem *adj* damp
nem *n* moisture
nemlendirmek *v* moisten, dampen
nemli *adj* humid
nerede *adv* where
neredeyse *adv* almost, nearly, virtually
nerelerde *n* whereabouts
neşe *n* bliss, joy
neşelendirici *adj* exhilarating
neşelendirmek *v* cheer up
neşeli *adj* blissful, joyful
neşeyle *adv* joyfully
nesil *n* generation
nesli tükenmek *v* die out
nesli tükenmiş *adj* extinct
net *adj* explicit
netameli *adj* sinister
netice *adj* consequent
netlik *n* clearness
nezaketsizlik *n* discourtesy
nezaret etmek *v* preside
nezle *n* influenza
nicelik *n* quantity
nihai *adj* ultimate
nihayet *adv* eventually
nikel *n* nickel
nikotin *n* nicotine
nine *n* granny
Nisan *n* April

nişancı *n* marksman
nişanlı *n* fiancé
nişasta *n* starch
nişastalı *adj* starchy
nitelik *n* quality
nitrojen *n* nitrogen
nöbet *n* guard; fit
nöbet tutma *n* vigil
nöbetçi *n* sentry
Noel *n* Christmas
Noel ilahisi *n* carol
noksan *n* shortcoming
nokta *n* dot, point
normal *adj* normal
normalde *adv* normally
Norveç *n* Norway
Norveçli *adj* Norwegian
nostalji *n* nostalgia
not *v* note
not defteri *n* notebook
not eklemek *v* annotate
not etmek *v* write down
noter *n* notary
nötr *adj* neutral
nüdist *n* nudist
nüfus *n* population
nüfus sayımı *n* census
nüfuz etmek *v* sink in
nüfuzlu *adj* influential
nükleer *adj* nuclear
nüksetmek *v* recur
nükte *n* wit
numara yapmak *v* feign
numune *n* specimen

o *adj* that
o da *adv* too
o erkeğin *pro* his
o erkek *pro* he
o kız *pro* she
o kıza *adj* her
o kızın *pro* hers
o yüzden *adv* therefore
o zaman *adv* then
obez *adj* obese
obje *n* object
obur *n* glutton
öbür tarafına *pre* across
öç *n* revenge
öç almak *v* revenge
ocak *n* furnace

Ocak *n* January
oda *n* room
odak *n* focus
odaklanmak *v* focus on
ödeme *n* pay, payment
ödemek *v* defray, pay
ödenecek *adj* payable
ödenek *n* grant
ödenen kişi *n* payee
odise *n* odyssey
ödül *n* award
ödüllendirmek *v* reward
ödünç *n* loan
ödünç almak *v* borrow
ödünç vermek *v* lend
ofis *n* office
öfke *n* rage
öfke nöbeti *n* tantrum
öfkelendirmek *v* enrage
öfkelenmek *v* rampage
öfkeli *adj* irate
öğe *n* item
oğlan *n* boy
öğle yemeği *n* lunch
öğleden sonra *n* afternoon
öğlen *n* noon
öğrenci *n* learner
öğrenme *n* learning
öğrenmek *v* learn
öğreti *n* doctrine
öğretim *n* tuition
öğretmek *v* teach
öğretmen *n* instructor
oğul *n* son
öğüt vermek *v* counsel
öğütmek *v* grind
ok *n* arrow
oklu kirpi *n* porcupine
okşama *n* caress
okşamak *v* caress
oksijen *n* oxygen
öksürmek *v* cough
öksürük *n* cough
okul *n* school
okuma *n* reading
okumak *v* read
okumamış *adj* illiterate
okumuş *adj* learned
okunaksız *adj* illegible
okunur *adj* legible
okuryazar *adj* literate
okutmak *v* instruct
okuyucu *n* reader
öküz *n* ox, oxen
okyanus *n* ocean
olabilir *v* may

olağanüstü *adj* prodigious
olanak *n* possibility
olanaksız *adj* unable
olarak *c* as
olası *adj* contingent
olasılık *n* chance
olay *n* event, issue
olaysız *adj* uneventful
ölçeklemek *v* scale
ölçmek *v* measure
ölçü *n* size
ölçülü *adj* metric
ölçüm *n* measurement
ölçüp biçmek *v* size up
olduğundan *c* since
oldukça *adv* quite
oldukça büyük *adj* sizable
öldürmek *v* assassinate
öldürücü *adj* lethal
olgun *adj* mature
olgunlaştırmak *v* mellow
olgunluk *n* maturity
olimpiyat *n* olympics
olmak *v* be
ölmek *v* die
ölmekte olan *adj* dying
olsa bile *c* even if
ölü *adj* dead
ölü sayısı *n* death toll
oluk *n* duct
ölüm *n* death
ölüm tuzağı *n* death trap
ölümcül *adj* deadly
olumlu *adj* affirmative
ölümlü *adj* mortal
olumsuz *adj* unfavorable
ölümsüz *adj* immortal
ölümsüzlük *n* immortality
olup çıkmak *v* end up
olup olmadığını *c* whether
oluş *n* occurrence
oluşmuş *adj* composed
ölüyü diriltmek *v* resuscitate
omlet *n* omelette
omur *n* vertebra
omurga *n* backbone
omuz *n* shoulder
omuz silkmek *v* shrug
on *adj* ten, front
ön *n* front
on bir *adj* eleven
on birinci *adj* eleventh
ön plan *n* forefront, foreground
on sekiz *adj* eighteen
on sent *n* dime
ön ürün *n* prototype

on yıl *n* decade
ona *pre* to
onaltı *adj* sixteen
onarılamaz *adj* irreparable
onarma *n* restitution
onarmak *v* fix
onay *n* approval
onaylama *n* ratification
onaylamak *v* approve
onaylamama *n* disapproval
onaylamamak *v* disapprove
onbaşı *n* corporal
onbeş *adj* fifteen
önce *adv* before
önce gelen *n* antecedent
önceden *adv* beforehand
önceki *adj* former
öncü *n* pioneer
öncülük etmek *v* spearhead
ondalık sayı *adj* decimal
öndeyiş *n* prologue
ondokuz *adj* nineteen
ondört *adj* fourteen
öne sürmek *v* assert
önek *n* prefix
önem *n* importance
önemli *adj* notable
önemli oranda *adj* considerable
önemsemek *v* heed
önemsememek *v* brush aside
önemsiz *adj* frivolous
öneri *n* suggestion
önermek *v* recommend
öngörmek *v* predict
öngörü *n* prediction
önhazırlık *n* groundwork
oniki *adj* twelve
onikinci *adj* twelfth
önizleme *n* preview
önkoşul *n* prerequisite
onlar *pro* they
önlem *n* precaution
önleme *n* prevention
önlemek *v* preempt
önleyici *adj* preventive
önlük *n* apron
ons *n* ounce
önsezi *n* hunch
önsöz *n* foreword
onu *adj* that
onüç *adj* thirteen
onun *pre* of
onuncu *n* tenth
önüne geçmek *v* pull ahead
onur *n* honor
onur kırıcı *adj* derogatory

onurlandırmak *v* dignify
önyargı *n* bias
önyargısız *adj* unbiased
onyedi *adj* seventeen
opak *adj* opaque
opera *n* opera
operasyon *n* operation
öpmek *v* kiss
optik *adj* optical
öpücük *n* kiss
orada *adv* there
orak *n* sickle
oran *n* proportion
orangutan *n* orangutan
ördek *n* duck
ordu *n* army
organ *n* organ
organizma *n* organism
orgcu *n* organist
orijinal *adj* original
orijinal olarak *adv* originally
orkestra *n* orchestra
orman *n* forest
örmek *v* knit
örnek *n* model
örnek olarak *adj* exemplary
örnek vermek *v* exemplify
örneklemek *v* illustrate
örs *n* anvil
orta *adj* medium
ortaçağ *adj* medieval
ortadirek *adj* grassroots
ortak *n* partner
ortak *adj* common
ortak merkezli *adj* concentric
ortak olarak *adv* jointly
ortaklık *n* partnership
ortalama *n* average
ortalamak *v* center
ortasına *pre* amid
ortaya çıkmak *v* arise
ortaya çıktı *v* arouse
örtbas etmek *v* hush up
örtülü *adj* shrouded
örülü *adj* woven
örümcek *n* spider
örümcek ağı *n* cobweb
ot *n* weed
ot yolmak *v* weed
otantik *adj* authentic
otantiklik *n* authenticity
ötede *adv* further
otel *n* hotel
ötelemek *v* shift
otlama *n* graze
otlamak *v* graze

oto *n* auto
otobüs *n* bus
otomatik *adj* automatic
otomobil *n* automobile
otonom *adj* autonomous
otonomi *n* autonomy
otopsi *n* autopsy
otorite *n* authority
otoriter *adj* authoritarian
otostop yapmak *n* hitchhike
otoyol *n* freeway
oturacak yer *n* seat
oturan *n* occupant
oturan kimse *n* inhabitant
oturma *n* sitting
oturma odası *n* living room
oturmak *v* sit
oturulur *adj* habitable
oturum açmak *v* log in
oturum kapatmak *v* log off
otuz *adj* thirty
oval *adj* oval
ovalamak *v* rub, scrub
övgü *n* praise
övgü dolu *adj* complimentary
övgüye değer *adj* praiseworthy
övmek *v* acclaim, praise
oy *n* vote
oy pusulası *n* ballot
oy vermek *v* vote
oybirliği *n* consensus
öykü *n* story
oylama *n* voting, poll
oynamak *v* wiggle
oyuk *n* burrow
oyun *n* game, play
oyun alanı *n* playground
oyun zarları *n* dice
oyunbaz *adj* playful
oyuncak *n* toy
oyuncak bebek *n* doll
oyuncu *n* player
öz *n* core
öz varlık *n* essence
özel *adj* fancy, special
özel ambalaj *n* wrapping
özel araba yolu *n* driveway
özel öğretmen *n* tutor
özel şoför *n* chauffeur
özelleşmek *v* specialize
özellik *n* feature, trait
özellikle *adv* especially
özen *n* diligence
özensiz *adj* slack
özerk *adj* sovereign
özerklik *n* sovereignty

özet *n* summary
özetlemek *v* summarize
özgün *adj* peculiar
özgür bırakmak *adj* free
özgür bırakmak *v* free
özgürlük *n* freedom
özlemek *v* long for, miss
özlü *adj* brief, concise
özne *n* subject
özsaygı *n* self-esteem
özür *n* apology
özür dilemek *v* apologize

P

pahalı *adj* expensive
pahalıya *adv* dearly
paket *n* package
paket postası *n* parcel post
paketlemek *v* pack
pakt *n* pact
palto *n* coat
palyaço *n* clown
pamuk *n* cotton
pancar *n* beet
panik *n* panic
pankart *n* placard
pankreas *n* pancreas
panorama *n* panorama
panter *n* panther
pantolon *n* trousers
Papa *n* Pope
papağan *n* parakeet
papalık *n* papacy
papatya *n* daisy
papaya ait *adj* apostolic
papaz *n* minister, friar
papazlık *n* priesthood
para *n* money
para basmak *v* mint
para harcamak *v* disburse
para hırsı *n* avarice
para yedirmek *v* buy off
paradoks *n* paradox
paragraf *n* paragraph
paralel *n* parallel
parametre *n* parameters
paranoyak *adj* paranoid
parantez *n* parenthesis
parasız *adj* penniless
paraşüt *n* parachute
parazit *n* parasite
parça *n* fragment, piece

parça başına *adv* apiece
parçalamak *v* rip, mangle
parçalanmak *v* part
parçalara ayırmak *v* dismantle
parfüm *n* perfume
parıldamak *v* gleam
parıltı *n* flare, glare
parıltılı *adj* flashy
parite *n* parity
park *n* park
park etmek *v* park
park yeri *n* parking
parke taşı *n* cobblestone
parlak *adj* bright, shiny
parlaklık *n* brightness
parlamak *v* blaze, glow
parlamento *n* parliament
parlatmak *v* brighten, shine
parmak *n* finger
parmak izi *n* fingerprint
parmak ucu *n* fingertip
parşömen *n* parchment
parti *n* party
partizan *n* partisan
pas *n* rust
pas tutmaz *adj* rust-proof
pasaport *n* passport
pasif *adj* passive
Paskalya *n* Easter
paslanmak *v* rust
paslı *adj* rusty
paspas yapmak *v* mop
patates *n* potato
patavatsız *adj* indiscreet
paten *n* skate
paten kaymak *v* skate
patent *n* patent
patentli *adj* patent
patika *n* alley
patlak verme *n* eruption
patlak vermek *v* break out
patlama *n* explosion
patlamak *v* burst, explode
patlamış mısır *n* popcorn
patlatıcı *n* detonator
patlatmak *v* blow up
patlayıcı *adj* explosive
patron *n* boss
pavyon *n* pavilion
pay *n* dividend
pay etmek *v* allot
payda *n* denominator
paylaşım *n* share
paylaşma *n* communion
paylaşmak *v* share
pazar *n* bazaar

Pazar *n* Sunday
pazarlık *n* bargain
pazarlık etmek *v* bargain
Pazartesi *n* Monday
peçe *n* veil
pedagoji *n* pedagogy
pedal *n* pedal
pejmürde *adj* shabby
pek çok *adv* highly
peki *adv* alright
pekiştirmek *v* consolidate
pelerin *n* cloak, cape
pelikan *n* pelican
pelüş *adj* plush
pembe *adj* pink, rosy
pembeleşmiş *n* claw, paw
pençe *n* claw
pençe vurmak *v* tap into
pencere *n* window
penguen *n* penguin
peni *n* penny
penisilin *n* penicillin
perçinlemek *v* clinch, rivet
perde *n* curtain
performans *n* performance
peri *n* fairy
perişan *adj* wretched
Perşembe *n* Thursday
personel *n* personnel
personel alma *n* recruitment
peruk *n* hairpiece
peşinat *n* down payment
peşine düşmek *v* chase away
peşine takılmak *v* tail
petal *n* petal
petrol *n* petroleum
peygamber *n* prophet
peynir *n* cheese
piç *n* bastard
pıhtı *n* clot
pıhtılaşma *n* coagulation
pıhtılaşmak *v* coagulate
pijama *n* pajamas
pike yapmak *v* nosedive
pil *n* battery
pilot *n* pilot
pinta *n* pint
piramit *n* pyramid
pire *n* flea
pırıldamak *v* glitter, wink
pırıltı *n* gleam
pirinç *n* rice
pırtlamak *v* protrude
pirzola *n* chop
pis *adj* filthy
pis kokan *adj* stinking

pis koku *n* stink
pis kokulu *adj* smelly
pısırık *adj* wimp
pişirmek *v* cook
piskopos *n* bishop, pontiff
pislik *n* contamination
pişman olmak *v* regret, repent
pişmanlık *n* contrition, regret
pist *n* runway
piston *n* plug
piton *n* python
piyadeler *n* infantry
piyango *n* lottery, raffle
piyanist *n* pianist
piyano *n* piano
plaj *n* beach
plak *n* record
plan *n* plan
planlamak *v* plan
plastik *n* plastic
platin *n* platinum
plütonyum *n* plutonium
polen *n* pollen
poliçe *n* policy
polis *n* policeman
politika *n* politics
Polonya *n* Poland
Polonyalı *adj* Polish
pompa *n* pump
popüler *adj* popular
porselen *n* porcelain
porsiyon *n* portion
portakal *n* orange
portatif merdiven *n* ladder
Portekiz *n* Portugal
Portekizli *adj* Portuguese
portre *n* portrait
posta *n* mail, post
posta damgası *n* postmark
posta kodu *n* zip code
posta kutusu *n* mailbox
posta ücreti *n* postage
postacı *n* mailman
postahane *n* post office
postalamak *v* mail
poster *n* poster
potansiyel *adj* potential
poz *n* pose
poz vermek *v* pose
pozisyon *n* position
pozitif *adj* positive
pratik *adj* practical
prens *n* prince
prenses *n* princess
prestij *n* prestige
prizden çekmek *v* unplug

prizma *n* prism
profesör *n* professor
profesyonel *adj* professional
program *n* program
programcı *n* programmer
proje *n* project, scheme
proje yapmak *v* project
projektör *n* floodlight
projektör ışığı *n* spotlight
propaganda *n* propaganda
prosedür *n* procedure
prostat *n* prostate
protein *n* protein
protesto *n* protest
protesto etmek *v* protest
protokol *n* protocol
prova *n* rehearsal
prova etmek *v* rehearse
pruva *n* prow
psikiyatri *n* psychiatry
psikiyatrist *n* psychiatrist
psikoloji *n* psychology
psikopat *n* psychopath
psişik *adj* psychic
puan *n* score
pudra *n* powder
pul *n* scale
pünez *n* tack
püre *n* puree
puro *n* cigar
pürüzsüz *adj* smooth
pürüzsüzlük *n* smoothness
püskürmek *v* erupt, spray
püskürtmek *v* sprinkle
pusuda beklemek *v* lurk
pusula *n* compass
putperest *adj* pagan
putperestlik *n* idolatry

R

radar *n* radar
radikal *adj* extremist, radical
radyasyon *n* radiation
radyatör *n* radiator
radyo *n* radio
rafine etmek *v* refine
rafineri *n* refinery
rağbet *n* vogue
rağmen *c* although
rahat *adj* cozy
rahatlama *n* relaxation
rahatlamak *v* chill out, relax

rahatlatıcı *adj* relaxing
rahatlık *n* ease
rahatlıklar *n* amenities
rahatsız *adj* ailing
rahatsız edici *adj* disturbing
rahatsız etmek *v* disturb, harass
rahatsızlık *n* discomfort
rahibe *n* nun
rahip *n* pastor, priest
rakam *n* figure
raket *n* racket
rakip *adj* competitive
rakip *n* rival
ralli *n* rally
rampa *n* ramp
randıman *n* spoils
ranza *n* berth, bunk bed
rapor *n* report, essay
raptiye *n* thumbtack
rastgele *adv* randomly
rasyonel *adj* rational
raydan çıkma *n* derailment
raydan çıkmak *v* derail
razı olmak *v* assent, settle for
reçel *n* jam
reddetmek *v* decline, reject
refah *n* affluence, welfare
refakatçi *n* escort
referandum *n* referendum
referans *n* reference
reform *n* reform
rehber *n* guidebook
rehin *n* pledge
rehine *n* hostage
rehine koyma *v* pawn
rehine koymak *v* pledge
reis *n* heading
rejenerasyon *n* regeneration
rejim *n* regime
rekabet *n* rivalry
rekabet etmek *v* compete
reklam *n* publicity
rekreasyon *n* recreation
rektör *n* chancellor
rektum *n* rectum
rengeyiği *n* reindeer
renk *n* color
renklendirmek *v* color
renkli *adj* colorful
resepsiyon *n* reception
resepsiyoncu *n* receptionist
resif *n* reef
resim *n* picture
resimlemek *v* picture
resimli örtü *n* tapestry
resmi *adj* formal, official

resmi olarak *adv* formally
resmi olmayan *adj* informal
resmileştirmek *v* formalize
resmiyet *n* formality
ressam *n* painter
restaurant *n* restaurant
restoran *n* diner
ret *n* refuse
reverans *n* bow
reverans yapmak *v* bow
revir *n* infirmary
revü *n* revue
rezervasyon *n* reservation
rica etmek *v* solicit
rıhtım *n* pier, dock
risale *n* epistle
risk *v* jeopardize
riske atmak *v* risk
riskli *adj* risky
ritim *n* rhythm
riyazet *n* abstinence
rıza *n* consent
rızasını almak *v* consent
roket *n* rocket
rolo yapmak *v* roll
rom *n* rum
romans *n* romance
romatizma *n* rheumatism
röntgen ışını *n* X-ray
rosto *n* roast
rota *n* route
rotasyon *n* rotation
rötuş yapmak *v* touch up
rozet *n* badge
ruh *n* soul, spirit
ruh hali *n* mood
ruh hastası *adj* lunatic
ruhani *adj* spiritual
ruhban *n* clergy
ruhsal *adv* inwards
rumuz *n* pseudonym
Rus *adj* Russian
rüşvet *n* bribery
rüşvet vermek *v* bribe
Rusya *n* Russia
rütbe *n* dignitary
rütbesini indirmek *v* degrade
rutin *n* routine
rutubet *n* humidity
rüya *n* dream
rüzgar *n* wind
rüzgar esmek *v* wind
rüzgar siperi *n* windshield
rüzgarlı *adj* windy

R

S

saat *n* clock, watch
saat üreticisi *n* watchmaker
saatlik *adv* hourly
sabah *n* morning
sabık *adj* preceding
sabır *n* patience
sabırla beklemek *v* hold out
sabırlı *adj* patient
sabırsız *adj* impatient
sabırsızlık *n* impatience
sabit *adj* constant
sabit olmak *n* standing
sabit ücret *n* toll
sabotaj *n* sabotage
sabote etmek *v* sabotage
saç *n* hair
saç fırçası *n* hairbrush
saç kepeği *n* dandruff
saç kesimi *n* haircut
saç şekli *n* hairdo
saçma *adj* absurd
saçmak *v* disseminate
sadaka *n* alms, handout
sadaka vermek *v* dole out
sadakat *n* allegiance
sadakatsiz *adj* unfaithful
sadakatsizlik *n* infidelity
sade *adj* simple, plain
sadece *adj* just
sadeleştirmek *v* simplify
sadelik *n* austerity
sadık *adj* loyal, staunch
sadist *n* sadist
saf *adj* gullible, naïve
safir *n* saphire
saflık *n* purity
safra kesesi *n* gall bladder
sağ *adj* right
sağ kalanlar *n* survivor
sağ salim *adj* unharmed
sağanak *n* downpour
sağda *adv* right
sağdıç *n* best man
sağduyu *n* discretion
sağgörü *n* prudence
sağır *adj* deaf
sağır edici *adj* deafening
sağır etmek *v* deafen
sağırlık *n* deafness
sağlam *adj* sturdy
sağlamak *v* provide
sağlamlaştırmak *v* brace for
sağlık *n* health

sağlıklı *adj* healthy
sağlıklı *n* fit
sağlıksız *adj* unhealthy
saha *n* range
şahadet *n* testimony
şahane *adj* splendid
sahibe *n* hostess
sahibi olmak *v* own
sahil *n* coast, shore
sahip olmak *v* possess, have
sahipsiz *adj* derelict
şahıs *n* person
şahit *n* witness
şahlanmış *adj* rampant
sahne *n* stage
sahnelemek *v* stage
sahra *v* desert
şahsi *adj* personal
sahte *adj* fake, phoney, counterfeit
sahtekar *adj* dishonest
sahtekarlık *n* dishonesty
sahtesini yapmak *v* forge
şair *n* poet
şaka *n* gag, hoax
şaka yapmak *v* joke
sakal *n* beard
sakallı *adj* bearded
sakat *adj* cripple
sakat etmek *v* cripple
sakatlamak *v* maim
sakatlık *adj* disabled
şakayla *adv* jokingly
sakin *adj* calm
sakin *n* calm
sakınca *n* drawback
sakinleşmek *v* calm down
sakinleştirmek *v* soothe
sakınmak *v* watch out
sakız *n* bubble gum
saklamak *v* preserve
saklamak *v* keep
saksı *n* flowerpot
sal *n* raft
şal *n* scarf
salata *n* salad
salatalık *n* cucumber
salça *n* sauce
saldırgan *adj* aggressive
saldırgan *n* aggressor
saldırı *n* assault, attack
saldırıp soymak *v* mug
saldırmak *v* assail, assault
şalgam *n* rape
salgı bezi *n* gland
salgın *n* epidemic
Salı *n* Tuesday

salım *n* emission
salıncak *n* swing
salıvermek *v* unleash
salkım *n* bunch
sallamak *v* sway, wag
sallamak *v* toss
sallanmak *v* waver, wobble
salmak *v* emit
saltanat *n* reign
salya *n* saliva
salyangoz *n* snail
saman *n* hay
saman sapı *n* haystack
saman tırmığı *n* pitchfork
şamandıra *n* buoy
şamata *n* commotion
samimi *adj* truthful
samimilik *n* intimacy
samimiyet *n* sincerity
şampiyon *n* champion
şan *n* glory
sanat *n* art
sanat çalışması *n* artwork
sanatçı *n* artist
sancı *n* gripe
sandal *n* sandal
sandal kıçı *n* stern
sandalye *n* chair
sandık *n* ark
sandviç *n* sandwich
şangırtı *n* crash
saniye *n* second
şanlı *adj* heroic
sanrı *n* illusion
şans *n* luck
sansasyon *n* sensation
şanslı *adj* fortunate
şanssız *adj* unlucky
sansür *n* censorship
şantaj *n* blackmail
şantaj yapmak *v* blackmail
santimetre *n* centimeter
sap *n* grip
şapel *n* chapel
sapık *adj* pervert
şapka *n* hat
şaplak atma *n* spanking
şaplak atmak *v* spank
saplama *n* stab
saplamak *v* plunge
saplantı *n* obsession
sapma *n* aberration
sapmak *v* depart, veer
sara *n* epilepsy
şarap *n* wine
şaraphane *n* winery

şarapnel *n* shrapnel
saray *n* palace
sardalye *n* sardine
sargı *n* dressing
sarhoş *adj* drunk
sarhoşluk *n* drunkenness
sarı *adj* yellow
sarılmış *adj* convoluted
sarımsak *n* garlic
sarışın *adj* blond
şarj *n* charge
şarj etmek *v* recharge
sarkaç *n* pendulum
şarkı *n* song
şarkı söylemek *v* sing
şarkı sözü *n* lyrics
şarkıcı *n* singer
sarkık *adj* baggy
sarkmak *v* dangle
sarmak *adj* involved
sarmalamak *v* wrap up
sarnıç *n* cistern
sarp *adj* steep
sarsılmış *adj* shaken
sarsıntı *n* convulsion
sarsmak *v* shake
şartıyla *c* providing that
şartlar *n* terms
şaşırtıcı *adj* amazing
şaşırtmak *v* amaze, baffle, bewilder
satıcı *n* salesman
satılıp biten *adj* sold-out
satın almak *v* buy
satış fişi *n* sale slip
satış yeri *n* outlet
satmak *v* sell
satranç *n* chess
savalı *n* defendant
savaş *n* battle, war
savaş gemisi *n* battleship
savaşçı *n* warrior
savaşım *n* warfare
savaşmak *v* battle
savcı *n* prosecutor
savunma *n* defense
savunmak *v* advocate
savunmasız *adj* defenseless
savunucu *n* defender
savurgan *adj* extravagant
sayaç *n* counter
saydam *adj* transparent
sayfa *n* page
saygı *n* respect
saygı duymak *v* respect
saygı göstermek *n* reverence

saygılar *n* regards
saygılı *adj* respectful
saygısız *adj* disrespectful
saygısızlık *n* disrespect
saygısızlık etmek *v* desecrate
sayı *n* number
sayısız *adj* countless
sayma *n* count
saymak *v* count
saz *n* reed
sebep *n* motive, reason
sebze *v* vegetable
seçenek *n* option
seçilebilir *adj* eligible
seçim *n* choice, election
seçip ayırmak *v* sort out
seçmek *v* choose, elect
sedye *n* stretcher
şef *n* chef, chief
şeffaf *adj* clear
şeffaf *n* compassion
şefkatli *adj* compassionate
şeftali *n* peach
seher *n* dawn
şehir *n* city
şehir dışı *n* suburb
şehirli *adj* civic
şehit *n* martyr
şehitlik *n* martyrdom
şeker *n* sugar, sweets
şekerleme *n* candy
şekerleme yapmak *v* doze
şekil *n* form, shape
şekillendirmek *v* shape
şekilsiz *adj* amorphous
sekiz *adj* eight
sekizinci *adj* eighth
sekreter *n* secretary
seksen *adj* eighty
sel *v* flood, torrent
sel basma *n* flooding
şelale *n* waterfall
selam *n* hail, hello
selamlama *n* greetings
selamlamak *v* greet, hail
semaver *n* urn
sembol *n* symbol
sembolik *adj* symbolic
semer *n* saddle
seminer *n* workshop
şempanze *n* chimpanzee
sempati *n* sympathy
sempatik *adj* congenial
semptom *n* symptom
şemsiye *n* umbrella
semt *n* ward

sen *pro* you
şen *adj* festive
senaryo *n* scenario
senato *n* senate
senatör *n* senator
senet *n* bond
senfoni *n* symphony
senin *adj* your
seninki *pro* yours
şenlik *n* festivity
şenlik ateşi *n* bonfire
sent *n* cent
sentez *n* synthesis
sepet *n* basket
sera *n* greenhouse
seramik *n* ceramic
serap *n* mirage
serbestlik *n* leisure
serçe *n* sparrow
şerefe *n* cheers
şerefli *adj* glorious
seremoni *n* ceremony
serenat *n* serenade
sergen *n* shelf
sergi *n* exhibition
sergilemek *v* exhibit
seri *n* string
serili *adj* tanned
serin *adj* chilly
serinkanlı *adj* cool
şerit *n* strip
sermaye *n* funds
sermaye bulmak *v* fund
sermek *v* lay
serpilmek *v* flourish
sersem *adj* dazed, dizzy
sersemletmek *v* daze
serseri *n* prowler
sert *adj* stark, strict
sert rüzgar *n* gale
sertifika *n* certificate
sertleşmek *v* stiffen
sertleştirmek *v* harden
sertlik *n* hardness
serum *n* serum
servi *n* cypress
servis *n* service
ses *n* tone, voice, sound
sesli *n* vowel
sessiz *adj* placid, quiet
sessizlik *n* quietness
set çekmek *v* foil
sevdirmek *v* ingratiate
sevecen *adj* loving
sevgi *n* love
sevgi dolu *adj* fond

sevgili *n* lover
sevimli *adj* amiable, cute
sevinç *n* pleasure
sevinçli *adj* elated
sevindirici *n* welcome
sevindirmek *v* delight
şevk *n* enthusiasm
şevk kırıcı *adj* discouraging
sevkiyat *n* consignment
sevmek *v* love
şey *n* thing
seyahat etmek *v* travel
seyir *n* navigation
seyirci *n* audience
seyirci kalan *n* bystander
seyrek *adj* infrequent
seyretmek *v* navigate
şeytan *n* demon, devil
şeytanca *adj* devious
sezgi *n* intuition
sezon *n* session
sıcak *adj* hot
sıcak dalgası *n* heatwave
sıçan *n* rat
sicile kaydetmek *n* enrollment
sicim *n* twist
sıçrama *n* leap, skip
sıçramak *n* bounce, skip
sıçrayış *n* jump
şiddet *n* violence
şiddetli *adj* intense, fierce
şiddetli sarsıntı *n* concussion
sıfat *n* adjective
sıfır *adj* null, zero
sıfırlamak *v* nullify
şifoniyer *n* dresser
şifre *n* password
şifre çözmek *v* decipher
sığ *adj* shallow
sigara *n* cigarette
sigara içen *n* smoker
sigara içmek *v* smoke
sigara içmeyen *n* nonsmoker
siğil *n* wart
sığınak *n* haven, refuge
sığınmak *v* shelter
sığır *n* cattle
sığır eti *n* beef
sığır filetosu *n* sirloin
sigorta *n* fuse; insurance
sigorta etmek *v* underwrite
sigorta olmak *v* insure
sihir *n* magic
sihirbaz *n* magician
sihirli *adj* magical
şiir *n* poem, poetry

sık *adj* frequent
sık uğramak *v* haunt
şikayet *n* complaint
şikayet etmek *v* complain
sıkı *adj* firm, tight
sıkı tutunmak *v* hang on
sıkıcı *adj* boring, tedious
sıkılaştırmak *v* tighten
sıkılık *n* firmness
sıkıntı *n* hardship
sıkıntılı dönem *n* downturn
sıkışmak *v* huddle
sıkıştırmak *v* squeeze in
sıkkın *adj* fed up
sıklık *n* frequency
sıklıkla *adv* often
siklon *n* cyclone
sıkmak *v* clench
silah *n* gun, weapon
silahı doğrultmak *v* muzzle
silahlanma *n* armaments
silahlanmak *v* arm
silahlı *adj* armed
silahsız *adj* unarmed
silgi *n* eraser
silindir *n* cylinder
silmek *v* delete, erase
şilte *n* mattress
siluet *n* silhouette
şımartmak *v* pamper
şimdi *adv* now
şimdiki *adj* present
şimdiye kadar *adv* hitherto
simetri *n* symmetry
simge *n* token
şimşek *n* lightning
sımsıkı tutmak *v* grip
simültane *adj* simultaneous
sinagog *n* synagogue
sınama *n* probing
sınamak *v* examine
sınav *n* examination
sınavda çakmak *v* flunk
sincap *n* squirrel
sindirim *n* digestion
sindirmek *v* digest; suppress
sinema *n* cinema
sınıf *n* classroom
sınıf arkadaşı *n* classmate
sınıflandırmak *v* classify
sinir *n* anger
sınır *adj* borderline
sinir bozukluğu *n* breakdown
sınırdışı *n* deportation
sınırdışı etmek *v* deport
sınırını aşmak *v* transcend

sınırlamak *v* constrain
sınırlandırmak *v* limit
sinirlendirmek *v* displease
sinirlenmek *v* anger
sinirli *adj* angry, furious
sınırsız *adj* boundless
sinmek *n* quail
sinod *n* synod
sinsice ilerlemek *v* sneak
sinyal *n* signal
siper *n* bulwark
siper etmek *n* shield
sıra *n* queue
sıradaki *adj* next
sıradan *adj* unpopular
sırasında *c* while
sırasında *pre* during
sıraya girmek *v* line up
sırdaş *n* confidant
siren *n* siren
şırınga *n* syringe
sirk *n* circus
sirke *n* vinegar
sırrını söylemek *v* confide
sırsıklam *adj* soggy
sırt çantası *n* backpack
sırtlan *n* hyena
sis *n* fog, haze
şiş *adj* bloated, swollen
şiş *n* bump
şişe *n* bottle
şişelemek *v* bottle
şişirmek *v* bloat, inflate
sıska *adj* skinny
şişkinlik *n* lump
sisli *adj* foggy
şişman *adj* corpulent
şişmanlamak *v* fatten
şişmek *v* swell
sistem *n* system
sistemli *adj* systematic
site *n* site
sıtma *n* malaria
sıva *n* plaster
sıva vurmak *v* plaster
sıvı *n* fluid, liquid
sıvılaştırma *n* liquidation
sıvılaştırmak *v* liquidate
sivilce *n* pimple
sivri *adj* pointed
sivrisinek *n* mosquito
siyah *adj* black
siyanür *n* cyanide
siyasetçi *n* politician
sıyırmak *v* skim
siz suz eki *pre* without

sızdırmak *v* extort
sızdırmazlık *n* leakage
sızmak *v* leak
skandal *n* scandal
skuter *n* scooter
slogan *n* slogan
soba *n* stove
sofra örtüsü *n* tablecloth
sofu *adj* ascetic
soğan *n* onion
soğuk *adj* cold, freezing
soğuk içecek *n* refreshment
soğuk ısırması *n* frostbite
soğukkanlılık *n* composure
soğukluk *n* coldness
soğukluk *v* cool, chill
söğüt *n* willow
soğutucu *adj* cooling
sohbet etmek *v* chat
şok *n* shock
sokak *n* street
sokak lambası *n* streetlight
şoke etmek *v* astound
şoke olmak *v* shock
sokmak *v* shove, sting
sokmamak *v* bar
sokuşturmak *v* squeeze in
solmak *v* wither
solucan *n* worm
soluk *adj* pale
solukluk *n* paleness
solumak *v* gasp
solunum *n* respiration
som balığı *n* salmon
sömestre *n* semester
şömine *n* fireplace; hearth
somun *n* loaf
sömürge *n* colony
sömürgeci *adj* colonial
sömürmek *v* exploit
somurtkan *adj* sullen
somut *adj* concrete
somut *n* concrete
son *adj* final, last
son *n* ending
son bulmak *v* culminate
son kısım *n* conclusion
son söz *n* envoy
son tarih *n* deadline
son zamanlarda *adv* lately
sona ermek *v* adjourn
Sonbahar *n* fall, autumn
söndürmek *v* extinguish
sonek *v* affix
sonlandırmak *v* end
sönmek *v* fade

sonra *pre* after
sonraki *adj* subsequent
sonraları *adv* later
sonsuz *adj* endless, everlasting, infinite
sonuç *n* consequence
sonuç çıkarmak *v* conclude
sönük *adj* faded, insipid
sopa *n* stick
sörf yapmak *v* surf
sorgulamak *v* question
sorguya çekmek *v* debrief
sormak *v* ask
şort *n* shorts
soru *n* question
sorumlu *adj* accountable, responsible
sorumluluk *n* responsibility
sorun *n* problem
sorunlu *adj* problematic
soruşturma *n* inquest
sos *n* gravy
sosis *n* sausage
sosyal *adj* sociable
sosyalist *adj* socialist
sosyalizm *n* socialism
sosyalleşmek *v* socialize
şövalye *n* knight
Sovyet *adj* soviet
soy *n* ancestry
soygun *n* heist
soyguncu *n* robber
soyisim *n* last name
soykırım *n* genocide
söylemek *v* say
söylenmek *v* grouch
söylenti *n* hearsay
soymak *v* pillage, rob
soysal *adj* generic
soyunma odası *n* locker room
soyunmak *v* undress
soyut *adj* abstract
söz vermek *v* stipulate
söz vermiş *adj* committed
sözde *adv* allegedly
sözle *adv* verbally
sözleşme *n* contract
sözleşmek *v* contract
sözlük *n* dictionary
sözünü kesmek *v* heckle
spazm *n* spasm
spekülasyon *n* speculation
sperm *n* sperm
sponsor *n* sponsor
spontane *adj* spontaneous
spor *n* fitness, sport
spor salonu *n* gymnasium
sporcu *n* sportsman

sportmen *adj* sporty
staj yapmak *v* intern
stajyer *n* trainee
standart *n* standard
steno *n* shorthand
steril *adj* sterile
sterilize etmek *v* sterilize
stoacı *adj* stoic
stok *n* inventory
stok yığını *n* stockpile
stoklama *n* stocking
strateji *n* strategy
stres *n* stress
stres verici *adj* stressful
su *n* water
şu anda *adv* currently
şu anki *adj* current
su basmak *v* inundate
su geçirmez *adj* waterproof
su götürmez *adj* indisputable
su hortumu *n* hose
su kabuklusu *n* shellfish
su kaybetmek *v* dehydrate
su samuru *n* otter
Şubat *n* February
şube *n* branch office
sübvansiyon *n* subsidy
suç *n* crime, guilt
suç ortağı *n* accomplice
suç ortaklığı *n* complicity
suçiçeği *n* chicken pox
suçlama *n* accusation
suçlamak *v* accuse, blame
suçlu *adj* criminal, guilty
suçlu *n* felon, culprit
suçluluk *n* delinquency
suçsuz *adj* blameless
suda yaşayan *adj* aquatic
suikast *n* assassination
suikastçı *n* assassin
suistimal *n* abuse
sukemeri *n* aqueduct
sükunet *n* tranquility
sulamak *v* water, irrigate
sulandırmak *v* dilute
sulu *adj* juicy
sülük *n* leech
sülün *n* pheasant
sunak *n* altar
sünger *n* sponge
süngü *n* bayonet
sunmak *v* present
sünnet *n* circumcision
sünnet etmek *v* circumcise
sunucu *n* announcer
sunum *n* presentation

süper *adj* superb
süper devletler *n* superpower
süpermarket *n* supermarket
şüphe *n* doubt
şüphe uyandıran *adj* fishy
şüpheci *adj* skeptic
şüphelenmek *v* doubt
şüpheli *adl* doubtful
şüphesiz *adv* undoubtedly
süpürge *n* broom
süpürmek *v* sweep
sürahi *n* jug
sürat *n* velocity
süre *n* times
süreç *n* process
sürekli *adj* continuous
süreklilik *n* continuity
süren *adj* ongoing
süresi bitmek *v* expire
suret çıkarmak *v* reprint
sureti *n* duplication
sürgü *n* bolt
sürgülemek *v* bolt
sürgün *n* exile
sürgüne yollamak *v* banish
sürmek *v* propel
sürpriz *n* surprise
sürpriz yapmak *v* surprise
sürtünme *n* friction
sürü *n* flock
sürücü *n* driver
sürüklemek *v* drag, drift
sürüklenmiş *adv* adrift
sürüm *n* edition, version
sürüngen *n* reptile
sürünmek *v* crawl
şurup *n* syrup
süs *n* embroidery
susamak *v* thirst
susamış *adj* thirsty
süslemek *v* adorn
susmak *v* silence
susturmak *v* gag, muffle
süt *n* milk
sütlü *adj* milky
sütun *n* column
sutyen *n* bra
süvari *n* cavalry
suya bastırmak *v* soak
suya daldırmak *v* duck
süzgeç *n* strainer
süzülmek *v* glide

T

taaffün *n* stench
taammüden *adv* willfully
tabak *n* plate
taban *n* sole
tabanca *n* handgun
tabiat *n* temper
tablo *n* painting
tabur *n* casket, coffin
taç *n* crown
taç giyme töreni *n* coronation
taç giymek *v* crown
tadilat yapmak *v* remodel
tafra *n* pomposity
tahammül *n* tolerance
tahıl *n* grain
tahliye ettirmek *v* evict
tahmin *n* estimation, guess
tahmin *v* forecast
tahmin etmek *v* guess
tahribat *n* devastation
tahrip etmek *v* raze
tahsis *n* allotment
taht *n* throne
tahta *n* wood
tahtadan *adj* wooden
takas etmek *v* exchange
takas yapmak *v* barter
takdir *n* admiration
takdir etmek *n* appreciation
takdir etmek *v* appreciate
takdire değer *adj* admirable
takibat *n* proceedings
takım *n* platoon; team
takımyıldız *n* constellation
takip etmek *v* follow, track
taklit *n* imitation
taklit *adj* counterfeit
taklit etmek *v* counterfeit
takma diş *n* dentures
takmak *v* insert
takoz *n* wedge
taksi *n* cab
taksit *n* installment
taktik *n* tactics
taktiksel *adj* tactical
takvim *n* calendar
takviye *n* reinforcements
takviye etmek *v* reinforce
talan edilmiş *adj* scrambled
talan etmek *v* plunder
talep *n* demand, claim
talep etmek *v* assess, demand
talep etmek *v* claim

talim *n* practice, training
talim ettirmek *v* train
talimat *n* prescription
talip olmak *v* aspire
tam *adj* absolute, complete, precise
tamahkar *adj* avaricious
tamam *adv* okay
tamamen *adv* completely
tamamıyla *adv* entirely
tamamlama *n* completion
tamamlamak *v* fulfill
tamir etmek *v* rehabilitate
tamirat *n* reparation
tampon *n* bumper
tane *n* pellet
tanecik *n* particle
tanıdık *adj* familiar
tanıklık etmek *v* testify
tanım *n* definition
tanıma *n* recognition
tanımak *v* recognize
tanımlamak *v* define
tanımlayıcı *adj* descriptive
tanıştırmak *v* introduce
tanıtım *n* advertising
tank *n* tank
tanrı *n* deity, God
tanrıça *n* goddess
tanrıtanımaz *adj* godless
tanrıya küfür *n* blasphemy
tapa *n* cork, tap
tapılası *adj* adorable
tapınak *n* temple, shrine
tapınma *n* adoration
tapmak *v* adore, worship
taraça *n* slab
taraf *n* side
tarafsız *adj* impartial
tarafsızlık *n* candor
tarak *n* comb
taramak *v* comb, scan
tarantula *n* tarantula
taravet *n* tenderness
tarçın *n* cinnamon
tarif *n* description
tarif etmek *v* describe
tarife *n* tariff
tarifsiz *adj* unspeakable
tarih *n* history
tarih koymak *v* date
tarihçi *n* historian
tarım *n* agriculture
tarım ilacı *n* pesticide
tarıma elverişli *adj* arable
tarımsal *adj* agricultural
tart *n* pie

tartaklamak *v* manhandle
tartar *n* tartar
tartışılabilir *adj* debatable
tartışılmaz *adj* undisputed
tartışma *n* argument
tartışmak *v* argue, debate
tartışmalı *adj* controversial
tartmak *v* weigh
taş *n* stone
tasa *n* preoccupation
tasarım *n* design
tasarlamak *v* devise
tasarruf etmek *v* economize
tasasız *adj* carefree
tasavvur etmek *v* envisage
tasdik *n* sanction
tasdik etmek *v* certify
tasdikli *adj* avowed
tasfiye *n* purge
taşıma *n* transfer
taşımak *v* cart, transport, carry
taşınabilir *adj* portable
taşıyıcı *n* bearer
taslak *n* sketch
taslak çizmek *v* sketch, draft
taşlamak *v* stone
tasma *n* leash
taşmak *v* boil over
taşocağı *n* quarry
taşralı *n* countryman
tasvip *n* approbation
tat *n* taste
tatil *n* holiday
tatlılaştırmak *v* sweeten
tatlılık *n* sweetness
tatmin edici *adj* rewarding
tatmin etmek *v* quench, satisfy
tatmin olmamış *adj* dissatisfied
tatminkar *adj* gratifying
tatsız *adj* distasteful
tava *n* frying pan
tavan *n* ceiling
tavanarası *n* attic
taverna *n* tavern
tavır *n* demeanor
tavşan *n* hare, rabbit
tavsiye *n* counsel
tavsiye etmek *v* advise
tavuk *n* chicken, hen
tavus kuşu *n* peacock
tay *n* colt
tayin *n* assignment
tayin etmek *v* appoint, assign
tayt *n* pantyhose
taze *adj* fresh
taze fasulye *n* green bean

T

tazelemek *v* brush up
tazeleyici *adj* refreshing
tazelik *n* freshness
tazı *n* greyhound
tazminat *n* indemnity
tazminat vermek *v* pay off
teberru *n* gratuity
tebeşir *n* chalk
tebliğ *n* bulletin
tebrik etmek *v* congratulate
tebrikler *n* congratulations
tecavüz etmek *v* rape
tecavüzcü *n* rapist
tedarik etmek *v* supply
tedarikçi *n* supplier
tedavi *n* treatment
tedavi etmek *n* cure
tedavi etmek *v* cure
tedavisi mümkün *adj* curable
tedbir *n* foresight
tedbirli *adj* discreet
tedirginlik *n* unrest
tefeci *n* pawnbroker
teftiş *n* inspection
teftiş etmek *v* supervise
teğet *n* tangent
teğmen *n* lieutenant
tehdit *n* threat
tehdit etmek *v* threaten
tehlike *n* danger, peril
tehlikeli *adj* dangerous
tehlikeli girişim *n* venture
tehlikeye sokmak *v* endanger
tek *adj* sole, unique
tek *n* single
tek elli *adj* singlehanded
tek eşlilik *n* monogamy
tek tük *adj* sporadic
tek yanlı *adj* unilateral
tekabül etmek *v* refer to
tekbiçimli *n* uniform
tekbiçimlilik *n* uniformity
tekerlek *n* wheel
tekerrür *n* recurrence
tekil *adj* singular
teklif *n* offer, proposal
teklif etmek *v* offer, propose
teklifsiz *n* informality
tekmelemek *v* kick
tekne *n* vessel
teknik *adj* technical
teknik *n* technique
teknik detay *n* technicality
teknik ressam *n* draftsman
teknisyen *n* technician
teknoloji *n* technology

tekrar *adv* again
tekrar *n* repetition, replay
tekrar yapmak *v* redo
tekrar yaşamak *v* relive
tekrarlamak *v* repeat
tel *n* wire
telaffuz etmek *v* pronounce
telafi etmek *v* compensate, recoup
telaşlı *adj* bustling
telefon *n* phone
telefon etmek *v* phone
telegram *n* telegram
telepati *n* telepathy
teleskop *n* telescope
televizyon *n* television
telgraf *n* wire
telif hakkı *n* copyright
telkin etmek *v* endorse
tema *n* theme
temas *n* contact
temas etmek *v* contact
tembel *adj* lazy
tembellik *n* laziness
tembih *n* admonition
tembih etmek *v* admonish
temel *adj* basic, essential
temel *n* base
temel bilgiler *n* basics
temelinde *adj* innate
temelsiz *adj* unfounded
temin etmek *v* assure
temiz *adj* clean
temizlemek *v* clean, purge
temizleyici madde *n* cleanser
temizlik *n* cleanliness
temkinli *adj* deliberate, wary
Temmuz *n* July
temsil etmek *v* appeal
temyiz etmek *v* appeal
ten rengi *n* complexion
teneke *n* tin
teneke kuru *n* canister, can
tenezzül etmek *v* deign
tenha *adj* secluded
tenha yer *n* retreat
tenis *n* tennis
tenkit *n* criticism
tenor *n* tenor
tensel *adj* sensual
tente *n* awning
teori *n* theory
tepe *n* hill
tepe üstü *n* hilltop
tepeden bakma *n* disdain
tepeden bakmak *v* look down
tepelik *adj* hilly

T

tepelik *n* crest
tepki *n* reaction
tepki vermek *v* react
tepsi *n* tray
ter *n* perspiration
terapi *n* therapy
teras *n* terrace
terbiyeci *n* trainer
terbiyesiz *adj* rude
terbiyesizlik *n* rudeness
tercih *n* preference
tercih etmek *v* prefer
tercüman *n* interpreter
tercüme *n* interpretation
tercüme etmek *v* interpret
tereddüt *n* hesitation, scruples
tereddüt etmek *v* falter, hesitate
tereddütlü *adj* hesitant
tereyağı *n* butter
terfi *n* promotion
terfi ettirmek *v* promote
terhis etmek *v* disband
terim *n* term
terk *n* abandonment
terk etmek *v* resign
terketmek *v* abandon, dump
terlemek *v* perspire, sweat
terlik *n* slipper
terminoloji *n* terminology
termit *n* termite
termometre *n* thermometer
termosifon *n* waterheater
termostat *n* thermostat
terör *n* terror
terörist *n* terrorist
terörizm *n* terrorism
tersane *n* shipyard
tersine *adv* conversely
tersine çevirme *n* reversal
tersyüz *adv* inside out
tertemiz *adj* immaculate
tertip *n* concoction
tertip etmek *v* concoct
terzi *n* tailor
tesadüf *n* coincidence
tesadüf etmek *v* coincide
tesadüfen *adj* casual
tesadüfen *adv* incidentally
teşbih *n* rosary
teşebbüs *n* attempt
teşebbüs etmek *v* attempt
teşekkür etmek *v* thank
teşekkürler *n* thanks
teselli *n* consolation
teselli etmek *v* console
teşhis *n* diagnosis

teşhis koymak *v* diagnose
tesirli *adj* telling
tesirlilik *n* effectiveness
tesis *n* foundation
tesis etmek *v* institute
tesisatçı *n* plumber
teşkil etmek *v* constitute
teslim *n* delivery
teslim etmek *v* hand in
teslim olmak *v* capitulate
teslimiyet *n* surrender
tespit etmek *v* identify
test *n* test
test etmek *v* test
testere *n* saw
teşvik etmek *v* exhort
tetik *n* trigger
tetiklemek *v* trigger
teyp kaydedici *n* tape recorder
tez *n* thesis
tezahürat *n* ovation
tezahürat yapmak *v* cheer
tezgah *n* counter
ticaret *n* trade
ticaret *n* commerce
ticaret yapmak *v* trade
ticari *adj* commercial
ticari marka *n* trademark
tıkamak *v* clog, seal off
tıkanıklık *n* congestion
tıkanma *n* blockage
tıkırdamak *v* rattle
tıkıştırmak *v* cram, stuff
tıklamak *v* click
tıklım tıklım *adj* congested
tıknaz *adj* plump
tiksindirici *adj* repulsive
tiksindirmek *v* sicken
tiksinmek *v* loathe
tiksinti *n* revulsion
tilki *n* fox
timsah *n* alligator
tipi *n* blizzard
tipik *adj* typical
tıpkısı *adj* identical
tıpkısı *adv* very
tırabzan *n* handrail
tıraş olmak *v* shave
tırmalamak *v* claw
tırmanma *n* climbing
tırmanmak *v* climb, mount
tırmık *n* rake
tiroit *n* thyroid
tırsmak *v* chicken out
tırtıl *n* caterpillar
tıslamak *v* hiss

titiz *adj* meticulous
titrek *adj* shaky
titremek *v* tremble
titreşim *n* vibration
titreşimli *adj* vibrant
titreşmek *v* flicker, vibrate
tiyatro *n* theater
tohum *n* seed
tohum ekmek *v* sow
toka *n* buckle
tokat *n* slap, smack
tokat atmak *v* smack
tokatlamak *v* slap
tökezlemek *v* stumble
toksin *n* toxin
toksinli *adj* toxic
toleranssızlık *n* intolerance
tomar *n* scroll
tombul *adj* chubby
tomurcuk *n* bud
ton *n* ton
tonbalığı *n* tuna
tonik *n* tonic
top *n* ball
topallamak *v* limp
toparlama *n* roundup
toplam *n* sum
toplama *n* congregation
toplamak *v* gather
toplamda *adv* overall
toplamda *n* aggression
toplanmak *v* convene
toplantı *n* gathering
toplu silah *n* cannon
topluluk *n* society
toplum *n* community
toprak *n* soil
toptan satış *n* wholesale
topuk *n* heel
tören *n* rite
tornacı *n* lather
tornavida *n* screwdriver
törpü *n* file
torun *n* descendant
tosbağa *n* tortoise
tost makinesi *n* toaster
totaliter *adj* totalitarian
tövbekar *n* penitent
toynak *n* hoof
toz *n* dust
tozlu *adj* dusty
trafik *n* traffic
trajedi *n* tragedy
trajik *adj* tragic
traktör *n* tractor
tramplen *n* springboard

tramvay *n* streetcar
transit *n* transit
travmatik *adj* traumatic
tren *n* train
tribün *n* grandstand
tromboz *n* thrombosis
tropik *adj* tropical
tüberküloz *n* tuberculosis
tüccar *n* merchant
tufan *n* cataclysm
tüfeğin gezi *n* hindsight
tüfek *n* rifle
tüfekçi *n* gunman
tugay *n* brigade
tuğla *n* brick
tuhaf *adj* cranky
tükenmeyen *adj* lasting
tüketici *n* consumer
tüketim *n* consumption
tüketmek *v* sap, deplete
tükürmek *v* spit
tümce *n* clause
tümen *n* legion
tümleyici *n* complement
tümör *n* tumor
tümsekli *adj* bumpy
tünel *n* subway, tunnel
tunik *n* tunic
tur *n* tour
tura *n* reel
türbin *n* turbine
türetmek *v* derive
türev *adj* derivative
turfanda *adj* precocious
turist *n* tourist
turizm *n* tourism
Türk *adj* Turk
Türkiye *n* Turkey
türlü *adj* various
turnuva *n* tournament
turp *n* radish
turta *n* tart
tutarlı *adj* consistent
tutarlılık *n* consistency
tutarsız *adj* inconsistent
tutku *n* passion
tutkulu *adj* passionate
tutmak *v* hold
tutsak *n* captive, prisoner
tutsak etmek *v* captivate
tutsaklık *n* captivity
tütsü *n* incense
tutucu *adj* conservative
tutuklama *n* arrest
tutuklamak *v* arrest
tutum *n* attitude

tutumlu *adj* frugal, thrifty
tutumluluk *n* frugality
tütün *n* tobacco
tutunmak *v* cling
tutuşma *n* combustion
tuvalet *n* rest room
tüy *n* feather
tüyleri kabarık *adj* furry
tüylü *adj* fuzzy
tuz *n* salt
tuzak *n* trap, snare
tuzlu *adj* salty

U

uç *n* edge, tip
üç *adj* three
üç ayda bir *adj* quarterly
uç nokta *n* extremities
uçağın konması *v* land
uçak *n* aeroplane
uçak kaçırmak *v* hijack
uçak pisti *n* airstrip
uçak postası *n* airmail
üçgen *n* triangle
üçlü *adj* triple
uçmak *v* fly
ücret *n* fee
uçucu *adj* volatile
üçüncü *adj* third
uçurtma *n* kite
uçurum *n* abyss, cliff
uçuş *n* fly, flight
uçuş ücreti *n* airfare
ucuz *adj* cheap
ucuz fiyat *n* bargaining
ucuzlatmak *v* depreciate
ufacık *adj* tiny
ufak ev *n* lodging
ufalamak *v* crumble
üflemek *v* blow
ufuk *n* horizon
üfürük *n* puff
üfürükçü *n* exorcist
uğramak *v* call on, stop by
uğraş *n* occupation
uğraşıp başarmak *v* thrive
uğraşmak *v* bother, molest
uğraştırıcı *adj* bothersome
uğursuz *adj* evil
ulaç *n* gerund
ulaş *n* attainment
ulaşılır *adj* attainable

ulaşmak *v* attain
ülke *n* country
ülkenin iç kısmı *adj* inland
ülser *n* ulcer
ültimatom *n* ultimatum
ültrason *n* ultrasound
ulu *adj* supreme
uluma *n* howl
ulumak *v* howl
ulus *n* nation
ulusal *adj* national
ümitle *adv* hopefully
ümitsiz *adj* hopeless
umudunu kırmak *v* dishearten
umursamaz *adj* reckless
umursamazca *adv* lightly
umurunda olmak *v* care
umut *n* prospect, hope
umut kırıcı *adj* disappointing
umutlu *adj* hopeful
umutsuz *adj* desperate
umutsuzluk *n* despair
un *n* flour
ün *n* fame
üniversite *n* university
ünlü *adj* famous
ünlü *n* celebrity
ünsüz *n* consonant
unutmak *v* forget
unutulmaz *adj* memorable
üremek *v* breed
üretim *n* production
üretken *adj* productive
üretmek *v* generate
ürkek *adj* timid
ürkeklik *n* timidity
ürkütücü *adj* dreadful
ürperme *n* tremor
ürpermek *v* quiver, shiver
ürperti *n* chill, shudder
ürün *n* produce, product
usanç *n* harassment
usandırmak *v* bore
üslup *n* wording
üst *adj* upper
üst giyecek *n* top
usta *n* master
ustabaşı *n* foreman
ustalık *n* ingenuity
ustalık isteyen *adj* tricky
üstelemek *v* persist
üstesinden gelmek *v* overcome
üstü kapalı *n* insinuation
üstün *adj* exquisite
üstün *n* distinction
üstün olmak *v* excel

üstünde *pre* above, over
üstünlük *n* excellence
üstünü çizmek *v* cross out
üstünü örtmek *v* cover up
üstüste binmek *v* overlap
usulüne uygun *adv* duly
üşüşmek *v* mob
utanç *n* chagrin, shame
utanç verici *adj* disgraceful
utandırmak *v* embarrass
utangaç *adj* bashful
utanmak *v* shame
utanmaz *adj* shameless
ütülemek *v* iron
üvey *adj* adoptive
üvey anne *n* stepmother
üvey baba *n* stepfather
üvey kız *n* stepdaughter
üvey kızkardeş *n* stepsister
uyandırmak *v* awake
uyanık *adj* awake
uyanış *v* award
uyanmak *v* wake up
uyarı *n* alert, caution
uyarıcı *n* stimulant
uyarıcı unsur *n* stimulus
uyarlamak *v* adapt
uyarlanabilen *adj* adaptable
uyarmak *v* alert, warn
uydu *n* satellite
uydurma *adj* untrue
uydurmak *v* fabricate
üye *n* member
üyelik *n* membership
uygulama *n* application
uygulamak *v* carry out
uygulanabilir *adj* applicable
uygun *adj* suitable
uygun davranış *n* decorum
uygun olmayan *adj* unfit
uygun şekilde *adv* properly
uygunluk *n* conformity
uygunsuz *adj* inept
uyku *n* sleep
uykuda *adj* asleep
uykulu *adj* drowsy
uykusuzluk *n* insomnia
uyluk *n* thigh
uymak *v* fit, obey
uymak *v* carve
uymamak *v* counter
uysal *adj* amenable
uysallık *n* docility
uyum *n* cohesion
uyumak *v* sleep
uyumlu *adj* compatible

uyumsuz *adj* discordant
uyuşmak *v* concur
uyuşmamak *v* conflict
uyuşmaz *adj* incompatible
uyuşmazlık *n* discord
uyuşuk *adj* numb
uyuşukluk *n* numbness
uyuyakalmak *v* drop off
uzak *adj* distant, remote
uzak durmak *v* shun
uzaklaşmak *v* pull out
uzaklık *n* distance
uzakta *adv* faraway
uzanmak *v* lie
uzanmış *adj* outstretched
uzatılmış *adj* protracted
uzatma *n* extension
uzatmak *v* extend, prolong
uzay *n* space
üzerine *pre* upon
üzerine titremek *v* cherish
üzgün *adj* sad, sorry
uzlaşma *n* compromise
uzlaşmak *v* compromise
uzman *adj* expert
uzmanlık alanı *n* specialty
üzmek *v* sadden
üzücü *adj* worrisome
üzülmek *v* worry
üzüm *n* grape
uzun *adj* long
uzun bank *n* pew
uzun boylu *adj* tall
uzun süreli *adj* long-term
uzunluk *n* length
üzüntü *n* distress, worry

V

vaat *n* commitment
vaaz *n* sermon
vaaz vermek *v* preach
vadi *n* valley
vaftiz *n* baptism
vaftiz etmek *v* baptize
vagon *n* wagon
vaha *n* oasis
vahim *adj* fateful
vahşet *n* atrocity
vahşi *adj* ferocious
vahşi doğa *n* wilderness
vahşi hayat *n* wildlife
vahşilik *n* ferocity, savagery

vaiz *n* chaplain
vaka *n* happening
vakit *n* time
vali *n* governor
valiz *n* suitcase
vals *n* waltz
vampir *n* vampire
van *n* van
vana *n* valve
vandal *n* vandal
vandalizm *n* vandalism
var olmak *v* exist
varis *n* successor
varış *n* arrival
varlık *n* existence
varmak *v* arrive
varsayılan *n* presupposition
varsayım *n* assumption
varsaymak *v* assume
vasıf *v* attribute
vasiyet etmek *v* bequeath
vat *n* watt
vatan haini *n* traitor
vatana ihanet *n* treason
vatandaş *n* citizen, compatriot
vatandaşlık *n* citizenship
vatansever *n* patriot
vazgeçmek *v* desist, renounce
vazo *n* vase
ve *c* and
vefa *n* constancy
vefasız *adj* disloyal, fickle
vefasızlık *n* disloyalty
vefat *n* demise
vejetaryen *v* vegetarian
vekaletname *n* proxy
veranda *n* porch
vergi *n* tax
veri *n* data
verimli *adj* fruitful, fertile
verimlilik *n* fertility
veritabanı *n* database
vermek *v* give
vernik *n* varnish
verniklemek *v* varnish
veteriner *n* veterinarian
veto etmek *v* veto
veya *c* or
veznedar *n* teller
vicdan *n* conscience
vicdan azabı *n* remorse
vicdanlı *adj* scrupulous
vida *n* screw
vidalamak *v* screw
vilayet *n* province
vinç *n* crane, hoist

virajlı *adj* crooked
virgül *n* comma
virüs *n* virus
vitamin *n* vitamin
viyadük *n* viaduct
vızıldamak *v* buzz
vızıldayan alet *n* buzzer
vızıltı *n* buzz
voleybol *n* volleyball
voltaj *n* voltage
vuku bulmak *v* occur
vurgu *n* emphasis
vurgulamak *v* emphasize
vurgun *n* killing
vurmak *v* strike, hit, zap
vuruş *n* throb, beat

yabancı *n* alien, foreigner
yabandomuzu *n* boar
yadsımak *v* disclaim
yağ *n* fat, oil
yağ çekmek *v* flatter
yağlamak *v* grease, anoint
yağlı *adj* fatty
yağlı *adj* greasy
yağmur *n* rain
yağmur yağmak *v* rain
yağmurlu *adj* rainy
yağmurluk *n* raincoat
yaka *n* collar
yakacak *n* firewood
yakalama *n* grasp
yakalamak *n* capture, catch
yakın *pre* close to, near
yakın ilişki *n* affiliation
yakında *adv* soon
yakından *adv* closely
yakınlarda *adj* nearby
yakınlaşma *n* approach
yakınlaşmak *v* approach
yakınlık *n* proximity
yakınma *n* grievance
yakınmak *v* beef up
yakınsamak *v* converge
yakışıklı *adj* good-looking
yakıt *n* fuel
yakıt almak *v* fuel, refuel
yaklaşık *adj* approximate
yaklaşılabilir *adj* approachable
yakmak *v* scorch
yakut *n* ruby

yalamak *v* lick
yalan *n* falsehood
yalan söylemek *v* lie
yalancı *adj* liar
yalanlamak *v* refute
yalıtım *n* insulation
yalıtmak *v* insulate
yalnız *adj* alone
yalnız *adv* only
yalnız *n* loner
yalnız başına *adv* lonely
yalnızca *adv* solely
yalnızlık *n* loneliness
yaltaklanmak *v* pander
yalvarmak *v* beg, beseech
yama *n* graft, patch
yamaç *n* hillside, slope
yamalamak *v* graft, patch
yamamak *v* darn
yamultmak *v* dent
yamyam *n* cannibal
yan *n* side
yan çizmek *v* shirk
yan kapı *adj* next door
yan ürün *n* by-product
yan yana *adj* adjoining
yan yana *adv* abreast
yanak *n* cheek
yanan *adv* alight
yanardağ *n* volcano
yanaşmak *v* dock
yandan *adv* sideways
yandaş *n* follower
yani *adv* namely
yanıcı *n* combustible
yanık *n* burn
yanılmak *v* err
yanılmaz *adj* infallible
yanıltıcı *adj* deceptive
yanıltmaca *n* fallacy
yanında *pre* along
yanında *pre* by
yankesicilik *n* pickpocket
yankı *n* echo
yanlış *adj* inaccurate, wrong
yanlış anlamak *v* misunderstand
yanlışlık yapmak *n* miscarriage
yanlışlıkla *adj* accidental
yanmak *v* burn
yansıma *v* bounce
yansımak *v* rebound
yansıtma *n* reflection
yansıtmak *v* reflect
yapabilmek *v* can
yapar görünmek *v* pretend
yapay *adj* artificial

yapayalnız *adj* lonesome
yapı *n* structure
yapı içi *adv* indoor
yapıcı *adj* constructive
yapım *n* make
yapışkan *adj* adhesive, sticky
yapıştırmak *v* stick, paste
yapmacık *n* sham
yapmak *v* do, make
yaprak *n* leaf
yara *n* wound
yara izi *n* scar
yaralamak *v* hurt
yaralanmak *v* wound
yaralı *adj* hurt
yaramaz *adj* naughty
yaramaz kimse *n* rascal
yararlı *adj* beneficial
yararsız *adj* useless
yarasa *n* bat
yaratıcı *adj* creative
yaratıcı *n* creator
yaratıcılık *n* creativity
yaratık *n* creature
yaratım *n* creation
yaratmak *v* create
yarda *n* yard
yardım *n* assistance, help, need
yardım etmek *v* assist, help
yardım istemek *v* invoke
yardıma muhtaç *adj* needy
yardımcı *n* aide, helper
yardımcı olmak *v* aid
yardımsever *adj* helpful
yargıç *n* magistrate
yarı *adj* half
yarı yarıya *adv* fifty-fifty
yarıçap *n* radius
yarıda kesmek *v* interrupt
yarık *n* cleft, crevice
yarıküre *n* hemisphere
yarım *n* half
yarım yamalak *adj* sloppy
yarımada *n* peninsula
yarın *adv* tomorrow
yarış *n* race
yarışma *n* match, competition
yarışmacı *n* competitor
yarışmak *v* race
yarıya bölmek *v* halve
yarmak *v* hack, slit
yas *n* mourning
yaş *n* age
yas tutmak *v* mourn
yasadışı *adj* illegal
yasak *n* prohibition

yasaklama *n* restraint
yasaklamak *v* ban, forbid
yasal *adj* legal
yasallaştırmak *v* legalize
yasallık *n* legality
yaşam *n* life
yaşam stili *n* lifestyle
yaşam süreci *adj* lifetime
yasama *n* legislation
yasama meclisi *n* legislature
yaşamak *v* live
yasemin *n* jasmine
yaslanmak *v* lean on
yaşlı *adj* old
yaşlı *n* elder
yaşlıca *adj* elderly
yaşlılık *n* old age
yastık *n* pillow
yastık kılıfı *n* pillowcase
yat *n* yacht
yatak *n* bed
yatak odası *n* bedroom
yatak örtüsü *n* bedspread
yatak takımı *n* bedding
yatakhane *n* dormitory
yatay *adj* horizontal
yatırım *n* investment
yatırım yapmak *v* invest
yatırımcı *n* investor
yatıştırıcı *adj* conciliatory
yatıştırılmaz *adj* implacable
yatıştırma *n* appeasement
yatıştırmak *v* appease
yatmak *v* repose
yavaş *adj* slow
yavaş yavaş *adv* piecemeal
yavaşça *adv* slowly
yavaşlamak *v* slow down
yavaşlatmak *v* slacken
yavuz *adj* stern
yay *n* arc, spring
yaya *n* pedestrian
yaya geçidi *n* crosswalk
yaygara *n* fuss
yaygara *v* clamor
yaygaracı *adj* fussy
yaygın *adj* prevalent
yayılıp yatmak *v* sprawl
yayılmak *v* emanate
yayımcı *n* broadcaster
yayımlamak *v* broadcast
yayın *n* publication
yayla *n* prairie, plateau
yaymak *v* propagate
yaz *n* summer
yaz ortası *n* midsummer

yazar *n* author, writer
yazarı bilinmeyiş *n* anonymity
yazdırmak *v* dictate
yazı *n* writing, letter
yazıcı *n* printer
yazıcıya ait *adj* clerical
yazılı *adj* written
yazmak *v* write
yedek *adj* spare
yedek *n* backup, substitute
yedek parça *n* spare part
yedi *adj* seven
yedinci *adj* seventh
yeğen *n* cousin, nephew
yel değirmeni *n* windmill
yelek *n* vest
yelken *n* sail
yelken açmak *v* sail
yelken iskotası *n* sheets
yelkenli *n* sailboat
yelpaze *n* fan
yem *n* bait
yeme *n* intake
yemek *n* food
yemek *v* eat
yemek borusu *n* esophagus
yemek odası *n* dining room
yemek tarifi *n* recipe
yemek yapma *n* cooking
yemin *n* oath
yemin etmek *v* vow
yemlemek *v* peck
yemlik *n* crib, manger
yengeç *n* crab
yeni *adj* new
yeni *adv* newly
yeni baskı *n* reprint
yeni doğmuş *n* newborn
yeni evli *adj* newlywed
yeni gelen *n* newcomer
yeniden *adv* afresh, anew
yeniden doğuş *n* rebirth
yeniden girme *n* reentry
yeniden saymak *v* recount
yeniden seçmek *v* reelect
yenilebilir *adj* edible
yenileme *n* renewal
yenilemek *v* renovate
yenilenmiş *adj* renowned
yenileştirmek *v* renew
yenilgi *n* defeat, beating
yenilik *n* innovation, novelty
yenilmez *adj* invincible
yenmek *v* defeat, prevail
yepisyeni *adj* brand-new
yer *n* room, place

yer değiştirmek *v* relocate
yer gösterici *n* usher
yeraltı *adj* underground
yeraltı sığınağı *n* bunker
yerçekimi *n* gravity
yerel *adj* local
yerfıstığı *n* peanut
yerinde *adj* relevant
yerinden çıkarmak *v* dislocate
yerinden oynatmak *v* dislodge
yerine *adv* instead
yerine koymak *v* replace
yerini almak *v* supersede
yerini belirlemek *v* locate
yerini değiştirmek *v* displace
yerleşik *adj* built-in
yerleşim bölgesi *n* enclave
yerleşme *n* relocation
yerleşmek *v* inhabit
yerleşmek *v* settle
yerleştirilmiş *adj* located
yerleştirmek *v* accommodate
yerli *adj* native
yeşil *adj* green
yetenek *n* ability
yetenekli *adj* capable
yeteri kadar *adv* enough
yeterli *adj* adequate
yetersiz *adj* inadequate
yetişkin *n* adult
yetişmek *v* catch up
yetiştirmek *v* bring up, rear
yetki aktarmak *v* delegate
yetki aktarmak *n* authorization
yetkilendirmek *v* authorize
yetmiş *adj* seventy
yığın *n* heap, pile
yığışmak *v* agglomerate
yiğit *adj* daring
yiğitlik *n* bravery
yığmak *v* amass, pile
yıkamak *v* wash
yıkanabilir *adj* washable
yıkıcı *adj* destructive
yıkılış *n* downfall
yıkılmak *v* collapse
yıkım *n* demolition
yıkmak *v* demolish
yıl *n* year
yıl boyu süren *adj* perennial
yılan *n* serpent, snake
yıldırım *n* thunderbolt
yıldırmak *v* terrorize
yıldız *n* star
yıldız imi *n* asterisk
yıldönümü *n* anniversary

yıllık *adj* annual
yıllık *adv* yearly
yılmaz *adj* intrepid
yine de *adv* nevertheless
yinelemek *v* reiterate
yıpranma payı *n* depreciation
yıpranmış *adj* decrepit
yirmi *adj* twenty
yirminci *adj* twentieth
yırtık pırtık *adj* ragged
yırtmak *v* tear
yiyecek *n* foodstuff
yiyip yutmak *v* devour
yobaz *adj* bigot
yobazlık *n* bigotry
yoğun *adj* intensive
yoğunlaştırmak *v* condense
yoğunluk *n* density
yok edici *n* destroyer
yok etmek *v* eradicate
yoklamak *v* ransack
yoksul *adj* destitute
yoksulluk *n* poverty
yoksun *adj* deprived
yoksun bırakmak *v* deprive
yokuş *adv* uphill
yokuş aşağı *adv* downhill
yol *n* path, road
yol açmak *v* cause
yol almak *v* head for
yol parası *n* fare
yol sayacı *n* odometer
yol şeridi *n* lane
yola çıkmak *v* set off
yolcu *n* traveler
yolcu rehberi *n* itinerary
yolcu uçağı *n* airliner
yolculuk *n* journey
yoldan çıkmak *v* stray
yoldan geçen *n* passer-by
yoldaş *n* companion
yoldaşlık *n* companionship
yön *n* direction
yön değiştirmek *v* avert
yönelmek *v* gravitate
yöneltmek *v* point
yönetici *n* director
yönetilir *adj* manageable
yönetim *n* executive
yönetim kurulu *n* board
yönetmek *v* govern
yonga *n* chip
yonga plakası *n* wafer
yönlendirmek *v* divert
yönlü *adj* oriented
yontmak *v* whittle

yorgan *n* quilt
yorgun *adj* tired, weary
yorgunluk *n* exhaustion
yormak *v* wear out
yorucu *adj* exhausting
yorum *n* comment
yorum yapmak *v* comment
yörünge *n* orbit
yosun *n* moss
yoz *adj* corrupt
yozlaşma *n* corruption
yozlaşmak *v* degenerate
yozlaşmış *v* corrupt
yüce *adj* sublime
yüceltmek *v* exalt, glorify
yudum *n* gulp, sip
yudumlamak *v* sip
yük *n* burden
yukarda *adv* upstairs
yukarı çekmek *v* hoist
yukarı çıkmak *v* ascend
yukarı kaldırmak *v* uphold
yukarı taşımak *v* move up
yukarıya doğru *adv* upwards
yüklemek *v* burden, load
yüklü *adj* burdensome
yüksek *adj* high, lofty
yüksek ses *adv* aloud
yüksek sesle *adv* loudly
yükseklik *n* altitude
yüksekten atmak *v* brag
yükseliş *n* upturn
yükselmek *v* go up, rise
yükselteç *n* amplifier
yükselti *n* elevation
yükseltmek *v* heighten
yulaf ezmesi *n* oatmeal
yumruk *n* fist
yumruklamak *v* punch
yumurta *n* egg
yumurta akı *n* egg white
yumurta sarısı *n* yolk
yumurtalık *n* ovary
yumuşak *adj* soft
yumuşaklık *n* softness
yumuşamak *v* relent
yumuşatıcı *adj* laxative
yumuşatmak *v* soften
yün *n* wool
yün ipliği *n* yam, yarn
Yunan *adj* Greek
Yunanistan *n* Greece
yünden *adj* woolen
yunus *n* dolphin
yürek *n* guts
yüreklendirmek *v* hearten

yürekli *adj* audacious
yürekten *adj* hearty
yurt *n* homeland
yurtdışında *adv* abroad
yurtsever *adj* patriotic
yürümek *v* pace, walk
yürütmek *v* execute
yürüyüş *n* hike, walk
yürüyüş yapmak *v* hike
yutmak *v* swallow
yuva *n* nest
yuvarlak *adj* circular, round
yuvarlak *n* circle
yuvarlanmak *v* tumble
yüz *adj* hundred
yüz *n* face
yüz *pre* facing
yüz ekşitme *n* grimace
yüz veren *adj* indulgent
yüz yüze gelmek *v* confront
yüzde *adv* percent
yüzdelik *n* percentage
yüzen *adv* afloat
yüzey *n* surface, facet
yüzgeç *n* fin
yüzkarası *n* disgrace
yüzleşme *n* confrontation
yüzme *n* swimming
yüzmek *v* swim
yüzsüz *adj* cheeky
yüzü kızarmak *v* blush
yüzücü *n* swimmer
yüzük *n* ring
yüzüncü *adj* hundredth
yüzyıl *n* century

Z

zaaf *n* frailty
zafer *n* triumph
zahmet *n* trouble
zahmet çekmek *v* toil
zahmetli *adj* inconvenient
zahmetsiz *adj* painless
zalim *adj* atrocious
zamanında *adj* timely
zamanlamak *v* time
zamansız *adj* untimely
zamir *n* pronoun
zamk *n* glue, paste
zamklamak *v* glue
zan *n* presumption
zanaat *n* craft

zanaatkar *n* craftsman
zannetmek *v* presume
zarafet *n* grace, elegance
zarar *n* damage
zarar veren *adj* damaging
zarar vermek *v* harm
zararlı *adj* harmful
zararsız *adj* harmless
zarf *n* adverb
zarif *adj* elegant
zaten *adv* already
zatürree *n* pneumonia
zavallı *adj* miserable
zayıf *adj* faint, weak, slim
zayıflatmak *v* weaken
zayıflık *n* weakness
zebra *n* zebra
zehir *n* poison
zehirlemek *v* poison
zehirleyen *n* poisoning
zehirli *adj* poisonous
zeka *n* mind
zeki *adj* intelligent
zemin *n* floor, ground
zemin kat *n* ground floor
zencefil *n* ginger
zengin *adj* wealthy
zenginleştirmek *v* enrich
zenginlik *n* wealth
zeval *n* decadence
zevk *n* gusto, zest
zevk almak *v* savor
zevk sahibi *adj* tasteful
zeytin *n* olive
zihninde tartmak *v* ponder
zihniyet *n* mentality
zil *n* bell
zillet *n* contempt
zımba *n* staple, stapler
zımbalamak *v* staple
zımpara kağıdı *n* sandpaper
zina *n* adultery
zincir *n* chain
zincirlemek *v* chain
zincirli testere *n* chainsaw
zindan *n* dungeon
zıpkın *n* harpoon
zıplamak *v* hop, jump
zırh *n* armor
zırhlı gemi *n* turret
zirve *n* apex, summit
ziyafet *n* banquet
ziyan *n* detriment
ziyaret *n* visit
ziyaret etmek *v* visit
ziyaretçi *n* visitor

zonklamak *v* throb
zooloji *n* zoology
zor *adj* difficult, hard
zoraki *adj* strained
zorba *adj* brutal
zorbalık *n* brutality
zorbalık etmek *v* brutalize
zorla *adv* hardly
zorla girme *n* intrusion
zorla girmek *v* intrude
zorlamak *v* coerce
zorlayıcı *adj* compelling
zorlu *adj* violent
zorluk *n* adversity
zorunlu *adj* mandatory
züccaciye *n* glassware
zulmetmek *v* persecute
zulüm *n* tyranny
zümre *n* class
zümrüt *n* emerald
zürafa *n* giraffe
zürriyet *n* posterity